DATE DUE

OCT 23 2000		MAR 3 1 2014	
JAN 26 2002			
MAR 10 2009			
MAR 24 2009			
MAR 19 2010			

A FISTFUL OF SUGAR

A FISTFUL OF SUGAR

☆ ☆

ALAN GOLDSTEIN

COWARD, McCANN & GEOGHEGAN

NEW YORK

The author gratefully acknowledges permission from the following publishers to reprint material in this book:

The New York Times for material written by Dave Anderson, copyright (c) 1980 The New York Times.

Random House, Inc., for lines from "Let Us Honor if We Can," in *W. H. Auden: Collected Poems* by W. H. Auden, edited by Edward Mendelson, copyright (c) 1934 and renewed 1962 by W. H. Auden.

Sports Illustrated for material written by Bill Nack, copyright (c) 1980 Sports Illustrated.

The Washington Star for material written by Betty Cuniberti, copyright (c) 1980 The Washington Star; and written by Moe Siegel, copyright (c) 1978 The Washington Star.

The Washington Post for material written by Tom Boswell, copyright (c) 1980 The Washington Post; by Ken Denlinger, copyright (c) 1979 The Washington Post; by David Kindred, copyright (c) 1980 The Washington Post; and by Judy Mann, copyright (c) 1980 The Washington Post.

Some material in this book appeared earlier in the Baltimore *Sun* in a different form.

Library of Congress Cataloging in Publication Data

Goldstein, Alan.
A fistful of Sugar.

1. Leonard, Sugar Ray. 2. Boxers (Sports)—United States—Biography. I. Title.
GV1132.L42G64 796.8'3'0924 [B] 80-27819
ISBN 0-698-11082-X

PRINTED IN THE UNITED STATES OF AMERICA

To my father, Harry, who first told me there was beauty to be found in the brutal sport of boxing.

And to Sugar Ray Leonard, who proved it was so.

Contents

Prologue 13
1 End of a Legend 17
2 From Choirboy to "Killer" 44
3 "My Journey's Ended" 61
4 Journey into Manhood 76
5 All in the Family 87
6 A Baptism Fit for a King 100
7 Reflections in a Looking Glass 112
8 Pussycats and Tigers 120
9 The Money Machine 137
10 Weighing Ray's Future 150
11 Waiting for Roberto 166
12 "War of the Wunderkinds" 172
13 Love: Lost and Found 194
14 The Empire Is Falling 201
15 The Unholy Alliance 213
16 "Manos de Piedra—Hands of Stone" 225
17 "Le Face-à-Face Historique" 233
18 The Man in the Mountain 243

19 Memories Are Made of This . . . 255
20 Fight Night 277
Epilogue 293
Appendix: Sugar Ray Leonard's Professional Record 297

"Strength undoubtedly is what a boxer ought to start with, but without art he will succeed but poorly."

—Pierce Egan, *Boxiana,* 1812

A FISTFUL OF SUGAR

★ Prologue ★

It was the winter of 1975, and the Washington Touchdown Club was holding its annual black-tie-and-tails sports banquet, attended by all the familiar Capitol Hill dignitaries and sports celebrities within shouting distance of the Washington Monument.

A special award—"Athlete of the Century"—was to be presented to then-heavyweight champion Muhammad Ali, but for weeks, dinner chairman Charley Brotman had searched in vain for a suitable person to make the historic presentation.

"I called a number of political bigshots, well-known boxing figures, ex-champions, and current professional stars," Brotman recalled, "but everyone, for some reason or another, claimed to be busy that particular night. Finally, after exhausting my original list, I told my committee members, 'I've found the perfect man for this job. Well, not exactly a man, but a kid you all know—Sugar Ray Leonard, who just won a gold medal in the Pan-American Games boxing competition.'

" 'It's a natural,' I said, trying to build my case. 'We'll

have the fighter of the future giving an award to the greatest fighter of our time.'

"But all I got in return was a bunch of blank stares," Brotman added. "Like a chorus, they all said, 'Ray Who?' and voted me down. But I overruled them, simply because I didn't have anyone else in mind, and the banquet was only a few days off. Frankly though, I was as worried as the rest of them. I hardly knew Leonard at the time, and I was afraid that we'd all be embarrassed by a tongue-tied teenager in awe of Ali."

Brotman needn't have worried. The incomparable Ali had met his match in the handsome, fresh-faced seventeen-year-old boxer sitting beside him on the dais.

With typical bravado, Ali needled Leonard throughout the affair, belittling the amateur ring accomplishments that had already stamped the youngster from Palmer Park, Maryland, as a future world-beater.

"Do you realize you're sitting next to the greatest fighter of all time?" Ali said with the appropriate theatrics.

Leonard nodded a silent reply.

"And do you realize that I was a two-time Golden Gloves champion?" Ali continued.

"So was I," replied his youthful companion, while devouring a huge salad.

"Mine were national titles," Muhammad growled.

"So were mine," Leonard smiled shyly.

"And I won two AAU titles, too," the heavyweight champ said, ignoring the interruption.

"Same here," replied the voice at his side.

"But I won an Olympic gold medal. Now I know you ain't done that," said Ali, playing his trump card.

"No, not yet," Leonard said, "but I will have by this time next year."

Ali finally let his guard down and emitted a loud laugh that rebounded off the back wall of the dining room.

"Yeah, you probably will," he said, playfully nudging Leonard in the ribs. "I saw you beat those Russian fighters last year. You showed me somethin'—the look of a champion. Yeah, you'll win an Olympic gold medal. And one day, you'll be a world champion just like me."

Muhammad, the prophet, had spoken. But Ali, if anything, had underestimated Sugar Ray Leonard. Little did he realize that in four short years the precocious Leonard would take his place not only as boxing's most familiar face, but also as the sport's top attraction, an incredible money-making machine who would earn over $20 million while twice laying claim to the welterweight crown.

And no one would ever again ask Charley Brotman, "Ray Who?"

★ 1 ★

END OF A LEGEND

Seven-year-old Ray Leonard, Jr., the image of his famous father, ran breathlessly through the corridors of his fashionable fourteen-room home in search of his mother, Juanita. He found her in the kitchen and proudly presented her with his latest artistic creation.

In broad, bold strokes, little Ray had etched a picture of his father fighting his old tormentor, Roberto Duran. Sugar Ray was depicted landing a straight right hand flush on Duran's bewhiskered chin. The balloon over Leonard's head said, "Take that!" while the obviously pained Panamanian shouted, "Ouch!"

"Ray, Jr., is going to New Orleans this time," the petite Mrs. Leonard said two weeks before the welterweight title rematch at the New Orleans Superdome. "He said his daddy lost in Montreal because he wasn't there to cheer for him."

Juanita Leonard wished she, too, had missed the first fight and all the ones that preceeded it. "Watching the fight in Montreal was a terrible experience for me," she said. "I started crying in the second round when Ray got hurt, and

I fainted in the fourth round. The tension was too much. Ray's sister, Sharon, kept slapping me, and when I finally opened my eyes, I remember telling her, 'OK, you can stop slapping me now. I'm up.' "

She would watch her husband endure eleven more rounds of savage fighting before Duran's fist was raised in triumph as the new welterweight champion. While the Panamanian fans leaped into the ring and began an orgiastic celebration, Leonard returned to his dressing room for a long look in the mirror.

He saw his handsome, boyish features covered with ugly bumps and bruises. His arms ached and his back was sore. There were even lumps on the back of his head, and his left ear, grotesquely swollen, bore the cauliflowered look of a washed-up club fighter. Sugar Ray turned to his wife and said, "That's it, no more. I gave it all I had, but this is it."

Juanita Leonard knew better. During a ten-day vacation in Hawaii following the fight, she waited patiently while Sugar Ray found a painless way of telling her that he had to challenge Duran again.

"For a week, Ray never mentioned what he planned to do next. But I knew it was on his mind," she said.

One afternoon, Ray sent Juanita on a shopping expedition. As soon as she had left, he began shadow-boxing in front of a full-length mirror. When she returned, he gave her a gentle kiss and said softly, "I've got something to tell you, sweetheart. I can't quit fighting."

"I just looked at him and smiled," Juanita recalled. " 'It took you a little time, didn't it?' " I said. "But I was expecting it. I knew there was no way he could quit fighting at twenty-four. It's his career, but that's not really it. Fighting is in Ray's blood, and he was going forward, not backward, and all I can do is stand behind him.

"In Montreal, Ray let his pride beat him. He had to prove to himself and everyone else that he was as tough as

Duran. If he had fought the way he knows best, he would have won. That's why this time, it will be different."

Yes, it would be different. Incredibly different. Unbelievable. Bizarre. An improbable ending that even O. Henry would have considered too preposterous.

In boxing's long and colorful history—a history full of stunning upsets, mob-inspired fixes and dubious decisions—nothing like this had ever happened before.

Roberto Duran, the ultimate "Macho Man," who once flattened a horse with a single punch to win a ten dollar bet; Roberto Duran, voted the "Fighter of the Seventies," who had won seventy-two of seventy-three previous fights while terrorizing lightweights and welterweights alike; Roberto Duran, the remorseless alley fighter seemingly impervious to pain, tossed in the towel and meekly surrendered his title without spilling a drop of blood.

For the better part of eight rounds, Sugar Ray Leonard would taunt, mock, and humiliate the Panamanian bully boy in much the same manner Muhammad Ali had teased and tormented malevolent Sonny Liston out of the heavyweight title seventeen years earlier. It was a boxing tour de force worthy of an Ali, Ray Robinson, and Kid Gavilan, three ring greats from whom Leonard had borrowed and honed his dazzling repertoire of ring tricks.

This time, Duran would not be able to trap him on the ropes, using his head as a battering ram and driving into Leonard with his hands of stone, shoulders, and knees. No, this time Sugar Ray used his quick feet and agility to spin off the ropes and take full advantage of the manueverability provided by a twenty-one-foot ring.

Time and again, he met Duran's bull-like charge with stinging jabs and right-hand counters. For every ploy or tactic the resourceful Duran attempted, Leonard found the proper antidote.

"I did everything I said I was going to do, and he couldn't accept it," Leonard would say later. "He had told everyone that he would knock me out this time. But I left him embarrassed and truly confused. Even his sneer was gone."

It was in the seventh round, however, that Leonard took both body and soul out of his belligerent foe, transforming "Duran the Lionhearted" into a confused kitten. Disparaged by the Duran camp as a synthetic creature of television and Madison Avenue hype, Leonard once more became the consummate showman that had gained him such incredible popularity in the States. For three uproarious minutes, he used Duran as his unwilling dupe. He dropped his hands to his side, daring the champion to hit him on his jutting, unprotected chin.

Amazingly, Duran seemed intimidated by Leonard's brazen clowning. This only encouraged Sugar Ray to become more mocking in his manner. He drew wild cheers from the crowd when he feigned a Popeye-like bolo, sweeping his right arm in windmill style. While a befuddled Duran looked on helplessly, Leonard quickly darted inside to slap his face with a crisp jab. It was the ultimate putdown for the proud champion. Not even Charlie Chaplin in *City Lights* had elevated boxing to such a comic art.

No real damage had been done. No telling blows had been struck. But far worse, Duran had been left naked and exposed in mid-ring by the same man he had bullied out of his title only five months before.

Still, no one expected Duran's submissive surrender. With eighteen seconds remaining in the eighth round and seven rounds to go, the crowd still waited for Duran to make his move. Instead, Duran gave a flip of his glove, abruptly turned his back on Leonard—and it was all over. Both Sugar Ray and referee Octavio Meyran were startled by the action. Wary of some trick, Leonard followed his reluctant rival to the ropes and delivered two solid hooks to the body. But Duran offered no resistance.

"Fight!" the referee admonished the champion. But

again Duran answered with a compliant wave of his glove and muttered, "*No más. No más.*" No more. No more.

"*Porque?*" asked Meyran, a Mexican native.

Duran shrugged once more and said, "*No más,* no more box."

For one incredulous second, Leonard stood, unbelieving. Then, realizing the full meaning of Duran's words, he raced across the ring, leaped on the ropes in a neutral corner, and raised his arms in triumph while emitting a joyful whoop that reverberated around the vast Superdome.

"*Porque?*" Why? The question would never be truly answered in the weeks and months of controversy that followed Leonard's return to the throne. There would be bitter cries of "Fix!" raised by both the big spenders that paid upward to $1,000 for ringside seats in New Orleans, as well as the hundreds of thousands who watched the outcome in disbelief on closed-circuit television in areas and theaters across the country.

In Panama, where Duran's past reputation of fearlessness had all but elevated him to sainthood, fresh grafitti appeared on the barrio walls branding their now badly tarnished hero a "TRAITOR!" Headlines in the country's major dailies reflected the shocked atmosphere and the deep grief of his worshipping countrymen. "PANAMA IS IN MOURNING," said *Critica.* "A SURPRISE ENDING BEYOND WHAT CAN BE IMAGINED," *La Estrella* said. And *La Prensa*'s front page cried: "OVERRUN BY LEONARD, DURAN ABANDONED EVERYTHING LAST NIGHT—IT IS THE END OF A LEGENDARY CAREER."

"Panama is a small country," said Luis Henriquez, Duran's confidant and interpreter. "There is no place to hide, especially for him."

Porque? Everyone searched for reasons, but none proved satisfactory. Duran blamed his demise on severe stomach cramps that began to sap his strength in the fifth round and left him all but paralyzed by the eighth and final round of the Leonard rematch.

Alibis and excuses were quickly incorporated into the routines of stand-up comics seizing on Duran's celebrated bellyache as fresh material. Johnny Carson said he considered having Duran appear on "The Tonight Show" to sing "The Twelve Days of Christmas," "but I'm afraid," the show host said, "he'll quit by the eighth day."

"If Duran had stomach cramps," offered another punster, "it must have been his guts shrinking."

And Leonard's attorney, Mike Trainer, repeated the most popular joke of the hour: "They're checking Duran's birth certificate in Panama. They think now he may be Guatemalan."

Ring historian Jim Jacobs showed more compassion and understanding for Duran's shocking capitulation. "Boxers don't refer to them as excuses, but as explanations," said Jacobs, who, only a month earlier, had heard the legendary Ali "explain" his tragically inept performance against heavyweight champion Larry Holmes on an overdose of thyroid drugs taken to enhance a crash diet.

And now it was time to fathom Duran's "explanations." But none seemed acceptable. True champions, the legend goes, are expected to be carried out on their shield, snarling, crawling and fighting to the bitter end until knocked out or saved by the final bell. Hadn't the late Marcel Cerdan, his shattered right arm hanging helplessly by his side, tried to retain his middleweight crown by fighting Jake LaMotta, the raging "Bronx Bull," one-handed? Hadn't Ali fought twelve rounds against Ken Norton with a broken jaw? And when Archie Moore, being bludgeoned into submission by Rocky Marciano, was asked by the referee if he wished to retire, hadn't gallant Archie responded, "No, I want to be counted out"?

And so Duran, retiring without a whimper, had left his extreme loyalists with a feeling of betrayal. There was no way to save face despite the somewhat ludicrous efforts of several members of his entourage.

"The water in New Orleans is bad," insisted Henriquez,

suggesting a reverse case of "Montezuma's revenge." "The water made Roberto sick, plus the hotel diet. He got tired of eating the same thing every day for over two weeks," Henriquez added, ignoring the obvious retort as to why the millionaire fighter hadn't simply arranged for a private chef to cater to his gastronomical whims.

Even more preposterous were the rumors that Duran was suffering from a mysterious heart ailment, a bit of popular gossip dating back to the first Leonard encounter in Montreal when the Panamanian was forced to undergo a four-hour examination after an EKG test had revealed "a squiggle" in the wrong place. Duran's supporters preferred believing there was something seriously wrong with their fallen idol rather than accept the story that he had surrendered to a bad case of indigestion.

"That story about having a bad heart is ridiculous," said Ray Arcel, Duran's eighty-one-year-old guru and chief cornerman. "He got a complete bill of health in Montreal, and his manager (Carlos Eleta) didn't want those stories cropping up again. He was afraid some publicity-crazy politician in New Orleans would capitalize on it. So he made Roberto take another battery of tests in Miami just before he came to New Orleans for the fight. We've got an affidavit saying Duran's heart is perfect."

Most of the explaining was left to Eleta, the Panamanian millionaire who has been a godfather to Duran since he purchased his ring contract from a jockey when Roberto was an unknown preliminary boy.

"You have to understand this about Roberto," Eleta told Dave Anderson of *The New York Times*. "In our country, he is like a god. Everybody is after him to do this or that, and he is very difficult to control. After he won the title from Leonard in Montreal and returned home to Panama, everyone invited him to parties and his home was turned into a hotel. Training in Panama became impossible. He was 183 pounds before we got him out of the country.

"We took him to Grossinger's Hotel in New York, but his

friends still wouldn't give him any peace. He must have invited at least sixty of them to the fight in New Orleans. When his trainers talked to him, Roberto's friends would say, 'Don't listen to them. You're fine.' And if he wanted to eat like a glutton, they'd encourage him. They didn't give a damn about him. All they want is Roberto's money. Meanwhile, they were destroying him.

"But Roberto didn't quit. He is no coward. In the eighth round, he just said to himself, 'Leonard is not going to make a fool of me.' He was just trying to do what his body wouldn't let him do, and finally he just said to hell with it. But later he was much ashamed, and he wept when we took him to the hospital."

But Freddie Brown and Ray Arcel, Duran's "two wise men," refused to accept the story of Duran's "tired blood."

"He just quit," said Brown, seventy-three, whose colorful, lopsided face was once described as resembling "a low club flush."

Arcel, Brown's octogenarian sidekick, was even more incredulous. In his time, Arcel had trained eighteen world champions, including the immortal Benny Leonard, Barney Ross, and Ezzard Charles. But Arcel considered none better than the indomitable Duran—he brought Duran out of a self-imposed retirement to train and polish him into a legendary fighter.

Of course, Arcel, in fifty years dedicated to fighting, also had his share of losers. In fact, he became known as "The Meat Wagon" after hauling fourteen victims of Joe Louis's back to their corner.

"Between the time we left the dressing room and walked the last mile to the ring and they played 'The National Anthem,' a strange thing happened to my guys going against Louis. Did you ever see a tulip wilt? I had to carry smelling salts and give them a sniff before the opening bell just to get them to stand up straight and look like an opponent."

But no Arcel fighter was ever allowed to quit of his own volition. "I had a fighter once who was getting clobbered and begged me to throw in the towel," he recalled. "The first time he came by the corner, he screamed, 'Ray, the towel!' The next time he staggered by, he yelled even louder, 'Ray, please, the towel!' The third time, it sounded like his last breath. 'Ray, pleeease throw the towel! I won't be around again.' "

But Arcel never thought he would see the day when an unbloodied Duran, the man alleged to have a heart to match that of his pet lion, would walk away from a fight.

"I've spent sixty-seven years in this business with hundreds, thousands of fighters, but to me, this is the most humiliating experience. This is terrible. The one man I had confidence in and looked up to for courage and determination had to quit. It's inexplicable. Maybe instead of a physical, they should give him a mental exam.

"Before the fight, if a guy had walked up to me and said, 'This guy will quit on you,' I'd have spit in his eye. But he *did* quit. I can't condemn him, but I can't accept it, either."

Porque? No one thought of asking Sugar Ray Leonard, who knew the answers better than anyone.

"I made Duran look like an amateur and now everyone is looking for excuses," he said. "There are no excuses. Why can't people accept it? I beat him mentally and physically. I made him lose his composure. People considered that impossible. Even some of my friends back in Maryland bet against me this time. They said I lacked the killer's instinct to beat a Roberto Duran. That's because everybody built up this myth about Duran, like when he walks past a snowbank, it's supposed to melt.

"But beating Duran was like a mission for me, just like winning that Olympic gold medal. Now I've proved myself to Duran and the world. I made him quit. To make a man quit, especially a Roberto Duran, was better than knocking him out."

The morning after, someone asked if Duran had simply taken the easy way out.

"No," Sugar Ray said. "He took the hard way out. He's got to go back to Panama now and face all those people."

Porque?

The first whys would be answered by the twenty-four-year-old Leonard in the days of deep soul-searching following the loss of his briefly held welterweight crown in Montreal, the same city where, four years earlier, he had first gained international acclaim with his spectacular march to an Olympic gold medal.

He had engaged Duran that cold, damp night at the Olympic Stadium in a brutal toe-to-toe slugfest and lost his title in proving his manhood.

"If Ray had fought any other way," his sister, Sharon, said, "people would have said, 'Oh. Duran could have knocked him out, but Leonard just ran all night.' "

Recalling that long, hard night in Montreal, Leonard told Bill Nack of *Sports Illustrated*, "My mind was on it. My mind was right up 'til fight night. I knew what I was going to do and I had to do. I was sitting there and it all vanished. All the adrenaline, all the momentum diminished. It was all going away.

"I walked into the ring and wasn't thinking of anything. I got into the ring and just held out my hands, and then I raised one hand toward Duran. That's not like me. I was like an android—I was just there, just senseless, no sense of who I am, just there . . .

"I got caught up in it all, the hype. It's like a spider's web. You fiddle around a little too much and all of a sudden you catch one of those sticky spots and then you become stationary."

Mike Trainer, the Maryland attorney whose shrewd negotiating had made Leonard a uniquely independent millionaire, made certain that his incorporated fighter would be free to concentrate solely on the act of fighting Duran in the rematch.

"Ray was intimidated by all the hoopla surrounding the first fight," Trainer said candidly. "He was in with the Tasmanian devil. He didn't know if Duran would breathe fire, if there'd be rockets on his shoes, if he'd hit Ray from thirty-two different places. The Montreal fight got such hype that for a couple of rounds, I believe Ray became an observer, sort of saying, 'Hey, this is really something. I wonder what's going to happen next?' "

But it was also the mind-boggling conception of earning $10 million for a single fight that made Leonard feel obligated in helping promote "Le Face-à-Face Historique" with Duran.

"I feel much better about the rematch, because Ray isn't doing it just for the money," said Trainer, who had assured Leonard another $7 million despite the fact that Duran now owned the title. "In the past, you might have wondered if the lure of the money wasn't more than the incentive of boxing itself.

"But Ray feels he has to prove himself. He has to show it wasn't the *real* Ray Leonard in Montreal. If he had waited too long to challenge Duran again, everybody would say he beat an old man, and it's very important for Ray to beat Duran at his peak. Some people wanted Ray to fight somebody else first. But Ray would never be satisfied to duck Duran. So after Montreal, I waited until Ray came to me and said, 'I want Duran again.' Then, I said, 'We'll see what we can do.' "

Both Leonard and Trainer learned valuable lessons from the defeat in Montreal. Leonard would be as cooperative as ever at the daily press conferences in New Orleans, but he kept his extracurricular activities to a minimum.

As Trainer told Ken Denlinger of *The Washington Post*, "To generate the money I thought Ray was entitled to the first time around, Ray became active in the promotion from a percentage standpoint. This time, when we sat down to negotiate, I had an idea what the fight would bring. So I cut out a significant chunk for Ray and said, 'Okay, you guys run with the rest. Divide it up any way you want, but this is what Ray's worth! It made it kind of nice. I stopped getting calls at one in the morning from people around the country saying, 'Hey, we can't get this or that theater for closed-circuit TV. What do I do now?' Or promotion men asking Ray to appear here, there, and everywhere.

"It's a lot quieter now. There's not as much anxiety. We made it clear Ray wouldn't be given responsibility to carry the promotional ball. Just because he's agreeable to the media is no reason to take advantage of him and say, 'The other guy's a jerk, so let's throw everything Ray's way.' For the first time, Ray had taken a more relaxed role."

In the gym, however, Leonard was more dedicated than ever. He established a businesslike attitude the day he opened training for the rematch in a Sheraton Hotel ballroom in New Carrollton, Maryland, just a short ride around the Capital Beltway from his new $850,000 home in Mitchellville, Maryland. He turned up wearing a blue stocking hat, making him look more like a factory worker carrying his lunch pail than a boxing aristocrat beginning another multimillion dollar challenge.

The first real evidence of a change in Leonard's approach to the fight was in the size, shape, and spirit of his sparring partners. For the first clash with Duran, Sugar Ray mistakenly massaged his ego daily by butchering a novice boxer who, after several days, began to resemble one of those pop-up clowns belabored by hyperactive children.

When even Leonard grew weary of assaulting the amateur, he would spar with his brother, Roger, a junior middleweight, or his cousin, O'Dell, another middleweight. But in boxing with his blood relatives, Sugar Ray appeared to be preparing more for a dance marathon than a welterweight world title match.

This time, however, Leonard would employ sparring partners mean in spirit and more suited to impersonate Duran's relentless "no-holds-barred" style of brawling. Chief among the impersonators was Dale Staley, alias "The American Assassin," a free-spirited, undisciplined middleweight, who, in his spotty professional career, had been disqualified several times for gouging and biting his opponent and otherwise thumbing his nose and gloves at the rules of ring etiquette.

"I'll do just about anything in the ring," boasted the unreformed Staley after a particularly rough sparring session. "I was really dirty, but Leonard is learning fast."

Very fast. One day, when Staley seemed to be taking his impersonation of the bullying Duran a bit too far while assaulting Leonard on the ropes with everything but a lead pipe, Sugar Ray suddenly spun away and, in judo fashion, lifted Staley by the crotch and tossed him to the canvas with a resounding thud. Such uncharacteristic roughhousing seemed foolhardy with the multimillion dollar rematch only a few days off. But it was Leonard's symbolic message to the fiery Panamanian that it would be "an eye for an eye" the second time around.

"The last time Duran mistook my decency for a sign of weakness," Leonard explained. "This time, I'll give back whatever I receive. I can be rough if I have to. I was always able to defend myself in street fights as a kid. I can change, but Duran can't. I want to make him look bad. I want to drive him crazy."

Angelo Dundee, who still carried the title of "manager" in Leonard's inner circle of advisors, but actually served as his principal trainer and cornerman, had been busy for months orchestrating the "game plan" for the rematch. But Dundee is also an acknowledged master of psychological warfare. He made everyone involved with "Leonard-

Duran II" cognizant of Duran's penchant for fighting by his own rules.

"Duran is the Svengali of boxing," Dundee advised everyone within earshot. "He's got everybody hoodwinked. He's got that same mystique as Sonny Liston, who scared everybody to death just by scowling. But the truth is that Duran is just a dirty fighter, and I want to make everyone aware of it. He looks like he's throwing a lot of punches, but it's a mirage. He gets the most out of the least.

"Check the films of the first fight with Ray," Dundee continued. "Duran looked real busy, but Ray landed all the clean shots and combinations. Duran is a very 'heady' fighter. That's because his head is his best weapon," laughed the trainer, enjoying his own brand of humor. "I've told the Louisiana officials to give Duran a third glove. One for each hand, and one for his head. He also makes good use of his shoulders and knees if the referee's not looking. But this time, if Duran wants to play games, we'll play games, too."

Dundee, based in Miami Beach where he serves as a booking agent and trainer for countless fighters who remember his long and profitable association with Muhammad Ali, had been called earlier than usual to oversee Leonard's training regimen. He was being asked to fill the void left by the controversial departure of Dave Jacobs, who had been in Sugar Ray's corner for ten years and 178 amateur and pro bouts.

Jacobs and Leonard had been inseparable from the day a scrawny, fourteen-year-old kid first walked into his gym and struck a comical fighting pose like John L. Sullivan. Jacobs would be the driving force, teacher, and soothsayer for Leonard on his meteoric march to the Olympics and his exhilarating climb through the professional ranks, capped by his first winning the welterweight crown from wily Wilfredo Benitez in the winter of 1979.

But from the day Leonard turned pro, the relationship began to suffer. Trophies, medals, and glory were no longer enough for a gifted, charismatic fighter who could demand and receive a staggering $40,000 purse for his pro baptism in a six-round fight.

There was now a need for a lawyer, manager, assistant trainer, personal public relations man, sparring partners, and countless "go-fors." The entourage seemed to grow proportionately with the size of Sugar Ray's purses, and with each new battle, Jacobs's soothing but persuasive voice grew softer and softer.

After Leonard earned his first million by whipping Benitez to win the WBC 147-pound title, Jacobs, who had heretofore been employed on a straight salary basis, asked to be paid the customary ten percent accorded to a full-time trainer. At first, he was rejected by Trainer, who guards the purse strings, but Leonard eventually interceded to maintain peace in his "second family."

Jacobs was back in Leonard's corner for the first Duran fight. Following the frustrated defeat, he strongly argued against an immediate rematch, suggesting Sugar Ray accept an easier challenge in order to regain his strength and confidence. But the advice went unheeded. Trainer was already drawing extensive plans for the lucrative return bout.

"I had to step down to say what I had to," Jacobs said, drained by the emotional impact of his decision. "It got to the point where I never knew what was going on unless I read the papers. It hurt me not to have a say after all those years we'd spent together.

"For over ten years, I made all the decisions for the boy. Now I found I was just along for the ride. They weren't around during the hard times when he was just learning to fight. They came along to enjoy the fruits, but they didn't make him. They just took the credit."

Jacobs insisted, however, that money was no longer an

issue in the separation. After the first falling out, he had reportedly settled for a guarantee estimated at $25,000 a fight.

"I never regarded Ray as my meal ticket," he said. "Actually, I was reluctant about continuing to train him as a pro, but if I didn't take the job, I would have spent the rest of my life worrying about him and second-guessing myself.

"I still regard Ray as the greatest fighter around today," Jacobs said, "but even a horse trainer with a super thoroughbred doesn't put him in a tough race every time out. Putting Ray right back in with Duran is a mistake. The last fight took a lot out of him, mentally and physically. If he were to lose to Duran again, it could destroy him."

There was, of course, another side to the story.

"Ray treated Jacobs well, probably better financially than any fight trainer in the country," said Mike Trainer, obviously distraught over the furor Jacobs's "resignation" had created in the hometown papers. "But life goes on. The thing to remember was that from the day Ray turned pro, Jacobs was never involved in the decision-making process outside of the realm of training Ray. But after Ray won the title, Jacobs wanted to change all that.

"People on the outside don't realize how smoothly things have operated for Ray. It's really not all that important at this stage in his career who gets his robes, gloves, and shoes ready. He's got to make the big decisions. The key to winning and losing is Ray himself.

"Losing to Duran was a growing experience for all of us," the attorney added. "I wasn't devastated by it. Duran defeated Jacobs, but he hasn't convinced Ray Leonard, and that's the whole bottom line on Jacobs. Duran took Jacobs's heart, not Ray's, and so what Jacobs did [resigning] was in the best interest of everybody. I just wish he would have ascribed the right reasons for it."

A short time after Jacobs's departure, Leonard was asked

if he would take his longtime trainer back in the fold should he have a change of heart. "No, he won't be back this time," the fighter said matter-of-factly. "I wouldn't want to destroy Jake's pride. It was pride that made him quit in the first place. He didn't want to have anything to do with the Duran rematch, and when he decided to quit, he didn't consult me first. It's over."

Janks Morton, his closest friend, would replace Jacobs in the corner and oversee the training program until Dundee was called to provide the finishing touches.

"People say, 'Janks can't train Ray,' and I say, 'Why not?' " said Leonard. "Janks has picked things up quickly. He knows the fundamentals. When I'm in the ring, I can't see my mistakes. I need somebody to correct them.

"Yeah, I'm sorry to see Jacobs go, but you can't stop going forward because one guy quits. It's like a toll bridge. If one guy quits, it doesn't mean the bridge shuts down completely. With Jake gone, it's just one less check."

It sounded unusually cold-blooded coming from Leonard, who had been portrayed in the media as possessing all the wholesome, endearing qualities of "the boy next door." But this time, he would not look back. Pride was his spur, and Jacobs's published remarks that he was not ready to again challenge the Panamanian bully boy only prodded Sugar Ray to work harder to prove his old trainer wrong.

Leonard did not have to work up a hatred for Duran. The sparks that flew between the two fighters whenever they came within sight of each other was not the usual transparent hype of developing a "grudge match" to increase ticket sales. No, this was a genuine dislike and was of nerves that had been raging between the two camps since Leonard and Duran first came face-to-face in the spring of 1980.

Several days before the rematch, a man asked Sugar Ray if he thought there might ever be a time he would consider Duran a friend. Leonard laughed loudly at the suggestion and said, "No, I don't think so. I doubt if we'll ever see each other socially. Even when we're broken, old men confined to wheelchairs, we'll probably be snarling and trying to hit each other."

"Why must you hate each other?" another reporter asked. "Aren't you brothers in mankind? If this man were your neighbor, I'm certain you would get along with him."

"If Duran was my neighbor, I'd move," cracked Leonard.

A strange love-hate relationship exists between fighters that has puzzled amateur psychologists throughout boxing's long and boisterous history. How, they ask, can two men who have tried to knock the other senseless for ten to fifteen rounds suddenly embrace in mutual respect after the final bell? Even the intense racial chasm that existed between Joe ("God Is on my Side") Louis and Max Schmeling, a living symbol of Hitler's Arian supremacy, was replaced by a deep affection after the two former heavyweight champions had retired from combat.

But the bristling hostility between Duran and Leonard was genuine, and they made a point of expressing their antagonism in public.

"I don't like anything about the man," Leonard said one day. "I dislike Duran for the way he is, and the way he carries himself. He's so macho, he has to be a bully. He never gives ground. He wants to prove he's the toughest man in the world. He tries to intimidate everyone, even the public. He insults people he doesn't even know, giving people in the street the finger, all because he believes what he is and can't respect himself. He wants to raise his hand and have you kneel down to him. I don't like him at all. He's a nerd."

Mike Trainer was even more harsh in his character evaluation of Duran.

"All the Duran mystique is so much bull," the attorney said. "I've never seen journalists go for something like that.

They're making a romantic figure out of the guy. If they ran into him in a bar, they'd throw up."

"But Duran is kind of unique," a *Los Angeles Times* reporter argued.

"There's nothing unique about him," Trainer replied brusquely. "Go into the South Bronx and you'll find hundreds of guys like Duran hanging around the street corners."

Promoter Don King, who had long championed Duran's cause, tried to maintain a posture of neutrality while insisting that the difference between Sugar Ray and Roberto was simply a matter of semantics.

"Here's what I mean," said King. "If Ray stole something and got caught, he'd be called a kleptomaniac. If Duran got caught stealing the same thing, he'd be called a thief. It's a matter of culture. Sugar Ray has what you call sophisticated insanity."

But Joe Frazier, the former heavyweight champion, was less subtle. After watching Duran strip Leonard of the title in Montreal, someone asked Frazier if he could compare the fiery Panamanian with any ring greats of the past. "No," said Frazier, "he reminds me of Charles Manson."

Even the fighter's wife became passionately involved in the extracurricular infighting. "Duran has no class," said Juanita Leonard. "I don't like the man at all. He's a great fighter, but he has no respect for anyone."

Respect. That most delicate part of a fighter's psyche. It can mean more to a proud fighter than untold wealth and the fawning affection of the public. Prick Duran's immense pride and you are inviting an invitation to living hell inside a ring or in an alleyway.

Duran's snarling distaste for Leonard stemmed from the day they met in New York's Waldorf Astoria in the spring of 1980 to announce their first battle, and Sugar Ray shook a fist under his nose and vowed, "I'll kill you."

"That was a terrible mistake," said Ray Arcel, Roberto's ageless guru. "Nobody, I mean nobody, ever treated Roberto so disrespectfully. Roberto is the killer, the assassin in the ring. Leonard? He's just a nice fighter who got rich too soon.

"You must remember," Arcel continued, "that Roberto has been fighting for himself all his life. He was literally raised in the streets of Panama City. His father deserted him, and his mother couldn't raise him. There are thousands of street urchins in Latin America like Roberto, and he was one of them. He learned to become a man in a hurry. But you have to live with a fighter to really understand him. Roberto is like a Jekyll and Hyde character. Inside the ring, he's as tough as they come. Outside, he's like a pussycat, a warm, beautiful human being."

Pride and the man. The tough guy image was so ingrained in the folklore surrounding Duran that any outward show of kindness was viewed as a sign of human frailty.

"Let me tell you a story," said Carlos Eleta, Duran's guardian angel and surrogate father. "Not long ago, I invited Roberto to my house to meet my young nephew. I wanted to take a funny picture of Roberto stretched out on the floor with my nephew standing over him. Well, Roberto thought about it for a few seconds and then said, 'No, no, I can't.' He is so proud."

Pride. Intense pride burning in his coal-black eyes. "Every fighter has that rage deep down inside," said Don Morgan, Duran's principal sparring partner, "but Roberto just expresses it more. It's the anguish built up from his days in the ghetto. He always wanted the better things in life, and now that he has them, he doesn't want to give them up."

But, Eleta insists, there is a soft underbelly to Duran's sinister exterior. "Roberto's heart is immense," Eleta said. "When we were leaving Panama to fly to New Orleans, he saw an old lady crying at the airport. She had lost her money and couldn't buy a ticket to visit her family in

Colombia. Roberto embraced her and gave her more money than she needed. That's so typical of his concern for people. One day he told me, 'I'd like to be like Robin Hood, helping all the poor people in Panama.' In many ways, he's like a child. Too soft."

The men closest to Duran claimed his reputation as an incorrigible guttersnipe was the direct result of his failure to communicate with the American press in English.

"Most of your reporters are white, middle-class, and well-educated," Henriquez, the interpreter, said. "He wouldn't be able to match wits with them speaking English, and Roberto doesn't like to lose at anything. He is always ready to challenge you."

Asked through Henriquez why he treated Leonard with such disdain, Duran said, "He wants to be an imitator. He wants to be another Muhammad Ali, and I don't like people who are not genuine. He is too much of a clown in the ring. Leonard is trying to make the American public believe he is the all-American boy. But he is no angel. He is a devil like the rest of us."

Jealousy was the main stimulus to the bad blood that ran between the two fighters. As Mike Trainer told a *Washington Post* reporter, "A lot of people would like to see Ray lose to Duran again. People are naturally jealous of third generation money and first generation talent. We all love to see the spoiled grandson squander the family fortune. We say, 'He couldn't invest in treasury bills.' So people looked at Ray getting so much so fast and said, 'Let him experience life like the rest of us.' That may not be fair, but that's the way it is."

Several weeks before the fight, Leonard and Duran reached a brief detente during the filming of a lucrative 7-UP commercial that included their sons, Ray, Jr., and Robertito. Before joining Duran at the studio, Leonard cautioned the producer that he would walk out the second his rival started acting the fool. As it developed, there were no harsh words, threats, or gestures, and, amusingly, when Leonard accidentally tripped over a rope, Duran was there to quickly help him back to his feet.

Asked about this uncharacteristic act of kindness, Duran mumbled, "It meant nothing. I still hate him."

"Does Duran truly hate Leonard?" a man asked Eleta.

"No, I don't think so," Eleta replied. "Roberto dislikes anyone who is a threat to him, and that means anyone he might be fighting. When the fighting ends, the hatred ends, too."

The tension and strategy sessions grew more intense as the rematch drew closer. One day, Leonard closed his workout to the media. It was more than a psychological ploy.

"When Ray works in public," Trainer explained, "he always wants to put on a show and win every round. But the workouts are strictly a learning experience. This time, Ray really got down to work. Both Janks and Angelo got in the ring with him and made him work on specific moves, like spinning off the ropes and nullifying the way Duran uses his head as a weapon.

"They made Ray do the same thing over and over again until they thought he had it right. It was just like a Hollywood producer trying to film the perfect scene. It was so quiet in the place, it reminded me of a classroom. The whole thing was fascinating to watch for a boxing novice like myself."

Leonard had learned his lessons well. The painful experience of Montreal had taught him the foolhardiness of retreating to the ropes whenever Duran mounted a charge.

"The way to avoid a truck isn't to keep going backwards," he told Tom Boswell of *The Washington Post*. "That way, the truck just builds up momentum. I've got to move side to side, not in and out. That way I can change Duran's rhythm and distract him."

Ray Arcel laughed sardonically when Leonard's change in strategy reached his ears.

"You can fool the world, but you can't fool yourself," said the eighty-one-year-old professor of boxing emeritus. "When great fighters meet, the outcome is always decided between the fighters' ears before the bell even sounds.

"Against Duran in Montreal, Leonard was like a boy against a man. Only he, himself, knows how badly he was beaten. That's the real key. How did this loss affect Leonard? How much mental damage did it do? After all, it's been less than six months since the last fight, and here they're at each other's throats again. This time, Leonard will walk into the ring knowing he can't win. I think he'll wilt just like my old fighters used to do against Joe Louis.

"In a way, it's a shame," Arcel said solicitously. "I'm really a great admirer of Leonard as a boxer, but I believe all those big purses retarded his progress. He had the makings of greatness when he left the amateurs, but he won the title too soon. Now everyone was waving millions at him. That's fine, if you think the only bottom line for a fighter is how much money he's making. But, at the same time, they stopped his natural development.

"That's why I say it doesn't matter how he changes his style. Duran can cope with any situation. It will be exactly the same as the first fight. Duran will not allow it to be otherwise. Only this time, Duran will make Leonard retire for good, and boxing will have lost a great talent."

The weigh-in ceremony in the ballroom of the plush Hyatt Regency the morning of the fight resembled a scene from *West Side Story*, the Sharks and Jets reassembled for a final showdown.

Duran arrived first, wearing a leather jacket that might have been discarded by one of the Hell's Angels and faded Wrangler jeans. He quickly stripped down to blue shorts and mounted the scale. A man from the Louisiana Athletic Commission shouted "One forty-six," and members of the champion's entourage applauded like "Weightwatchers" saluting a reformed fat man.

Duran smiled and immediately began gulping down a thermos of beef consommé, topped off by two king-sized oranges.

"He's overweight," Angelo Dundee whispered to a confidant. "Didja watch how quickly he gulped that stuff down? The man's been starving himself to make weight. He's trained down too fine. I'll have Ray go to his body right away."

Duran and his legion of admirers exited from one door just as Sugar Ray entered from another, bedecked in a tailored tan leather jacket and expensive designer jeans. He seemed totally relaxed as he stepped on the scale and the man again shouted, "One forty-six."

"This time, I'm going in with a full tank of gas," he said. "The last time I was only three-quarters full."

In the final countdown to fight time, Duran would overfill his "tank." After subjecting his body to an agonizing diet to make the welterweight (147) limit, he was now trying to overcompensate by ravenously devouring two steak dinners in the next five hours, tearing at the food with the same impatience of his pet lion. The cramps would follow or so he said. In retrospect, his personal physician, Dr. Orlando Nunez, said, "Roberto wasn't beaten by Sugar Ray Leonard. He was beaten by two sirloin steaks."

It was eight P.M., New Orleans time. The fighters and their respective clans were now gathered in their dressing rooms, joking and making idle chatter to kill the tension in the air.

Leonard, who, since his Olympic gold medal days had favored a red, white, and blue ensemble from his trunks down to his tasseled sneakers, was now surprisingly dressed in stark black with gold trimming. His low-cut sneakers looked as if they had been salvaged from a trash heap. He bore the look of an old-time fight. No show biz.

Strictly business. Sugar the Sweet had become Ivan the Terrible.

As he headed for the door, Mike Trainer remarked, "You look like a cross between the Grim Reaper and an assassin."

"Good," said Leonard.

He made his long walk to the Superdome ring to the lilting disco beat of his personal theme song, "Hey, hey, Sugar Ray." Duran, in turn, was accompanied by an incessant salsa rhythm. The fighters and the crowd then stood for the playing of the upbeat Panamanian anthem that seemingly took longer than the entire preliminary card.

If you believe in omens, the first signs pointed Sugar Ray's way when Ray Charles, the beloved blues singer for whom he was named, stepped to the microphone and gave a moving, soulful rendition of "America the Beautiful" that was greeted by a standing ovation from the pro-American crowd. All the tension was gone now, and Leonard's face lit up like a Christmas tree as he embraced Ray Charles before the opening bell.

From the first minute, Leonard firmly established the pace, darting and moving from side to side as promised, pausing just long enough to catch Duran with his rediscovered jab. By round two, it was evident that Roberto's bullying tactics were no longer effective.

Sly smiles passed between the two fighters in round three, but Duran was already making signs of frustration. It only heightened when, one time, Leonard nimbly sidestepped one of his mad charges and the Panamanian embarrassingly fell through the ropes.

"That's beautiful, kid, just beautiful," shouted Dundee. "Make him miss and tag him!"

Meanwhile, across the ring, Arcel was admonishing the champion, "Keep him on the ropes. Be the boss!"

In the fifth round, Duran began to resemble his old, belligerent self. He pushed and bullied Leonard against the ropes, one time brazenly shoving Sugar Ray on the seat of his pants. The familiar look of arrogance was returning and, after the round ended, Dundee chastised his man, "Don't give away any rounds."

Leonard was back on his toes in the sixth round, countering and jabbing, but Duran was persistent as ever in his pursuit, showing no signs of the discomfit he would complain about later.

Round seven: Leonard would now keep his prefight pledge to "drive Duran crazy." Bug-eyed like an old baggy-panted vaudevillian, Sugar Ray would unleash his Ali pantomine complete with the "Ali Shuffle" fake bolo, strut-away, and jutting jaw. The "Macho Man" was reduced to the "pie in the face" foil. When Sugar Ray's sideshow ended to wild applause, Duran answered with a derisive wave of his glove.

Less than three minutes later, he would give a farewell wave. He would fight his way or not at all. He would surrender his title rather than be a laughingstock.

Surprisingly, there was no malice in Duran's face when Leonard would later warmly embrace him in his corner. The fury was gone. Shortly thereafter, Duran would try to explain his actions to hundreds of puzzled reporters. He talked about the cramps, and said he was through fighting. Period.

He then climbed into a waiting van that would carry him back to the hotel and later to the hospital. He peered out the front window and spotted Leonard on his way to the interview room. Leonard waved and Duran, with an embarrassed smile, gave a wave in return. Total surrender.

The morning after, everyone was still trying to put the pieces together. No one seemed ready to accept Duran's excuse of a bellyache.

"The word 'quit' bothers me," said Dundee, on behalf of the fallen champion. "You shouldn't use that word with a great fighter like Roberto Duran. In Europe, they use a different word: 'retire.' "

Again, just a matter of semantics. The "Macho Man" had fallen from grace. No more "Stone Hands." Just another ex-champion. In one implausible night, his aura of invincibility had vanished. A ring legend had died. But another was about to begin.

★ 2 ★

FROM CHOIRBOY TO "KILLER"

> "Drummers and boxers, to acquire excellence, must begin young. There is a peculiar nimbleness of the wrist and exercise of the shoulder required that is only obtained from growth pattern."
> —Pierce Egan, *Boxiana*, 1812

It was one of Sugar Ray Leonard's frequent public appearances in the whirlwind weeks following his triumph in the 1976 Olympics. This day, he was speaking at Dodge Park Elementary School in Washington's inner-city ghetto. Sugar Ray was clearly one who had escaped the squalor, a shining example for the adolescents gathered in the assembly room.

Sugar Ray could remember quite vividly when the roles were reversed. But now he was a confident young man, riding the crest of public adulation.

A huge sign on the stage said, "WELCOME, SUGAR RAY LEONARD" and the school principal presented him with a cake decorated with chocolate figurines in boxing shorts and gloves. The champ was home.

"Nothing comes easy in life," he told the students. "Make yourself someone. Whatever path you take, make sure it's the right one. Don't try to be like someone else. Be yourself, but be the best you can be. Be somebody in life."

His inspirational message over, Leonard then answered the perfunctory questions about how it felt to win a gold medal, what it was like to be interviewed by Howard Cosell, and did he plan on becoming a millionaire?

Finally, a little girl in pigtails, seated in the rear of the hall, raised her hand tentatively.

"Yes?" said Leonard.

"How old were you when you were born?" she asked.

"I was about ten," said Leonard, flashing that boyish grin that had captivated both kids and adults across the country.

Yes, it seems quite possible that Sugar Ray Leonard had a sizable jump on the rest of us mere mortals. How else to explain his meteoric march through the professional ranks that made him a certified millionaire by the age of twenty-one and the owner of a world title.

But, indeed, there was a beginning—a rather humble one for Ray Charles Leonard in Wilmington, North Carolina, on May 17, 1956, as the fifth of seven children born to Getha and Cicero Leonard. He was christened Ray Charles, for his mother had ambitions of her number four son one day emulating the famous blues singer.

But fighting bloodlines run deep in the Leonard clan. First, there was grandpa Bidge, a giant of a man (six-foot-four and 240 pounds) with a Bunyanesque reputation for brute strength. He reputedly brought a reluctant mule to its knees with a single punch.

Bidge, a South Carolina sharecropper, fathered a dozen children, one of them Cicero, who grew to more modest proportions. But Cicero was a born fighter. Back in the Thirties, while young Cicero pushed his father's mule, Belle, through the fields of peanuts, okra, sweet potatoes, and tobacco, he dreamed of becoming another Joe Louis, who had come from a similar hard scrabble background to become the heavyweight champion of the world.

On nights when Louis defended his title, the entire Leonard clan would gather around the radio, and between the static, Cicero, in pantomine, would mock each move and mannerism of "The Brown Bomber."

On weekends, the fights were real. Saturday nights, the farm work done, young Cicero would string his boxing gloves over his shoulder and head for Clyde Davis's near-by farm, where there was always some rawboned kid to challenge him.

Sundays, the action would swing back to the Leonards' front yard, where Cicero had improvised a boxing ring out of iron spikes and plowlines, with a sturdy oak serving as a ballast. And here, Cicero, a muscular five-foot and 150 pounds whose lust for fighting belied his otherwise gentle disposition, would take on three or four rivals in an hour's time, regardless of size. But he would always walk away the winner.

An understanding mother would fondle the bruises and wash away the blood before packing the entire family off to the Sunday meeting at the Pleasant Grove Baptist Church in Mullins, South Carolina.

By the time he was twelve, however, Cicero had quit school to work as a ribbon binder. These were Depression days, leaving little time for a boy to dream of better things.

"We were making out all right," Cicero remembered, "but we did all our farming the old way. We didn't own a tractor or anything like that. And I just got sick and tired of walking behind that damn mule."

Cicero first left the farm in 1942 to join the Navy, spending most of his service hitch landside while campaigning as a first-rank amateur boxer in military competition.

"I was a middleweight, and a pretty good one," he said, without false modesty. "I had close to seventy fights in the service and lost only one—to a guy named 'Little Red' from Philadelphia."

But any intention he had of turning professional after his discharge ended when he married Getha and soon had a family to support. He left the farm behind and took a job as an assembly worker in a Coca-Cola plant in Wilmington.

"Ray was too young to remember anything about Wilmington, except what we've told him," said Cicero, a stocky man with soft puppy eyes. "He's strictly a Washingtonian."

Ray Charles was four when Cicero packed his family into his '57 Mercury and headed north for the nation's capital. They would first crowd into an apartment on "L" Street in the District. But by 1967, the family numbered four boys—Roy, Kenny, Roger, and Ray—and three girls—Linda, Sandy, and Sharon. Cicero decided his family needed more breathing room and relocated in Seat Pleasant, a Maryland suburb east of Washington. A year later, they would finally settle in Palmer Park, a lower-middle-class, predominantly black enclave just minutes from the Capital Beltway.

With Cicero working as a night manager at a supermarket and Getha working days as a nurse, they earned enough to foot the mortgage for a modest single-story home some thirty minutes from the Washington Monument.

Palmer Park is light years removed from the fancy homes of the nouveaux riches in the affluent bedroom communities surrounding the Capital. But it is also a far cry from the rat-infested slums of the inner city.

Yet again, the verdant suburban setting belied a mounting crime rate, particularly in the nearby Landover Shopping Center, the neighborhood hub where trafficking in drugs became as lively a business as the selling of the customary department store wares.

"There were a lot of temptations out there for a teenager—drugs, petty crime, prostitutes," Leonard would say, "but I was just lucky to keep clear of all that."

As Ollie Dunlap, who was instrumental in the building of the area recreation center, told Bill Nack of *Sports Illustrated*: "Palmer Park is not a ghetto, but on a scale of one to ten, it's a two. When we built the rec center, we were trying to bring self-pride to the community. It was a dog-eat-dog atmosphere. It was just after the 1968 riots, and there was still hostility in the air."

It was more than self-discipline that kept Leonard from becoming a delinquent. He had a guardian angel in his brother, Roger, three years his senior.

"I was always getting him out of scrapes when he was young," recalls Roger, now a promising junior middleweight. "Older guys were always trying to pick on him in school, but if they messed with Ray, they knew they'd have to tangle with me, too."

Even away from the schoolgrounds, Ray relied on Roger to watch over him. "One time," Roger said, "we had a terrible flood when we were still living in Seat Pleasant. We were playing down by the creek when the water just came gushing down. Ray grabbed on to a branch, and I just managed to pull him ashore."

Because of his natural shyness, Ray spent most of his after-school hours around the house reading and re-reading comic books. "He was real quiet," his sister, Sandy, said. "Ray wouldn't say anything to anyone unless they asked him a specific question. He'd just sit and look at you and smile."

Remembering his early adolescence, Ray said, "My brothers and friends were always after me to try something—gymnastics, basketball, roller-skating—you name it. But I was a loner back then and never really had my heart in anything.

"Oh, I wrestled for awhile in school and I ran cross-country in junior high school. That was the only time pain made me stop competing. I pulled a thigh muscle, and that pain went through me like a dagger. I just quit the team after that."

His lack of initiative and motivation soon became a concern to his parents.

"Ray was a funny sort of kid," his father reflected. "He never gave us a bit of trouble in or out of school. He was always kind of hanging back. It used to worry me some. All my other three sons, and even my three daughters, were always getting into some sort of mischief or athletic activity. But Ray didn't like doing anything physical."

To which Getha, Ray's mother, added, "Ray was singing in the church choir until he was fourteen. He had a real pure voice, and I figured singing was something he'd be doing for the rest of his life, just like Ray Charles."

But first puberty and then brother Roger ended Ray's singing career. Goaded by Roger, who had already collected several amateur trophies for boxing, Ray would follow his brother to the gym. No doubt, Hollywood would have this shy, introspective youngster undergo a lightning metamorphosis into a fighting machine the first time he donned a pair of boxing gloves. But Leonard had as much love for fighting as a sworn pacifist.

"I remember when I was seven or eight, I tagged after Roger when he was taking boxing lessons at the Police Boys Club in Washington. Everytime he got hit, it made me sick. I couldn't stand to watch it."

Even six years later, Ray shrank from the prospect of having his nose bloodied by another kid. Fighting in the streets was a matter of survival, but fighting in a gym without provocation seemed utterly senseless.

"It wasn't only a matter of courage," he said. "It was more a matter of confidence, and feeling like I was somebody. I was always wearing my older brothers' hand-me-down clothes and never had any spending money of my own. We were never real poor. But we just never had that extra dollar to waste on foolish things."

When his classmates took field trips to the city museums, Sugar Ray would excuse himself. "It might have meant spending as little as a dollar to make the trip, but we needed it to pay the bills at home. That's why I spent so much time hanging around the house."

But there is no stronger influence on a teen-ager than peer pressure, and it took only gentle prodding by Ray's closest friend, Derrik Holmes, to persuade him to return to the gym and overcome the repulsion he had felt initially.

"Ray and I were best friends," said Holmes, now a contender in the featherweight division. We went to the same school (Parkdale High), came from the same neighborhood, and hung out together all the time.

"But when I heard they were starting a boxing team at Palmer Park, I decided to join, and I'd head for the gym right after school. That kind of put Ray on the spot. He could either join me at the gym or head home by himself. He decided to stick with me, and, I guess, that started it all."

Ray Leonard could see the Palmer Park Recreation Center from the front lawn of his house on Barlowe Road. Years later, flushed with his Olympic success, he gazed down at the rambling building and said, "One day, I'll be rich and famous and they'll rename it the 'Sugar Ray Leonard Recreation Center.' " And, indeed, they would.

In retrospect, the community center seemed an unlikely place to launch the boxing career of a fourteen-year-old youngster, who, within two short years, would be hailed by AAU Boxing Chairman Rollie Schwartz as "the greatest amateur fighter of all time."

In fact, when the facility was first opened in 1970, not a single penny was alloted to furnish equipment for a "brutal sport" like boxing. And that situation would persist for five years until Ollie Dunlap, the recreation director, and Dave (Jake) Jacobs, then an unpaid volunteer, begged and borrowed to launch a boxing program for the neighborhood kids.

"We started up with basketball and things like that," said Mary Wells, a Maryland Park and Planning Commission official, "and then the kids told us they wanted boxing.

Well, we started experimenting without any proper equipment, and then this ex-boxer volunteered to coach the kids, and it just took off from there."

The "ex-boxer," of course, was Dave Jacobs. He had won the District AAU featherweight title in 1949, and developed into a highly promising middleweight as a professional until family pressure forced him to quit fighting and accept a "regular" job as a delivery man for a pharmacy in Annandale, Virginia.

After moving to Palmer Park in 1970, Jacobs began spending so much time as a volunteer in the recreation center that it soon became a full-time vocation.

"The early Seventies were hardly the best time to be starting a boxing program," said Jacobs, now forty-seven. "A lot of people felt boxing was as good as dead and parents were afraid their kids would get hurt fighting.

"But when we first started, it was never with the idea of producing future Olympians. The main thing on our mind was getting the kids off the street and out of trouble. If a young man has boxing on his mind, he usually doesn't have time to steal cars."

Interesting the kids in fighting was the easy part. The hard part was finding money to finance the ring program, a job that fell squarely on the shoulders of Dunlap and Jacobs.

"If it's fund-raising you're talking about, you name it, I've tried it," said Dunlap, who had a brief fling with the Washington Redskins as a member of their "taxi squad." "But the people of Palmer Park, particularly the businessmen, have always been good to us. I've always been able to raise money when I needed it."

When the boxing budget grew tight, Jacobs's effusive wife, Memphis, would spring into action.

"Sometimes," she said, "I felt like I was cooking for an army. My stove was going nonstop from Wednesday through Friday. We'd buy a gross of hamhocks, thirty pounds of collard greens, and cases of chicken and ribs.

When that was done, we'd start baking cakes, cookies, just about anything we could sell on the weekends so that the boxers would have money for equipment and to make trips to tournaments."

Still, Jacobs and his ring protégés got by with the bare essentials. "We never had a real boxing gym at Palmer Park," he said, "but somehow we kept producing champions. In the first place, they only gave us half the gym for boxing. The other half was used for basketball. And when it was time for the basketball tourney, we couldn't box at all."

When the Palmer Park fighters started bringing home trophies from around the state, the gym policy changed. Each day, from one P.M. to five P.M. was reserved for boxing exclusively. But it was still more pantomime and shadowboxing than actual combat.

Jacobs fashioned a makeshift ring by taping boundary lines on the basketball court. "That's why the first thing I taught the boys was balance," he said. "If they had good balance, they didn't have to worry about getting knocked down and banging their heads on the hardwood floor. That was our 'ring' the whole time Sugar Ray trained there. That, plus two heavy bags and the speed bags we bought when the Park Commission gave us a forty-five dollar budget for boxing. I found an old dresser mirror in a junkyard, and that's what the kids used for their shadowboxing.

"We took the few things they gave us and turned it into pure gold," said the moon-faced Jacobs. "That's why I don't accept excuses. When someone says to me, 'We want to start a community project but we don't have any money,' I tell them, 'Start with what you have and make it do.' If you want to achieve anything in life, first you have to start."

Preaching the virtues of hard work and clean living was as much a part of Jacobs's technique as the tutoring of a stiff left jab and a right thrown straight from the shoulder.

Aphorisms in big block letters cover the gym walls: "DO UNTO OTHERS AS YOU HAVE THEM DO UNTO YOU," "ANY MAN WHO BELIEVES IN GOD IS A WINNER," and "DON'T FORGET THE BRIDGE YOU CROSS. YOU MAY HAVE TO CROSS IT AGAIN."

It was in these Spartan surroundings that Leonard, barely fourteen, had his first acquaintance with boxing in 1971.

"He was painfully bashful and not very coordinated," said Jacobs. "Just a bag of bones, maybe a hundred pounds soaking wet. Derrik Holmes started a week or so earlier, but neither one of them knew the first thing about boxing. We started both of them with the basics.

"I asked Ray to strike a fighting pose, and he carried his hands real high like one of those old pictures you see of John L. Sullivan. He was so shy at the start, he couldn't even look me in the eye. But after a few weeks in the gym, you could see boxing was in his blood. He was what we call a 'natural.'

"The kid just learned everything so quickly. If you showed him a move once, he was doing it like a pro the next day. And you could see he wanted to make something of himself. I'd have the kids do roadwork every morning at five A.M. They'd run around the ballfield right behind Ray's house, but he was always outside waiting for them to show up.

"The kid was really too good to be true," Jacobs added. "I remember after he'd been in the gym only three or four months, I took him aside and told him, 'If you stick with it, you'll be a world champ one day.' I went home that night and told my wife what I'd said to Ray. I figured she'd laugh in my face. But she just looked at me for awhile and finally said, 'You know, Jake, I think you're right.' "

Leonard had a much tougher time convincing his parents of his promising future as a fighter. He accepted the daily bruises and bloody lips as part of his learning process. His mother thought otherwise.

"Ray would come home with a black eye or some other

ugly bruise on his face once or twice a week," she said. "I'd try to keep my composure. I'd say to him, 'Ray, don't you want to quit before you get hurt real bad?' and he'd look at me with that baby face and real sad eyes and say, 'No, Momma, I'm gonna stick with it.' And then I'd go back to my room and cry for my boy."

Ray's father was the last to be convinced that he had a future champion living under his roof. Cicero's skepticism remained until his son came home one night to inform him that he was fighting that weekend in the local amateur tourney and wanted his father to lend his vocal support.

"You're not really fighting, are you?" his father said in astonishment. "Roger, yeah, I can believe that. But not you, Ray Charles."

But Ray pressed the matter, and that Saturday night Cicero Leonard came home shaking his head in wonderment. "Lordy, he was good," the father said. "I couldn't believe my eyes. He gave some boy an awful beating. But it was more than that. You could see right away he had something special. He never had to ask me to watch him again."

For Jacobs, the first real proof that he had a truly gifted fighter on his hands came in the spring of 1971 when Ray, who had since added twenty-five pounds and noticeable muscle to his bony skeleton, was matched against featherweight Bobby Magruder.

"At the time," said Jacobs, "Magruder was not only the best featherweight, but the best amateur in our area, no matter what the weight. But Ray handled him without too much trouble, and now everyone in Palmer Park, clear down to Washington, started talking about this new kid, Ray Leonard."

By the end of his first full year in the gym, Leonard was dominating the regional tournaments and seeking more challenging competition. And he proved he was ready to move up in class by winning the National Golden Gloves

132-pound title in 1972 and later that same year advancing to the quarterfinals of the National AAU Tournament.

Ray was only sixteen—a year short of the required age for the Olympic trials, but Jacobs was ready to test his prodigy against the best amateurs in the country. While preparing for the trials, Leonard would also catch the eye of Sarge Johnson, the assistant coach for the U.S. boxing squad. Watching Ray's dazzling hand and foot speed in a sparring session, Johnson whispered in Jacobs's ear, "That kid of yours is sweeter than sugar." And Leonard would be known as Sugar Ray from that day forward.

"I never worried about anyone comparing him to Ray Robinson," said Jacobs. "It didn't put any added pressure on the kid. He just took to the nickname 'Sugar Ray' naturally."

Nor did the "real Sugar Ray" take umbrage at some promising young fighter borrowing his famous "nom de clout." "It's a good feeling that the kid thinks that much of me," Robinson noted.

Johnson thought enough of the new Sugar Ray to make him a full-fledged member of the American team that would compete against a number of European teams in 1972. At sixteen, Leonard was already embarrassing international fighters five to ten years older, with hundreds of fights behind them.

"The first time I met Leonard in 'Seventy-two," recalled AAU Boxing Chairman Rollie Schwartz, "was in an international meet with the Russians. To fight in international competition, you've got to be seventeen. I looked at the choir boy face of this kid and I had a sneaking suspicion he wasn't quite that old.

"I asked him how old he was, and he said, 'I'm seventeen, sir,' without batting an eye. We let him fight anyway, because, quite simply, he was the best amateur lightweight in the States. He was matched against the Russian champion, who had to be twenty-two or twenty-three, a real seasoned fighter. The opening bell sounded, Ray threw a short left hook, and the Russian fell flat on his face. They didn't even bother to count. That's why, to this day, I laugh whenever someone says, 'Sugar Ray can't punch,' " Schwartz said.

It was during that same visit by the Russians to Las Vegas that Leonard, himself, first had the experience of being knocked off his feet.

"I was fighting this Russian named Valery Lov, and he caught me with my guard down," Ray remembered. "The next thing I knew, I was on the floor and the referee was counting. I looked around ringside and saw Joe Louis and Redd Foxx laughing at me. I was part mad and part embarrassed. I got up real quick, and I stopped Lov in the third round."

Owing to his strong showing against the Russians, the precocious sixteen-year-old was favored to win the 132-pound division in the 1972 Eastern Olympic Trials in Cincinnati. Leonard, however, would lose in the semifinals to Greg Whaley, a hometown boy. It was the most unpopular and disputed decision of the tourney. For Leonard had administered such a severe beating to his opponent that Whaley was not only unable to continue in the Olympic Trials but would never fight again.

"Back then," Ray said, "I was living in a dream world. I was seeing places and famous people I'd only dreamed about. Like one day I'm saying to myself, 'It would be great to go to Las Vegas,' and then I wake up the next morning and I'm right there, mingling with all those stars.

"But that first loss in the Trials was a real 'bummer.' I gave that kid Whaley an awful beating. Even so, I didn't feel that depressed about it until everyone started grabbing me in the street and saying, 'Wow, man, you could have gone to the Olympics.' Maybe I was just too young to put the Olympics and what it meant to be part of it into focus. But I remember Sarge Johnson telling me, 'Don't worry, Ray, you'll be there in 'Seventy-six.' "

Leonard, however, was given a second chance to win a berth on the '72 Olympic team. "You could get in the final 'box-off' for the Olympics," said Jacobs, "if you represented one of the service teams. We worked it out that Ray would be on the Army team and sent him down for the final competition at Texas Christian University.

"But the day before Ray was scheduled to fight," Jacobs added, "he was doing roadwork at the college track and just passed out. It was sheer exhaustion. He was trying to get down too fine. I took him to the team doctor, and he disqualified him from fighting. The next day, though, Ray was feeling great and complaining that they wouldn't let him fight.

"He was really disappointed and, I guess, if I'd have kept my mouth shut and kept him away from the doctor, he would have been OK to fight the next day and would have probably won, too. But since he was only sixteen, somebody would have said something and he would have been disqualified anyway. It all happened for the best, though, because this gave Sugar Ray a real goal to shoot for in the next four years."

By 1976, Sugar Ray Leonard was the undisputed amateur king of America. Most amateurs are all but ignored by the public, save for those fans from the fighter's home town. But Leonard was a shining exception. His crackling power and silky-smooth style made him an Ali in miniature and the subject of several *Sports Illustrated* articles in that Olympic year.

But in the four years leading up to the '76 Olympic Games, Leonard more than once entertained thoughts about ending his personal crusade.

"All my friends would be partying or playing around," he said, "and I'd be stuck in that gym every night. I seriously thought about quitting in 1974. I was a big ball of confusion. But some people talked me out of it."

The most influential voice belonged to Janks Morton, a former pro football player who was an assistant trainer at the Palmer Park Recreation Center and would, over the years, become Leonard's most trusted confidant.

"Ray had already laid the foundation," said Morton. "He had all the potential in the world. It took a little while for that to dwell on him, that he had too much talent to throw everything away."

But Leonard's doubts were more than mental. More perplexing was the chronic condition of his delicate hands that gave him repeated pain and concern over whether they would hold up long enough to gain an Olympic berth.

The wily Jacobs tried to remedy the problem by putting protective pads on Leonard's vulnerable fists, but amateur regulations disallowed any covering, save for a thin strip of gauze.

"I first hurt my hands in 1973," Ray said. "They'd swell up on me, but I think it was mostly the result of having to fight as often as five or six times in a couple of days during the tournaments. It's something like what happens to a marathon runner. After all that punishment, his body just swells up.

"I tried just about everything—Epsom salts, Ben-Gay, rubbing alcohol. Nothing really worked. After awhile, I just learned to blot out the pain from my mind because I loved fighting too much to give it up."

And fight he did, with incredible success, winning all but five of his one hundred fifty amateur tests leading to Montreal and the Olympics. He lost to Randy Shields in the 1974 AAU finals, but would avenge that defeat as a professional five years later.

In 1974, he fought Russian champion Anatoli Kamnev in Moscow. The judges voted for Kamnev, but when his countrymen howled in protest, Kamnev walked across the ring, and, with a diplomatic bow, presented the winning trophy to Leonard.

Sugar Ray would lose another questionable decision to

Kazimier Szczerba of Poland on Szczerba's home turf. He dropped his Polish rival three times in the final round, and Szczerba failed to beat the count the last time. But the Polish referee ruled that Leonard had delivered the knockout punch after the bell had sounded, and awarded the decision to Szczerba, who had to be propped up to accept the winning medal.

That dubious setback would mark the fifth and last defeat for Sugar Ray in a total of one hundred and fifty amateur bouts. And it also taught him a valuable lesson. He would no longer fight the system. Henceforth, he would dispose of all his crowd-pleasing tricks. He would forgo the "Ali Shuffle," Kid Gavilan's flashy bolo punch, and the big, innocent smile he mustered to distract an overly confident opponent.

"I'm putting aside all the tricks," he said. "From now on, I'm going to give the amateur judges a stand-up, classic boxing style that they seem to appreciate. Forget the smile while I'm tattooing some dude. A couple of American officials told me, 'Ray you're too good for that. People will think you're showboating.' Well, from now on, I won't let them think that no more."

But there would be other obstacles and distractions before Leonard would reach Montreal in August, 1976. Promoters, who dealt mainly in flesh and blood, were already eyeing the charismatic Sugar Ray as a prize catch.

The first to come calling was Eddie Hrica, a personal emissary for Baltimore boxing impresario Eli Hanover.

"At sixteen," said Hrica, who now serves as a matchmaker for the Capital Centre, "Ray Leonard was better than almost all the pros fighting in our area.

"At the time," Hrica continued, "we had five world-rated fighters in heavyweight Larry Middleton, junior middleweights Ralph Palladin and Alvin Anderson, welterweight Johnny Gant, and featherweight Ronnie McGarvey, plus a world champion in light-heavyweight Bob Foster. But I was convinced that, after ten or fifteen fights, Sugar Ray would be better than all of them.

"Besides," said Hrica, "Leonard had that all-American boy glow about him. Everybody loved the kid, just like apple pie and baseball. You could see that he had tremendous box-office appeal."

So Hanover dispatched Hrica with a $5,000 check as an initial offering for Leonard to turn pro. But Hrica got no further than Dave Jacobs.

"I never really got to finish my sales pitch," Hrica said. "Jacobs cut me short. He said, 'Sugar Ray will not turn pro. He is going to win the Olympics in 1976.' The way he said it, the look in his eye, you knew he was sincere."

Jacobs and Leonard had come too far to be dissuaded by a few bags of money. A shiny gold medal still represented the whole world to Sugar Ray.

☆ 3 ☆

"MY JOURNEY'S ENDED"

Howard Cosell is a scholarly man with a strong sense of history. After the 1960 Olympic Games in Rome, he was the first to trumpet the untapped potential of a gold medal winner named Cassius Clay. And he would studiously follow each dramatic step of the young heavyweight's tempestuous career, a fortunate decision that would forever link him with the future world champion.

By the summer of '76, Cosell needed no crystal ball to inform him that this once glorious fighting machine, now known to the world as Muhammad Ali, had only a few fights left in his now distended body. It was clearly time for Cosell to hitch himself to a new shooting star. And this he found at the Montreal Olympics in Sugar Ray Leonard, a fresh-faced junior welterweight who lit up the television screen with his lightning fists and feet and his captivating smile.

Before the army of media men swooped down on the Olympic Village, Cosell received a call from Roone Arledge, his boss at ABC sports.

"Roone asked me if we had a fighter with a unique

personality," Cosell said. "I immediately thought of Leonard. I said at the time that he would be the Olga Korbut of the 'Seventy-six Olympics, a statement for which I was reviled and derided by certain members of the press corps. But the statement was borne out. As you know, I always tell it like it is."

Cosell, of course, would remind the world of his farsightedness that July day in the Maurice Richard Arena when the kid from Palmer Park, Maryland, with the "made-for-television" face thoroughly whipped Andres Aldama of Cuba to win a gold medal.

In all, five American fighters would win championships at Montreal. But the gold rush north of the border was anything but accidental. The United States boxers, once regarded as the most finely skilled ringmen in the world, had been greatly embarrassed at the 1972 Olympics in Munich when junior welterweight Ray Seales was the lone American representative to win a title.

It was time for the U.S. amateur boxing officials to realistically reappraise the coaching and training methods in use in our country. The investigation revealed what everyone knew already—that we had fallen significantly behind the Europeans in preparing fighters for intense international competition.

A major revamping of the training system was in order, and the man chosen for the job was Rollie Schwartz, a white-maned native of Cincinnati. In his role as president of the AAU Boxing Commission, he would initiate—over the protests of several hardline coaches—a "Four Year Plan" aimed at grooming a U.S. squad that could make a strong showing in 1976.

As Schwartz told Paul Attner of *The Washington Post*, "We had to start doing things on a grander scale. The coaches screamed and kicked about having to change the way they'd always done things. But they finally realized this was the only way we were going to win in the Olympics.

"We took on everyone," Schwartz added. "We fought the Russians and the East German teams four times. We took on the Poles, Hungarians, and Yugoslavs, anyone who would fight us."

When not actually competing, the American boxers were busy in classrooms studying films of European boxers and dutifully breaking down their strengths and weaknesses much like football coaches formulating a game plan.

Out of all this classwork evolved an American style that Schwartz labeled "esoteric boxing"—a combination of eye-catching hand and foot speed coupled with the stamina to withstand the assault of the rugged Europeans, who were trained to save their best for the final round.

But Schwartz and head boxing coach Pat Nappi did not turn their newly conditioned fighters completely loose in the four years leading up to the '76 Olympics. They sent their students on thirty-three overseas missions, but never once did the American squad include more than a handful of its best boxers.

"We didn't want to show anyone how good we really were," said Schwartz. "We wanted to spring a few surprises at Montreal."

It was more than a few. In addition to Leonard, a pre-Olympic favorite to bring home a gold medal, titles were also won by the two Spinks brothers, Michael (160 pounds) and snaggle-toothed Leon (175), stylish Howard Davis (132), a smaller version of the flamboyant Leonard, and flyweight Leo Randolph.

Leonard, however, was the indisputable star, a dazzling boxer with a fluid style and enough Ali-like showmanship to bring a special excitement to each of his six Olympic appearances.

And, in the bold manner of Ali, who had forecast his victory as a light-heavyweight in the '60 Games, Sugar Ray flatly predicted he would return to Maryland with a gold medal hanging around his neck.

Before the first blow was struck in anger, Sugar Ray told the assembled press, "The only pressure I feel here is the pressure I put on myself. I've been aiming for the Olympics since 1972. I went to the Olympic Trials that year, but I was just too young and inexperienced.

"It's taken me four long years of sacrificing to get this far," he added somberly. "I didn't party. I didn't run the streets. I didn't vacation at the beach. There were no late hours. My whole mind has been focused on winning a gold medal at Montreal. My expectations are high, and I expect to live up to them."

With Cosell supplying most of the prefight ballyhoo, Leonard would become the focal point of the Olympic boxing competition. But while the twenty-year-old wunderkind was rolling over a Swede, Russian, Briton, East German, Pole, and Cuban on his way to the victory stand, Cosell did not dwell on the story behind the two small pictures affixed to his sneakers—one of a teen-age girl dressed in a graduation cap and gown, the other of a bright-faced two-year-old boy.

It would be explained in passing that, quite simply, the girl was Leonard's high school sweetheart, Juanita Wilkinson, and the boy, Ray, Jr., was their child born out of wedlock. No one earnestly pursued the story during the Olympics. But it would not end there. For a few days after his celebrated triumph, the whole story would explode in Leonard's face like a delayed time bomb.

But the Games in Montreal were not a time for gossiping and innuendo. The Olympics were meant for furious flag-waving, rampant patriotism, and rallying around the boys dressed in red, white, and blue jumpsuits.

Leonard, however, was excused from marching behind the flag in the exhilarating, but also exhausting two-hour pageantry that heralded the opening of the Games. Schwartz, who like Cosell had made the Marylander his personal "pet," wanted Sugar Ray fresh for his preliminary match against Ulf Carlsson, of Sweden.

"I'm glad to fight right away," he said, "because the longer you have to wait, the more pressure builds up inside and the more tense you get."

He looked totally relaxed against Carlsson, clowning, miming and intimidating the Swede with all the tricks he had mastered in a boxing style that combined Ali, Ray Robinson, and Kid Gavilan. At times, he would display the "Ali Shuffle," follow with the blinding combinations of a Robinson, and cap a furious rally with a sweeping bolo punch à la Gavilan.

Following his three-round tour de force, Leonard said, "People think when I do the shuffle and drop my hands, it's for show. It's not. That's the way I box. Everything I do is for a reason. I don't call that 'hot-dogging.' I'm trying to 'psyche' out my opponent. Give him something to think about.

"When I drop my hands, they relax, and then I pop them. I know I surprised the Swede because I came out fighting straight up. But I make each fight different. I want people to respect me for a lot of reasons."

The Russian, Valery Limasov, would be next, and, as in all American-Soviet confrontations, this fight would take on added significance. A capacity crowd jammed the boxing arena to see how the flashy Yank would handle the experience of the Soviet southpaw, who was well-schooled and effectively awkward.

"Left-handers are hard to fight," Leonard said. "They can make you look bad, real bad by being so unorthodox."

But Sugar Ray had no cause for concern. A consummate boxer in his opening night victory over Carlsson, Leonard turned into a stalking tiger against Limasov, a miniature Joe Frazier. A minute into the bout, he stunned his opponent by reaching the Russian's chin with a rapid-fire combination. The pro-American crowd began to chant, "Sugar Ray, Sugar Ray," and he responded to the cheers with another blistering salvo to close out the round.

In the second round, Leonard repeatedly caught Limasov flatfooted with right-hand leads until it became as routine as a kid hitting a pop-up bag.

He now had a commanding lead, but his coach, Pat Nappi, had warned him that the Russians prided themselves on their stamina and endurance, and he could expect Limasov to come charging out of his corner at the start of the final round.

Instead, Leonard met Limasov head-on in mid-ring, quickly taking the initiative away from the Russian and forcing him to give ground under a heavy fusillade of blows. There was no need to await the decision. At the sound of the final bell, Sugar Ray was already flashing the victory salute to his parents and friends watching at home.

"I hit him with some fantastic shots," he said in the press tent. "I couldn't understand what kept him up. But I admire the Russian's courage. I remember catching him with a solid right in the second round. I smiled at him, but he smiled right back at me."

Before leaving the arena, Sugar Ray was picked by Olympic officials for a random drug test which took him longer to pass than the Russian. "That was tougher than the fight," he joked with reporters.

To celebrate his lopsided victory over Limasov, Leonard, to the surprise of the crowd, unfurled the red-and-white flag of Prince Georges County, Maryland, where Palmer Park, his home town, was located. The flag-waving was not an impromptu act, but rather a clever political ploy conceived by county executive Winfield M. Kelly.

"Three weeks ago," said Kelly, "we asked Ray if he would take the flag to Montreal for us. I guess we got a little carried away. But we suggested he unfold it to show all the people watching him fight the beautiful area of the country he comes from. We're pretty proud of this young man, but there's a lot more to him than just boxing. I guess he's just as proud of us as we are of him, if that's possible."

The county flag bore a crusader's cross and the official seal, inscribed with the Latin motto, "*Semper Eadem.*"

"Who knows Latin?" asked sports columnist Dave Israel. "What does this mean?"

No one spoke in the crowd, all hoping Leonard might supply the answer.

"It means 'G-O-O-O-O-D,' " he cooed. "That's what it means."

Actually, the Latin inscription meant "Always the Same," but that would hardly apply to Leonard, who, in one brilliant performance, had shown the Russians more boxing tricks than they could hope to steal.

In a few short days, Sugar Ray had taken Montreal by storm. An army of reporters followed his every footstep, seeking any tidbit of information about the American wunderkind to relay to their audience at home. Leonard, in a few words, was too good to be true. But none of the American ring officials were ready to concede his mortality. Quite the contrary, the press discovered.

"Pound for pound," said assistant coach Sarge Johnson, "Leonard is the finest fighter I've seen in thirty years of working with the amateurs."

That was almost faint praise compared to what followed from head coach Pat Nappi, regarded as the Angelo Dundee among amateur fight trainers.

"Sugar Ray is the best amateur I've ever seen, and that includes Muhammad Ali," Nappi told columnist Bob Maisel of the *Baltimore Sun.*

Noticing the raised eyebrows, Nappi quickly added, "I know. I know. I always get that same reaction when I say that. But I've been in this business for thirty-eight years, and my opinion should stand for something.

"People think I'm some sort of a nut or just popping off when I put Leonard ahead of Ali. But that's because they're projecting Ali's development as a professional. That's not what I'm talking about. I traveled with Ali when he won the light-heavyweight title at Rome. But back then, he was strictly a two-punch fighter—left jab and straight right. That was his stock in trade, plus the movement. He always had the quick feet.

"But this Leonard kid has all that and more," Nappi said emphatically. "He throws better combinations than Ali, he has a professional left hook, a sharp jab, and throws the right from a dozen different angles. Then, of course, he also has the great legs. And remember, he's just twenty, but already a tremendously poised fighter as an amateur. If he ever chooses to turn pro, there's no telling how far he might go."

Despite the unstinting praise of his coach, Leonard still had four more obstacles in his path to the Olympic gold medal. And the supremely confident young fighter was mildly shocked three days later to hear scattered boos and catcalls from the crowd that did not appreciate his unspectacular third-round victory over Clinton McKenzie.

Several ringside critics suggested that Leonard should have displayed less style and more substance in disposing of his English rival. But the chilly reception was hard to comprehend. For Sugar Ray had fought a battle best appreciated by the connoisseurs of "The Sweet Science" of boxing in dominating McKenzie from the opening bell. It was not a fight for the bloodthirsty, but rather one to be savored for its ring artistry.

Leonard seized control quickly and finished the first round with a blistering barrage that lasted for a full ten seconds. He also landed all the telling punches in round two, and, by the third round, McKenzie was in desperate shape. Another whirlwind volley left the Englishman barely hanging on as the final bell sounded. But by this time, boos were mingled with cheers for the American winner.

"Sure I'm disappointed by the boos," said Leonard, "but I'm not really surprised. Some of these people who boo and criticize you don't know what's going on in the ring. They don't understand what international boxing is all about.

"They're used to the 1920s style of fighting, a slugfest. I'm trying to prove a point, that boxing can be scientific. You just don't keep punching until somebody falls. You try to outbox your opponent and confuse him. No, I don't feel bad about the booing. It just makes me more determined."

He would hear no boos in his next two Olympic tests. He easily outpointed Ulrich Beyer of East Germany in the quarterfinals and then gained a measure of revenge in the semifinals when he soundly whipped Kazimier Szczerba, the Pole who had accounted for his last loss as an amateur on a disqualification in Warsaw in 1974, when Sugar Ray landed a knockout punch just as the final bell sounded.

This time, Leonard outpointed Szczerba without fully extending himself. "I conserved myself as much as I could," he said. "I wanted to make sure I was in good condition for the championship match."

But despite his easy triumph over Szczerba, there was genuine concern by the American boxing officials over the condition of Leonard's fragile fists, particularly his somewhat swollen right hand.

"I first hurt that hand in the 1973 Golden Gloves," he recalled, "and it's never really had a chance to heal properly. After every fight, my knuckles would swell, especially the middle one. Sometimes, I could hardly make a fist."

The problem was diagnosed an inflammation of the synovial membrane—an extremely painful deposit of calcium on the tissues of the knuckle. And now, on the threshold of a fight he had dreamed about for most of his adolescent years, Ray's hands were hurting again. Ice packs helped kill the pain, but it was more a case of Leonard blotting it from his mind.

Throughout his Olympic ordeal, the pressures had been far more mental than physical. He grew terribly homesick, missing the familiar faces and surroundings of his little piece of Maryland. He felt like a prisoner in the Olympic Village, living with fifteen teammates in the dormitory-style rooms and constantly being checked and supervised by the small army of security personnel, being doubly cautious to avoid a repeat of the 1972 debacle in Munich. His dejection was heightened when his call home was unanswered following his semifinal victory over Szczerba. He returned to the Olympic Village feeling more alone than ever.

The next day, however, his depression would change to sudden elation. "I was going out to do some light roadwork," he said, "when I looked up, and there were my parents, my brother, my sisters, my coach, Dave Jacobs, and several friends. There were ten of them piled in this van that's supposed to hold only six. I couldn't believe it."

The trip had been planned by Jacobs, the moon-faced man who first introduced Leonard to boxing at Palmer Park and had so splendidly prepared him for his ultimate test in the '76 Olympics.

"It was the only way we could afford to take his parents and the rest of us to Montreal," said Jacobs, who would be cheerfully christened "King Sardine" by the rest of the Leonard clan for taking up most of the sleeping space in the overcrowded van with the women finally taking refuge in a budget motel. But no one complained about the less than luxurious accommodations.

"It was better coming here than staying home," said Mrs. Leonard, who watched her son fight with great reluctance. "Back home, I couldn't get any sleep. The phone wouldn't stop ringing and people were always dropping by to ask about Ray. And our phone bill was getting out of sight. It was bad enough when he fought in the Pan-Am Games. That cost us $279. But I don't even want to see the bill from the Olympics," Getha laughed.

Her husband, Cicero, had made the trip despite a warning from his boss at the supermarket that he would be docked for any time missed. "I told him I was going anyway," Mr. Leonard said. "This is a once-in-a-lifetime thing. You can't put a price tag on it."

Packed into the van with Ray's parents and Jacobs were his older brother, Roger, his two younger sisters, Sharon and Linda, his girl friend, Juanita Wilkinson, and two high school friends—Joe Broddie and Eddie Jenkins.

They had driven all night to assure their arrival in Montreal in time for Ray's championship match with Cuba's Andres Aldama. The trip had taken longer than necessary. Mr. Leonard had taken a wrong turn after crossing the Canadian border, pointing the van west to Toronto.

"We were almost in Toronto when I'd realized what I'd done," Cicero said sheepishly. "The rest of 'em haven't let me forget it, either."

The "Sugar Ray Leonard Fan Club" was ensconsed in a $10-a-day parking lot directly across from the boxing arena. Pictures of their personal hero adorned the windows of the van and a sign stretched across its flank read: "WE'VE COME A LONG WAY TO SEE SUGAR RAY WIN THE GOLD MEDAL—ALL THE WAY FROM PALMER PARK, MD., PRINCE GEORGES COUNTY, U.S.A."

The colorful van would attract a continuous flow of curious tourists and autograph seekers, sticking their heads inside without even a polite knock, hoping to catch a glimpse of the twenty-year-old tyro who had turned the Olympics into a one-man demolition derby.

Several of the uninvited guests mistook Roger for his younger brother, although the brothers bear only a slight family resemblance. Roger, however, had impressive boxing credentials of his own. On leave from the Air Force, he had won two Inter-Service crowns and suffered a frustrating loss in his bid for the Olympic team.

"I was going to compete at 139 pounds," Roger said, "but there was no way I could see myself competing against Ray. So I fought at 147 pounds, and lost in the semifinals of the Olympic Trials to Clint Jackson. That dude's beaten me seven times. I guess, he's just got my number.

"But I've got no doubts that Ray is going all the way," Roger added. "Ray has tremendous drive. He just keeps pushing himself 'til he gets there."

"That's right," Jacobs chimed in. "Ray's dedicated himself to being the best. It didn't make any difference what sport he got into—gymnastics, wrestling, or whatever. He was going to be successful because of his attitude."

A reporter in the crowd asked if Ray might also have been successful if he had fulfilled his mother's wish and become a popular blues singer.

"Oh, I used to hope so," Mrs. Leonard laughed. "When he was singing in the church choir, he had a beautiful soprano voice. He sounded just like Sam Cooke. Now he sounds just awful."

"Yeah," said Roger. "Once Ray's voice started to crack, that was it. He came home one day and told us, 'I'm changing from singing to swinging.' "

The laughter almost made the overflowing van rock. But no one was enjoying the Olympic scene more than the once-skeptical Cicero Leonard, who had now become his son's number one cheerleader.

"He's changed all our lives," Cicero said, "and I don't think they will ever be the same for a long, long time. I'm glad we're here in Montreal, because Ray has been away from home for so long, and now we're going to get him back with us again. But I'm sad in a way, too," Mr. Leonard added, "because I just love to watch my boy fight. He's that good."

A visitor asked Cicero if he would be satisfied with his son winning a silver medal. Mr. Leonard gave the man a curious look.

"See that?" he said, pointing to a gold medal hanging above the driver's seat in the van. "That's what Ray won in the Pan-Am Games. And we don't want anything less than the gold from these Games, and neither does Ray."

There were a few shouts of "Right on" from the back of

the van. For the fast-growing Sugar Ray Leonard Fan Club, winning the gold seemed a mere formality. But getting to see their favorite son accomplish the job was a different matter—a logistical problem of the first order.

"We got real lucky," Mrs. Leonard said later. "We met this couple from New Jersey outside the trailer, and we told them about our problem in getting enough tickets for the family.

"They couldn't understand how the Olympic people hadn't taken care of us. So they took us around to the VIP entrance of the arena, and we all started talking to one of the guards. He grabbed his walkie-talkie and started speaking in French. After awhile, he asked me how many tickets we needed.

"I got real bold," Getha said, " 'How about five?' I asked him. He asked how long it would take to get all my people together. I told him, 'No more than three minutes,' and I ran all the way to the van and back. Well, they gave us the royal treatment. We all got seats in the VIP section at ringside. It was great," Mrs. Leonard said.

Back in the dressing room, Leonard soothed his throbbing fists in ice packs. He had fought six times in a thirteen day span and the pain was now becoming almost unbearable.

"One more fight, then it's over," he said. "I've been fighting with one hand up to now. Now I'll let go with everything I have. What do I have to lose?"

But Leonard would fight an uncharacteristic battle against Aldama, the Cuban slugger who had dispatched his four previous Olympic foes in a total of eighteen minutes. The strategy decided upon before the fight was to have Leonard move inside and smother Aldama's awesome firepower, while attacking the Cuban's body.

This choice of tactics surprised ringsiders, who had so often seen Sugar Ray play the part of a skillful matador, picking and probing at his charging opponent before moving in for the kill.

This time it was the slender American who marched

forward throughout the first round and a half, giving his rival scant punching room as a frustrated Aldama missed repeatedly with his lethal left hook.

Midway through the second round, Leonard unleashed a lightning flurry of blows and Aldama was forced to give ground. A minute later, Aldama, mistakenly thinking the referee had ordered a break, dropped his guard, only to be hit flush on the chin by a whistling left hook. The Cuban dropped to one knee and took an eight count.

The third and final round was all Leonard's. Responding to the rhythmic chanting of "Sugar Ray, Sugar Ray," he became the picture-perfect fighter that had made him the darling of the Olympic competition.

Aldama, now desperately trying for a knockout, began swinging wildly. But Leonard adroitly slipped the looping punches and caught the lunging Cuban with a head-spinning five-punch salvo. Aldama retreated and the referee gave him a standing eight count. Sensing the kill, Leonard moved quickly to the attack and bombarded Aldama with both hands. Again, the Cuban was forced to take a standing count that was interrupted by the sound of the final bell and the frenzied cheers of the pro-American crowd.

The cheers were still ringing in Sugar Ray's ears as Howard Cosell, in his grandiloquent manner, predicted a waiting world of riches for the newly crowned Olympic champion as soon as he elected to turn professional killer.

But as Cosell droned on, Leonard silently shook his head in dissent.

"No, I'm finished," he said. "I've fought my last fight. My journey has ended. My dream is fulfilled."

His single-mindedness and zealous dedication to winning a gold medal had left him both physically and mentally drained. It was time to start a new life.

"When they finally put that medal around my neck, I was in shock," he said. "Everything was spinning around. All I wanted to do was go home."

In this strange mixture of euphoria and utter exhaustion, Leonard left his family behind in the Olympic boxing arena and wandered out into the night. They would fan out across the Olympic Village searching for him, until Jacobs suggested they try looking in the family van. And there he was, waiting and anxious to point the van toward Palmer Park, where it had all started.

"Leave everything here," he told Jacobs. "Let's go home right now. I want to be there by tomorrow."

Jacobs nodded in agreement and began gathering the Leonard clan for the return trip. Cicero planted the new gold medal over the dashboard and then revved up the motor.

Sugar Ray was going home. But his journey had not ended. In fact, it had just begun.

☆ 4 ☆

JOURNEY INTO MANHOOD

The conquering hero was home. The rented van carrying the Leonard clan home from the Olympic Games in Montreal had just turned on to the Capital Beltway for the final leg of the journey when it was overtaken by a wailing police cruiser, closely followed by a limousine packed with county executives.

Sugar Ray would travel in grand style the final few miles to a gala neighborhood celebration characterized by a *Washington Post* reporter as "an explosive mixture of hero adulation and old-fashioned politics."

Everyone wanted to rub elbows with the charismatic twenty-year-old kid who had introduced the world to Palmer Park, Md., his personal piece of turf. But Leonard, still trying to unwind from the Olympic ordeal that had left him both mentally and physically drained, preferred leaving the festivities behind, to find a quiet place where he could begin to sort things out. He had, after all, to prepare for a future without fighting.

"I can't tell you how I feel," he told the convoy of area reporters who dogged his footsteps. "I'm still in a state of shock. It's like a dream. Every sacrifice I made to reach a single goal—a gold medal. I've got it, and now it's over, and I'll never box again."

Friends and neighbors crowded forward to shake his hand. A politician placed a king-sized paper crown on Sugar Ray's head, and he posed for hundreds of pictures with his "queen"—his high school sweetheart Juanita Wilkinson, and their two-year-old son, Ray, Jr., born out of wedlock.

"In my heart," he said, "this medal is all I ever wanted. That, and a chance at a straight life. But this medal belongs to the whole community of Palmer Park, and all the people from here were part of my Olympic experience.

"With my girl friend and family in Montreal to cheer me on, I couldn't let them down. But now I want to set an example for all the kids on the streets. I always remember what Muhammad Ali once said. He told a group of boys not to go into boxing until they had an education. And that's what I plan to do now. I've had my share of glory. My name will always be in the record books, and my family can be proud that I came up the hard way and accomplished something most people aren't capable of. But I'll never be a professional fighter. I promise you that. It's time I started a new life."

Leonard then announced his plans to accept a congressional scholarship to the University of Maryland, where he would major in communications and recreation, hoping ultimately to work with the kids in his neighborhood.

School, however, was still a month away, enough time for the whirlwind to subside.

"Things are coming at me so fast," he said. "Everyone wants my ear. I feel like I'm being pulled in a hundred different directions."

A mountain of mail sat on the living room table of the Leonards' modest ranch house. "They're from all over the world—Germany, Italy, and Poland," Ray said. "Some of these letters are unbelievable. Mostly from kids. But this is what kept me motivated in Montreal. Those two months of training were like living in a prison, but these letters helped break the monotony."

Some of the correspondence, however, wasn't from idolizing teen-agers or young ladies hoping for a chance meeting. A number were from fast-buck operators and politicians hoping to quickly capitalize on Leonard's newly won fame.

"The politicians are coming out of their bags," he said with a note of exasperation. "Why are they all coming around now? Obviously, they're trying to get something out of me. They want to attract attention, and they do it in a sly way.

"But my true friends are really coming through now," he added. "They're helping me to settle down and figure things out."

On the long trip home from Montreal, Sugar Ray spent a lot of time daydreaming about all the benefits he would reap from his celebrated Olympic triumph. He could envision himself appearing on talk shows with Johnny Carson, being invited to the White House, and in short time, having his image appear on cereal boxes and billboards advertising national products in the same way as Bruce Jenner and Mark Spitz, the two outstanding American competitors in the 1972 Olympics. All Ray had to do was sit back and wait for the money to begin rolling in.

But only two days after his triumphant return, Leonard's fragile fantasy world came tumbling down like a house of cards. Indeed, he found his name emblazoned in front-page headlines, but not in tribute. The *Washington Star* instead chose this method to inform the public that the Olympic hero had been named in a paternity suit.

The newspaper had learned that Juanita had filed an application to receive $156-a-month in welfare payments to help support Ray, Jr., and the county, in turn, had filed a paternity suit against the father, Sugar Ray. In a matter of hours, the news became a *cause célèbre* in Washington, which nurtures itself on daily scandals.

At first, Leonard reacted to the story with blind rage. "Here I bring the county flag to the Olympics and give them their share of glory," he said, "and what do I get?—a paternity suit.

"The worst thing about it is that all the kids here look up to me, and then this thing blows up in my face. It will destroy me. I wouldn't want the kids to see me in a different light. But life comes in all ways and all angles. All I can say is I'm sorry. I wish it hadn't happened at this particular time."

When tempers cooled, Leonard wondered aloud why the politicians had chosen this particular time to make his personal problems public. He had made no attempt to deny the truth, and had, in effect, told the whole world by wearing both a picture of Juanita and his infant son on his sneakers throughout the Olympic competition.

"I never denied my son," he said. "I've always been proud of Ray, Jr. But I was still an amateur fighter when the baby was born in 1973. I had no money and no time for a job. The Olympics were a dream I had to fulfill even though I knew it meant neglecting Ray, Jr., somewhat. I thought that I was doing something that one day would make him especially proud of his father. And I also thought that I was being patriotic by fighting in the Olympics for my country. But this story made everything turn sour."

The welfare officials, of course, denied any malicious intent. They explained that Leonard was simply the victim of legal machinery and a new law that was enacted in 1975 because of wholesale welfare cheating.

"There is nothing criminal about fathering a child—it's a privilege," said assistant county state's attorney Karen Silver. "But by law, we must establish in court who the father is and if he can provide support. It makes no difference if he says he is the father publicly."

But Leonard was more concerned over what effect the uproar over the paternity suit would have on Juanita than his own personal discomfort.

"The papers made it look like Juanita was trying to cash in on my Olympic success," he said. "But she was told that there would be no child care benefits unless she filed a complaint against me. But I think it was all blown out of proportion because this was something that happened to us three years ago when we were both still very young.

"The way Juanita acted when the story broke, I thought she was going to have a nervous breakdown," he said soulfully, "and I almost had one myself. I was catching hell in my hometown papers and getting hate mail from as far away as Germany."

If anything, these traumatic days helped bring Ray and Juanita closer together. And Leonard, now more mature, was beginning to understand that Juanita's personal sacrifice had, perhaps, been even greater than his own through his Olympic ordeal.

Juanita dropped out of high school her senior year and went on welfare to support the child while Ray finished his schooling and pursued his amateur boxing career.

"There was never any question about my having the baby," Juanita would later tell Judy Mann of *The Washington Post*. "It wasn't meant to be, but it happened and we had to deal with it.

"We were going to do our best, to do what was right," Juanita said. "We tried to be adult about it, but at age seventeen, how adult can you be? We had nothing to hide, though. Ray simply had no money to give me.

"But I didn't tell him I was filing for welfare. I knew how much the Olympics meant to him, so I never asked for financial support. I just kept living at home with my father. But when that story in the paper came out, I felt like everybody suddenly turned against me, like they thought I was trying to hurt Ray through the papers. But I've never done anything to hurt him."

Juanita and Ray had first met as students at Parkdale High School. Her girl friend had introduced her to Ray, a bony, rather shy teen-ager with a mini-Afro. They lived around the corner from each other, but it was hardly a case of Juanita falling in love with the boy next door.

In fact, it took a great deal of peer pressure to bring them together, with Juanita's friends constantly reminding her that Ray was already a neighborhood celebrity of sorts through his amateur ring accomplishments. That, in itself, was worth a casual date.

Their first phone conversation would last into the wee hours of the morning until Ray, growing in confidence, informed his new girl friend, "You've met your match."

They would go "steady" while Leonard pursued his Olympic dream, but lengthy separations led to occasional disenchantment. After Ray, Jr., was born on November 22, 1973, they decided to stay together for the sake of the child. Juanita would stay in her father's home and Ray would continue to live with his parents. And the situation would remain unchanged until the scandal caused by the paternity suit story.

Ironically, the same day the *Washington Star* broke the story, Leonard and his parents were being invited to meet President Ford in the White House, where he would receive a special commendation for his Olympic performance.

"Ray had tears in his eyes when he read the newspaper story," his mother said. "Juanita hadn't said anything to us before. We would have helped her some way like we'd always tried to in the past. But is it a disgrace for an eighteen-year-old girl to need assistance in raising a child?"

The public would share Getha Leonard's sentiments. The Washington papers were bombarded with letters protesting the lack of compassion in treating the story, which the majority of correspondents thought was unnecessarily sensationalized.

But the damage had been done. Leonard's dream of converting his gold medal into a post-Olympic fortune quickly vanished. The decision-makers on Madison Avenue decided the fighter with the $1 million smile no longer projected the image of the all-American boy.

"It killed every commercial he would have gotten," Ray's closest friend and advisor, Janks Morton, told the *Post*'s Tom Boswell. "Bruce Jenner puts his face on the cereal box. Mark Spitz holds up an after-shave bottle. All he has to do is make sure not to drop it. But Ray, who's a natural actor, had to wait four years after the Olympics to start getting major commerical offers.

"Oh, yes, he might have got a chance to sell some roach powder, but that's the end of the line. You just degrade yourself. We wanted Ray to start with quality products, but first Ray had to go through this time of trial."

Throughout these trying times, Janks Morton, a self-employed insurance man who had become the young fighter's "father-confessor" from his early days in the Palmer Park gym, would be there with advice for his young friend.

"These were the little bumps that made a man out of Ray," Morton would say. "He saw what could happen to his dreams, what had happened, what life was all about."

While Leonard tried to free himself from "this web of confusion," he would often accompany Morton on his business trips. On one visit, Morton made a point of introducing Sugar Ray to a prospective client. But all he got was a blank stare in reply.

"You know, this is Sugar Ray Leonard, the Olympic boxing champ," Morton said emphatically, hoping to stir the man's memory.

"Oh, yeah," the man said a bit sheepishly. "*That* Sugar Ray."

But this was hardly an isolated incident. A few short

weeks after the Olympics, Morton encouraged Ray to participate in an experiment. They would stand on a busy intersection in the nation's capital and count the numbers of passersby who recognized Leonard with some form of greeting. It was a sobering experience for Howard Cosell's personal "pet."

"I was expecting all kinds of people to say, 'Hey, there's Sugar Ray.' " Leonard recalled the incident. "But people kept passing right by without a word. I never thought of myself as a celebrity, so it didn't bug me. But it made me think a lot. A few weeks after the Olympics. Boom. Nothing."

More than anything, it forced Leonard to re-think his priorities. His private world had turned topsy-turvy. Glamorous dreams of self-fulfillment had now changed into clouds of self-doubt.

"Sure, it hurt Ray's ego," said Morton. "But it also showed him that life is no fairy tale. He couldn't expect people to come flocking to him the same way they did to Jenner and Spitz. It was a real rough period for Ray, but it made a man of him. He discovered that he had to start making his own decisions."

The pressure to resume his boxing career as a professional was mounting every day. Offers came from both fast-buck operators hoping to capitalize on Leonard's name, and legitimate fight promoters who viewed the popular Olympic champion as a likely successor to Ali as boxing's new box-office king.

Most of the offers, legitimate and otherwise, filtered down to Dave Jacobs, who had served as Ray's trainer throughout his amateur career. Jacobs, for one, felt the next step up the boxing ladder was inevitable.

"As soon as the air clears, I'm sure he'll turn pro," Jacobs confided to a newspaper friend one day. "I know Ray's first love is still boxing. He loves fighting and the public acclaim that goes with it. He worked so hard the past five years of his life to get where he is. Now that he has a chance to make some big money, he won't turn his back on it."

During this discouraging period of limbo, Jacobs did his best to keep Leonard busy. One night they made a trip to Utica to see George Foreman fight Scott Ledoux. "Ray got a much bigger hand than either of the heavyweights," Jacobs remembered, "and I think he started getting that old feeling back again.

"I know he talked about going to college," the fight trainer added, "but I think that was to keep a lot of the wheeler-dealers off his back. When they'd start talking real fast, Ray'd tell them, 'Go talk to my coach.' I had about twenty different offers for him to turn pro since he got back from Montreal, and some of them went as high as $125,000 just to sign a contract. Most of them sounded legitimate, too.

"But all these guys figure they can get closer to Ray through me. But I'm not instigating anything or putting him under any pressure. The decision to turn pro is strictly his own. I've only advised him that he has to make a move one way or the other now if he wants to keep his name before the public."

Expectedly, all of the big-name fight promoters offered opinions on Leonard's future and his best course of action. Very little of the pressure was subtle.

One of the first callers was flamboyant Don King, the man with the electrified Afro and the fast-talking glibness of a snakeoil salesman. At the time, he was serving as matchmaker for the Capital Centre, little more than an overhand right from Leonard's front doorstep.

King offered an attractive multiyear contract, but all the renewable options favored the promoter when, and if, Sugar Ray found himself included in the Top Ten rankings. King's heavy-handedness at the outset ultimately left him salivating on the sidelines, thinking of what fortunes might have been reaped out of a more equitable agreement.

King, of course, had plenty of competition. Another frontrunner was Teddy Brenner, then the powerful matchmaker for Madison Square Garden, still considered by many the mecca of the boxing world.

"Of all the 1976 Olympic champions," noted Brenner, "I like Leonard's chances of succeeding as a professional best. He's got both the ability and the charisma. But he's got to be careful of guys flashing a lot of money in his face. If someone is going to make you rich real quick, he's looking to get his money back just as fast. He probably wouldn't work in the boxer's best interest.

"But the big thing is that Leonard can't wait that long to make up his mind," Brenner added, sharing Jacobs's sentiments. "Ron Harris was a gold medal winner in 1972—the same year as George Foreman. Harris was a hell of a lightweight. But he sat around two years before turning pro. People forgot about him, and he never made the money he should've. It seems a great waste of talent."

By now, everyone was ready to offer Leonard advice on how to spend his time and money—mostly on their own terms.

"I'd get calls at three and four in the morning from people who wanted me to endorse this or that, or make an appearance somewhere, but usually for free," Ray said. "People I never met before would come banging on my door. My parents' home was filled with strangers almost every day. I thought I was going crazy. I honestly didn't know what to do."

The troubled Leonard then paid a visit to Charley Brotman, the best-known public relations man in Washington.

"I think when Ray first talked about college," said Brotman, "he didn't take into consideration where the money for everyday living would come from. He had this specific goal—winning an Olympic gold medal—but the rest of his life lacked direction.

"I think he finally realized that he would have to start making decisions that would alter his life," Brotman noted. "So I laid out all these things in front of him. 'What do you want to do?' 'Where are you going?' I told him, 'We're talking specifics now, not generalities.' But underneath it all, I think he realized he had a God-given gift for boxing and didn't want to throw it away."

But soon, Sugar Ray Leonard ran out of options. His mother was stricken by two mild heart attacks, and his father, who had been the main breadwinner, was hospitalized with spinal meningitis. All eyes now seemed to turn on the twenty-year-old Leonard, who was unofficially appointed the "man" of the family. And no one needed to tell him what had to be done to put bread back on the table.

Reflecting on his decision, he said: "I was really sincere during and after the Olympics when I said I didn't want to turn pro. The decision wasn't easy. I know that's what I'm supposed to say, but I'm not fooling anyone. It's just suddenly that there's a lot of things for me to consider—my family, Juanita, my son, and myself. But most of all, I saw that the family wasn't moving. I said to myself, 'Ray, you have to get back out there.'

"But I was ready to fight again. Boxing was still in my blood, and I couldn't stay away from the gym for very long. But I didn't like the idea of having somebody else 'own' me. I'd always remembered Ali telling me, 'If you ever turn pro, hold on to everything you've got. Don't be like me.' "

With Ali's advice ringing in his head, Ray Charles Leonard was ready to resume his fighting career. But first, he would have to find himself a "new family."

✯ 5 ✯

ALL IN THE FAMILY

"No bad habits in this family," said Angelo Dundee, glancing around Sugar Ray Leonard's dressing room. "This is strictly 'home cooking.' Everyone in this room has been with Ray right from the start. And that's the way it stays. We're a team," said the renowned fight trainer, sounding more like a football coach.

Yes, the "Leonard family" was truly unique in the sordid history of boxing—a sport where trust and loyalty are generally measured by the size of the fighter's bankroll. By its very essence, few sports are more individualistic than boxing. But no self-respecting prizefighter ever made it to the top without a coterie of sycophants to constantly massage his ego. Ring champions have always attracted parasites, but colorful Sugar Ray Robinson set the modern trend. When the former middleweight king journeyed to Europe in 1951 to battle England's Randy Turpin, he headed a small army of flunkies, including a barber and masseur.

But Robinson was a mere amateur compared to the conspicuous extravagances of Muhammad Ali, whose regular traveling party numbered three trainers, a masseur, a "witch doctor" (Bundini Brown), photographer, biographer, armed bodyguard, and a half-dozen other followers with no discernible job description. As fight time drew near, the Ali entourage quickly swelled to include pimps, fast-buck operators, magicians, sociologists, and psychologists, all bidding for the champion's attention and charity. At times, the "infighting" between the parasites provided more action than Ali on fight night.

Chaos was the order of the day among Ali's palace guard with Bundini ("Float Like a Butterfly, Sting Like a Bee") Brown usually leading the tumult. The bearlike Bundini, who served as the "Dr. Bones" in the heavyweight champion's minstrel show, once hocked Muhammad's championship belt when financially pressed. When Ali discovered it missing, Bundini crawled back on hands and knees to beg forgiveness for fear of being removed from his rich benefactor's list of dependents.

There is the story, perhaps apocryphal, that during an early-morning fire at a hotel where Ali's troops were encamped, Dundee, the first to smell the smoke, ran from door to door shouting, "Fire!" But when he arrived in front of Bundini's room, the best he could summons was a loud whisper.

"What Ali had was a necessity," said Dundee, who was also with Ali at the beginning of his pro career. "Ali was always on stage, and you had to keep pampering his ego. He loved it. Whatever all those guys around him did, I still don't know. Nobody knows. But it worked for Ali, didn't it? So who's to say it was wrong?

"But it won't happen to Sugar Ray," Dundee added. "This kid is something else. The big guy always needed people to fuss over him. But Ray is basically a family man. Ali is a 'street person.' He loves the crowds and the adulation. Ray is a homebody."

Ironically, Dundee would find himself the lone "outsider" in Leonard's second family, composed entirely of trusted friends and advisors from his home town and neighboring communities.

"What happened to Ali will never happen here," said Dave Jacobs, Ray's trainer during his amateur and early pro career. "We've got everything we need to help him. There's always people popping up and saying, 'I can be a sparring partner.' 'I can be a bodyguard.' 'I can do this and that.' But Ray don't need no bodyguard. Everybody loves him."

Leonard, who experiences fits of homesickness whenever an out-of-town fight removes him from his familiar Maryland surroundings for more than a week's time, prefers the closeness of his "inner circle." It includes Janks Morton, his old friend and confidant; Mike Trainer, his plain-talking attorney and financial wizard; Dundee, his titular manager with the ready smile and wit; Charley Brotman, his personal public relations man; Julius ("Juice") Gatling, an unofficial valet and a ready foil for Ray's practical jokes; cousin O'Dell, his favorite sparring partner; and Ollie Dunlap, the director of the Palmer Park Recreation Center where it all began.

Throughout his quick-step march to the welterweight title, the Leonard family displayed more togetherness and true harmony than the 1979 world champion Pittsburgh Pirates, who lived by the lyrical message of Sister Sledge wailing "We Are Fam-il-ee." It was worthy of the *Good Housekeeping* seal of approval—a "love-in" that would last until Leonard assumed the throne.

From the day he declared himself ready to fight professionally, Leonard, despite his tender years, would be his own boss. No one would own a single piece of him, a fact of life that sent shock waves through the entrenched boxing establishment of fast-talking wheeler-dealers not accustomed to being shown the door by a neophyte with a Pepsodent smile.

They came with their talk of rainbows filled with overflowing pots of gold. Some, in fact, were legitimate, offering as much as $200,000 to obtain the Olympic champion's signature on a long-term contract.

"It started in Montreal," Ray recalled. "Guys kept sneaking up to me and telling me what wonderful things they could do for me if I signed with them. I spent a lot of my time at the Olympics trying to duck these guys. I'd say, 'Talk to me later, man. Not now.' But they kept on coming. They were driving me crazy. The offers kept coming and I didn't know what to do."

The best offer came from Don King, the street kid who had risen to become a millionaire through his skillful maneuvering in boxing's maze of intrigue and double-dealing. King, acting as a spokesman for Abe Pollin, the proprietor of the lavish 20,000-seat Capital Centre in Leonard's "backyard," promised $200,000 up front if Sugar Ray would become his headliner on a series of boxing shows.

"It would have locked Ray in tight," Trainer would say in retrospect. "The money wasn't *that* good. It gave King all the options when the contract expired."

But, for a young man, who once didn't have enough spending money to accompany his school class on field trips to downtown Washington, it seemed like all the money in the world.

"It was tempting," Ray admitted, "and I had to think about it for several days. To me, it sounded like a fortune. But the more I thought about it, the less I liked the idea of someone owning a part of me.

"I wanted to have a unique operation as a pro. I didn't want to go into the record books as just an ordinary fighter. So I had to be super-selective about the people I chose. . . . If you're good, and you have good people around you, it's a lot easier to win that title."

Fortunately, Leonard was able to bank on the street smarts of Janks Morton, whose personal dream of glory as a professional football player was quickly shattered, and Mike Trainer, the hard-nosed, pragmatic Silver Spring attorney who would counsel Sugar Ray throughout this period of indecision.

"I had seen athletes gypped and forgotten all my life," said Morton, who became a self-employed insurance man after flunking his NFL trial. "I have a high school buddy who played thirteen years in the NFL and even made All-Pro. Now he's working in a car wash. For once, in Ray's case, I didn't want the world to win."

Morton and Leonard first met when Janks was serving as a volunteer coach at Palmer Park and Ray was learning boxing's ABCs. "Ray and I have always been close," said Morton, "but it wasn't anything like a father-and-son relationship. Ray has been a man for some time. I just helped him get over some of the rough spots."

Janks, however, was not in a position to handle Leonard's financial affairs. For this, he turned to Trainer, a teammate on an informal softball team sponsored by a gas station.

"I told Ray I'd trust Mike with everything I own," said Morton, and delivered the young fighter to Trainer's unpretentious office in Silver Spring, an upper-middle-class suburb of Washington.

Recalling their first meeting, Trainer said, "At first, I actually encouraged Ray to go to college like he had originally planned after the Olympics. But the longer we talked, the more it seemed like he really wanted to get back to fighting. It was in his blood."

When Leonard continued to vacillate, Trainer took him aside and said, "Ray, I'll never push you into anything. But consider this: Few people ever have a chance to prove they're the best at what they do. But you have a chance to prove you're the best fighter in the world, only you can't afford to wait to do it."

Sugar Ray would accept the challenge, but it was left to Trainer to decide just how to launch his pro career.

"I had to chase a lot of fast-buck operators out of my

office," he said. "Everyone had a gimmick. They all made big promises, but they all wanted a piece of Ray, from one-third to one-half of his future ring earnings. A few, like Don King, were talking about a lot of money, but still wanted to tie him up.

"We didn't want Ray to go to the promoters with his hat in his hand like an orphan," Trainer added. "And we didn't want him winding up on his heels as some greeter in a gambling casino. Frankly, I thought Ray deserved a chance to do it on his own, and I tried to explain all his options.

"First, I had to convince him that he was a valuable piece of property and that he could go in a number of ways. He could take a big bonus from an established promoter or go it alone. But I told him I had a lot of personal friends who were willing to help him get started and it would be a community-oriented investment organization. They'd lend him the money, but he'd own himself.

"I felt very strongly about it, because I had stood on my own two feet going through law school and getting a practice started. I wanted to do the same for Ray. Nobody would own him, now or ever."

And so "Sugar Ray Leonard, Inc." was born with a thirty-five-dollar fee to the state of Maryland for incorporation papers. There would be twenty-four sponsors—most of them softball teammates of Trainer. They were salesmen, insurance men, barkeepers, lawyers, jewelers, and gas station owners, all contributing to a $21,000 ante to launch Leonard's pro career.

The twenty-year-old boxer would own one hundred percent of the company stock as both president and chairman of the board. He, in turn, pledged to pay back the loan with eight percent interest in four years time. In fact, Leonard would pay off his debt after his first pro fight in which he earned $40,000 for pinning back the ears of one Luis ("The Bull") Vega.

"It was a terrible investment," Trainer would say two

years later after his client was a certified millionaire. "They only got back $1,000, plus forty dollars in interest. But these people weren't in it to make a killing. It was just a nice gesture to get a well-meaning kid a start in his profession."

At the time Trainer rallied his friends around Leonard, he had no idea of the fighter's earning potential. As he told *Sports Illustrated*'s Bill Nack, "This may sound absurd, but I even considered getting Ray a part-time job to help pay off the loan. I said to Ray, 'Look, it might take as long as eighteen months to build you up to a big-money fight.' But, as things worked out, we never had to spend a nickel of the $21,000."

Admittedly, both Morton and Trainer were novices when it came to the ruthless business of boxing. They needed to find a true professional to safely guide their promising protégé through a boxing jungle infested with sharp-toothed predators.

"The only way I could see Ray being sidetracked," said Trainer, "was if he got snookered. We needed someone who knew the business from every angle. We wanted every edge we could get."

Placed in charge of finding the man who would handle Leonard's boxing affairs was Charley Brotman, a well-connected Washington public relations director who had earned the reputation as a skillful navigator in the Capital's murky political waters.

In Leonard's case, Brotman had to bring order out of chaos. Sugar Ray first called on Brotman in the weeks following his Olympic triumph when he was beseiged with hundreds of requests for personal appearances, with only a few of them offering money for his time.

"Ray had phone numbers scribbled on napkins, the back of envelopes, matchboxes, and scraps of paper. It was unbelievable," said Brotman. "He had tried to do all this on his own, but found himself promising two, or three different people that he'd make appearances at the same time. So, the first thing I did was to get him a desk calendar where he could keep track of everything. That was the easy part."

Brotman then started calling some of the numbers. "A lot of the people were just trying to take advantage of Ray," he said. "But he hadn't learned to say 'No.' I remember one guy, in particular. He kept leaving his number, and begged Ray to call him back. I finally reached him and said, 'Do you want Ray to do some work for you?' He said, 'Oh, no. I just want him to come to a party with me.' "

In a matter of a few days, Brotman managed to separate the freeloaders from the legitimate businessmen and bonafide charities bidding for Leonard's services. But now Trainer had given Brotman a new assignment—one, he admitted, that was completely out of his sphere of influence.

"I wasn't fooling anyone," he said. "I was a complete novice when it came to boxing. But I figured the best approach to finding a manager for Ray was to be completely candid.

"I spent over three weeks canvassing the country. I must have sounded awfully naive. I'd get on the phone and say, 'Hello, I'm Charley Brotman, and I've been authorized to find a manager for Sugar Ray Leonard's professional career. Are you interested? If not, can you recommend someone?'

"A lot of guys made big promises I knew they could never keep," Brotman added. "We wanted someone who wasn't going to put Ray in over his head just for the sake of a big pay day."

The more Brotman called, the more he kept hearing the same three names—Eddie Futch, Gil Clancy, and Angelo Dundee. All three had handled champions in their time and, in a cutthroat business, were considered exceptions to the rule—honest men with compassion for their fighters' welfare. But Futch wanted Leonard to train in Philadelphia, where most of his other fighters were located, and

Clancy campaigned to secure the dual role of Ray's trainer and manager.

"Ray had too much loyalty to Dave Jacobs, who has always been his trainer," Brotman explained, "and he wanted him to remain as part of his pro setup.

"When we talked to Dundee, he told us that he'd be happy to work along with Jacobs. In the long run, he figured to be the best man for the job. He'd traveled all over the world with Ali and knew all the promoters and managers in the business. We knew how thoroughly he scouted other fighters. There would be no chance of Angelo overmatching Ray."

The owl-eyed Dundee, who has trained or managed eleven world champions, including Ali, Carmen Basilio, Luis Rodriguez, Willie Pastrano, and Ralph Dupas, made his debut as Leonard's manager at the National Press Club on November 18, 1976.

In a room where the world's leading diplomats and political figures usually held court, Dundee insisted that he hadn't sought the office despite Leonard's unlimited potential.

"I've never approached a fighter in my life," he said. "Brotman called me one day and told me the whole story about how twenty-four guys had bankrolled Sugar Ray. I was really intrigued. I couldn't believe that there were some people who were willing to put up money for an athlete without trying to make a killing.

"But now I see Leonard's situation isn't anything like the deal Ali had with those Louisville millionaires when he first turned pro. They were looking to make a fat profit, just like the guys who backed Joe Frazier when he came out of the sixty-eight Olympics. But all the people here are strictly looking out for Sugar Ray. There's no guarantee they'll get their money back, but they don't seem to care."

In his agreement with Trainer, Dundee would receive fifteen percent for each of Leonard's fights. ("If I'd had that same kind of deal with Ali, I'd be a millionaire by now," he later confided.) Nominally, Dundee would serve as Ray's manager. More precisely, he was an all-purpose Svengali who would beautifully orchestrate Leonard's march to the title without the slightest misstep.

As always, Angelo had dutifully done his "homework." He had thoroughly scouted Leonard, and reduced the fighter to all his essentials, down to such seemingly trivial information as to how he hits a speed bag and skips rope.

"He's luminous," Angelo gushed. "He lit up the TV screen during the Olympics. You could see he had the goods even then. He had the great attitude to go along with the God-given gifts—the tremendous hand and foot speed and the ability to alter his style according to the man he's fighting. Only the great ones can shift gears like that. That's what champions are made of."

Despite Leonard's precociousness, Dundee would adhere strictly to his philosophy of "slow-teach" in assuming command of the Olympic champion.

"Used to be that people said if you don't want to work, be a boxer," Dundee said. "Guys who believed that last about a day. There's no shortcuts in this business, believe me.

"Ray is going to start out as a six-round fighter just like Ali did. We'll let him get his feet wet first. But I'm not going to match him against any stiffs. We'll put Ray in with guys of comparable talent. And, if he happens to lose, it won't be a catastrophe. When I managed Pastrano and Dupas, they lost fights early in their careers. Fighters have to learn to react to adversity, even an Ali. The ones who can't, don't make it.

Dundee, himself, started in "kindergarten" as a fight trainer and struggled for a number of years just to survive. "There were a lot of hungry days and lonely hotel rooms," he remembered. "For a long time, I was sleeping in my brother Chris's office in the Capitol Hotel. But why complain? I was right around the corner from Madison Square Garden."

A small, swarthy man with gentle brown eyes, Dundee needed only a few fights to convince himself that, if he was going to make any money in the fight business, it wouldn't be through his own blood, sweat, and tears.

"I never got past the amateur ranks," he said. "I fought in the Air Force only so that I could eat ham instead of spam. But sometimes, it wasn't worth the beatings. The only real fighter in our family was my brother, Joe. He worked on a garbage truck, so naturally the press dubbed him 'The Fighting Ash Man.' Today, I'm sure they'd call him 'The Fighting Sanitation Man,' " Angelo laughed.

After his service discharge, Angelo returned to his old South Philadelphia neighborhood and became a handyman around the gym and fight clubs for brother Chris, already an established manager and fight promoter.

"Chris was handling stickout fighters like Georgie Abrams, Tommy Bell, and Jimmy Webb, and I was handling the water bucket. Back then, I didn't even know how to wrap a fighter's hands. But I learned the tricks of the trade from the very best—Ray Arcel, Whitey Bimstein, Freddie Brown, and Chickie Ferrera. Watching them was a real education, and they didn't mind passing their wisdom along to a greenhorn like me."

Dundee's puppy eyes grew wider than ever the night one of Arcel's fighters scored a last-round knockdown. Arcel was already throwing the robe across his fighter's shoulders while the referee was halfway through the count. It was enough of a distraction for the referee to skip a few numbers on the way to "ten."

A year later, Dundee borrowed the old robe trick while working in the corner of featherweight Billy Bossio. "Yeah," he smiled at the memory, "I had the robe on Billy's back and I was already cutting his gloves off while the other guy was still falling. The referee messed up half the count, and the other corner was screaming, but, by that time, we were halfway to the dressing room."

Over some four decades in the fight racket, Angelo has

also discovered the wisdom of maintaining a low profile at the right time.

"I pride myself in never messing in a fighter's religion (Ali's conversion to the Muslim faith) or his personal life," he said. "I learned my lesson a long time ago. I had a promising preliminary fighter. He came to me crying one night that he'd just had a terrible fight with his wife. I gave him some sympathy, and he goes back and tells his wife. 'See, Angie said I was right.' That was the last I saw of him in the gym, and I never stuck my nose in again."

More than anything, Dundee learned that no two fighters are alike, and that applying the right psychology can often mean more than teaching a young pug to double up with his hook.

"Fighters are as different as night and day," he said. "Some fighters, I almost had to drag in the ring. Take Willie Pastrano, my light-heavy champ. When he was right—moving, dancing, flicking that snakelike jab, nobody could touch the son-of-a-gun.

"But Willie was the type who believed in all the zodiac signs and astrology charts," Angelo continued. "If everything wasn't in the right 'house' or 'moon' or whatever the night he was scheduled to fight, then Willie was scared to death.

"Well, we were fighting Gregorio Peralta for the title down in New Orleans in 1964, but all day long Willie is weeping, 'I can't fight tonight, Angie. The stars are all wrong.' I told him, 'Willie, maybe you're not reading those charts right. Maybe the Milky Way's got you confused.'

"We spend the whole day arguing about Scorpio and Aquarius when we should be worrying about Peralta. I had to push Willie out of the corner that night. But, you know, he surprised everyone, especially himself, by knocking out Peralta."

Someone asked Angelo about Tony Alongi, a stringbean heavyweight he managed who reportedly once lost a fight to a shadow.

"Yeah, Alongi was somethin' special," Dundee said. "He was a pretty fair fighter, but he had no confidence. Two weeks before a fight, he'd start feeling sick. First headaches. Then sniffles. Then the flu and the grippe. By the day of the fight, he was sure he had malaria or double pneumonia. He'd beg me to take him to the hospital so he could die in peace.

"The biggest fight for Alongi was that walk from the dressing room to the ring. Have you ever tried pushing a piano uphill? Alongi was twice as tough, believe me.

"One night, we're fighting George Chuvalo, the tough Canadian, and Tony's crying like a sick dog. I almost carried him into the ring. I shoved him out of the corner each round, and he boxes Chuvalo's ears off and gets a draw. That might have been my greatest triumph as a manager."

But Dundee has a way of belittling his contributions, particularly in regard to Ali's unprecedented three reigns as heavyweight king. On at least two occasions, he rescued the crown for Muhammad, the first time as a title challenger against Sonny Liston in 1964.

"They say Ali was ready to quit in the fifth round of that first fight with Liston when he couldn't see, and a lot of people were ready to brand him a coward. But it was just frustration," Dundee insisted.

"To this day, I don't know what got in his eye. It could have been salve they used on Sonny's eye or liniment from his body, but it blinded Ali. He didn't want to fight as a blindman, and when he came back to the corner, he was screaming, 'It's foul play.'

"I told him, 'Forget all this bullbleep. This is your chance to win the title. Liston's dead tired. Just go out, run around until your eye clears.' I half-pushed him out of the corner, but his eye cleared up, and two rounds later, Liston threw in the towel."

Ali also needed Dundee's "expertise" in his 1966 fight with Henry Cooper in London. Badly embarrassed for three rounds, "Our'Enry" landed a picture left hook flush on the champion's chin in the fourth round and an astonished Ali found himself sprawled across the canvas. He beat the count, but he was still groggy when he returned to the corner.

Almost magically, a slit appeared in Ali's left glove between rounds. "They had to find new gloves," Dundee said, his voice dripping with innocence. "The promoter searched half of London before he came back and said, 'We can't find a pair anywhere.' By this time Ali's head had cleared, so I said, 'OK, we'll just have to fight with these,' and he knocked Cooper out in the sixth."

Angelo also learned some valuable lessons out of the ring from his wily brother, Chris, who still promotes fights in Miami Beach.

Dundee tells of the time Chris got a collect call from a former fighter of his who had a serious case of the shorts. The fighter kept yelling into the phone, 'All I need is two hundred dollars,' and Chris, on the other end, kept saying, 'What? What's that?' Finally, the operator broke in and said, 'I can hear him fine.' To which Chris quickly countered, 'OK, then you pay him the two hundred dollars.' "

When Dundee finished his round of spellbinding tales for the press, Brotman and Trainer were convinced they had found the right man for the job of steering Leonard as a pro. But a few outsiders expressed skepticism over whether Dundee could coexist with Jacobs. They speculated aloud that as soon as Angie got his foot in the front door, Jacobs would be leaving by the back one.

Dundee did his best to quickly quash this rumor. "I'm not about to come in and change things just to prove a point," he said. "Why change a good thing? Didn't Sugar Ray win an Olympic gold medal with Jacobs behind him?

"People figured that right off the bat I'd move Leonard down to Miami so that I could supervise his daily training. But that would have been downright stupid," Angelo added. "Ray's always had a great working relationship with Jacobs. He keeps Ray in excellent shape, and Ray always feels more relaxed when he's close to home."

More than once during Leonard's rapid climb to the head of the welterweight class, Jacobs, with good intention, would question Dundee's choice of opponents. But, for the most part, he maintained a low profile while Angelo continued to draw the attention of the media, who could always count on him for a new story about his latest ring wunderkind.

"Look," Jacobs confided to a friend, "I don't have to carry the ball all the time. I'm no glory hound. I know what I did for the boy and God knows what I did. I've got nothing to prove to anyone. I'm getting my dues."

In time, however, this model boxing family began to show the signs of natural stress and tension of a real family. It led to some bitter infighting that would leave some of them with mental scars that would never truly heal.

Ultimately, the real decision-makers in the Leonard family would number only two—Trainer, who had learned to talk in megabucks, and Morton, who would continue to serve as Leonard's most trusted friend. "Without Janks," the fighter would say, "there wouldn't be a Sugar Ray Leonard."

But, for the moment, all was peace and harmony. And, in the words of Angelo Dundee, Sugar Ray was ready to take his first baby steps as a professional.

Before his trumpeted debut, Leonard said, "I know professional boxing's not like the Olympics. As an amateur, you're doing something for yourself and your country and people seem to respect you more. Money changes a person's way of thinking. People tend to get jealous.

"I know boxing is a brutal business. But life is pretty brutal, too. Look at all the people out of work."

But Sugar Ray Leonard wasn't one of them. He had chosen his profession, and now he was ready to prove that he was the very best at his line of work.

☆ 6 ☆

A BAPTISM FIT FOR A KING

It was a Hollywood-like setting befitting a visiting potentate. Buffet tables overflowed with delicacies. Baltimore Mayor William Donald Schaefer stood ready to present the key to his city. TV personalities, photographers, and reporters jockeyed for position around the boxing ring on the Civic Center floor.

The houselights dimmed and the arena was now filled with the inspiring sound of the Olympic theme. A spotlight flashed across the stage, silhouetting the figure of Sugar Ray Leonard, bedecked in his bright red Olympic robe as he shadow-boxed his way down the aisle to a spontaneous roar of approval.

This was no fanfare for the common man. This was strictly a day for royalty. The city of Baltimore had rolled out the red carpet for the dynamic twenty-year-old welterweight from Palmer Park, Maryland, a glorious welcome that hopefully would make Leonard momentarily forget that his roots were much closer to the more cosmopolitan Washington that usually reserved such treatment for foreign dignitaries.

With Mayor Schaefer's blessing, Baltimore's Civic Center Commission, led by energetic Lou Grasmick, a born promoter who had the gift and persuasion to make big events happen in his home town, was able to outbid the plush Capital Centre, located only a roundhouse right from Leonard's backyard.

Leonard would be guaranteed $10,000 for his six-round pro debut, plus a matching amount from CBS-TV. In addition, he would receive considerable bonuses, swelling to fifty percent if the live gate exceeded $40,000.

Tuning in to all the hoopla and splendor that surrounded his appearance, Leonard said, "I used to think only heavyweights could create this kind of excitement. But, I guess, I'm the exception."

Sugar Ray was as right as his lightning jab. His actual baptism—February 5, 1977—was still some six weeks away, but none of the old-time fighters and fans in the assemblage that day could remember such a lavish christening, especially for a nonheavyweight. Not even Muhammad Ali, boxing's all-time money-maker, made such an auspicious bow.

In fact, the then-Cassius Marcellus Clay, fresh from winning a gold medal as a light-heavyweight in the 1960 Olympic Games in Rome, earned only two hundred dollars in his first pro fight against Tunney Hunsaker, even though it was fought in Cassius's hometown of Louisville. And it would take another twelve scuffles before he would earn as much as $15,000 for fighting Alejandro Lavorante—less than one-half the amount Leonard would ultimately net for his "coming-out party."

"That's right," said Angelo Dundee, who served as Ali's trainer and was now appointed to manage Leonard's ring affairs. "I wasn't at Ali's first fight, but I understand there wasn't that much of a fuss over it. I've never seen anything like the reaction this kid gets.

"But you have to remember, this is the TV era, and Sugar Ray is a product of the medium that made him a worldwide figure thanks to the 'Seventy-six Olympics. Besides, this is a special occasion. Here you've got a whole city interested in promoting his debut. Sugar Ray is very salable, and he's 'homecooking,' a home town boy who made good.

"A lot of fighters," noted Dundee, "never made it big because they'd didn't have a home town that cared. Jimmy Ellis was a heckuva fighter, but he was from Louisville, and Louisville's never been a good fight town."

Baltimore, at one time, had been an exceptional fight town, a spawning ground for five world champions, including the incomparable Joe Gans, Kid Williams, Harry Jeffra, and Joe and Vince Dundee.

In the late Forties, there would be as many as three professional fight cards a week in different sections of a city that was dotted with distinctive ethnic neighborhoods. But the glut of free boxing on TV in the Fifties would kill the small clubs in Baltimore, as well as elsewhere.

In the words of the late fight promoter Eli Hanover, Baltimore became a *My Fair Lady* town. Translated, it meant that the boxing fans would only support the big-name attractions. Club fighters, no matter how determined and appealing, could not draw enough to cover the arena rent and printing of tickets and publicity posters.

But Mayor Schaefer, who was instrumental in transforming Baltimore's once gray and dreary image into that of an upwardly mobile "all-American city," was certain that Leonard had that *My Fair Lady* appeal, and he was willing to support that notion with municipal funds. The mayor, however, was admittedly unfamiliar with the fight game's lexicon. In welcoming Sugar Ray, he said he was proud to be a part of Leonard's "debate."

There was, in fact, a lively debate going on between members of the press and Schaefer's city hall staff as to whether the city had the authority to act as fight promoters in place of legitimate sports entrepreneurs.

The Civic Center Commission, headed at the time by

attorney Robert Hillman, had made an effort to find a man more familiar with the territory. It interviewed both wrestling promoter Phil Zacko and fight promoter Deacon Brown about the possibility of launching Leonard's pro career.

Brown, a man of average means who had backed a couple of low-budget ring shows, was quickly frightened off when Hillman requested $40,000 in "good faith" money to cover Leonard's purse and possible expenses. Zacko, more accustomed to promoting the likes of Bruno Sammartino and Andre the Giant, followed on Brown's heels, after wondering who had decided that the bidding for Leonard's services would start at $10,000. Zacko had also made a habit of sharing the TV revenue, which, in this case, was strictly earmarked for the fighter.

Finally, Grasmick, a well-heeled lumberman, stepped forward and agreed to underwrite the fight for the city, although Hillman's name would appear on the athletic commission contracts as the "official" promoter.

"Yes, it's a precedent," Hillman said. "We've never actually acted as a sports promoter before. But I don't think we really need anything but the approval of the Board of Estimate.

"We can't worry about losing money, even though I see little chance of it happening. We want to keep the Civic Center as busy as possible. If it stays empty, we're losing money because of the overhead. But Lou Grasmick assured us he'll personally assume fifty percent of any losses that should occur."

Hillman, of course, had no reason for concern. The day before the fight, there was already $40,000 in the Civic Center till, assuring the city of a profit, not to mention Leonard, who would himself ultimately take home $40,000 from the record Baltimore house of $73,000. It would stand as a record for first-fight earnings until converted football player Ed (Too Tall) Jones grabbed $70,000 in his ring inaugural.

But, then again, no one has ever matched the almost royal treatment accorded to Leonard on the eve of the bout. The week of the fight, downtown Baltimore was awash with likenesses of Sugar Ray. Wherever the eye turned, it found billboards, banners, placards, and posters hanging from buildings and buses. "Big Brother" never had it so good.

The marquee at the Civic Center advertised, "PRO DEBUT OF SUGAR RAY LEONARD, SATURDAY, FEBRUARY 5, 4 P.M." There was no mention of his ring foe—one Luis ("The Bull") Vega. This was strictly a "one-man show." Vega, who had signed for $650—a figure that would later become somewhat of an embarrassment to the fledgling city promoters in view of the princely ransom they were paying for Leonard's services—was, quite simply, "the opponent."

Vega, a native of Puerto Rico, who had resettled in Reading, Pennsylvania, was a glorified club fighter with an uninspiring 14-8-3 record. He was depicted by his manager as "a tough, rice-and-beans" fighter. But throughout the prefight ballyhoo, he would remain as obscure as a spear-carrier in an opera scene with Pavarotti.

Even Leonard's public workouts became daily "happenings." Close to one thousand spectators would turn out to see the wunderkind in the flesh. TV camera whirred. Politicians plotted. Pens scribbled. And teen-age girls giggled in delight.

The prefight "weigh-in," a nonevent usually attended by only the fighters, athletic commission staff, and reporters assigned to the match, evolved into a major media event, reminiscent of the circuslike atmosphere that always surrounded an Ali physical, a time in which the heavyweight champion would begin his "psyching" in earnest.

Leonard found himself surrounded by an army of media men, while Vega and his manager, Vic Santoro, sat in a corner all but ignored by the madding crowd.

"The money we're getting—$650—qualifies as no more

than a tip," said Santoro, a steelworker, who had discovered Vega fighting in a Police Boys Club in Reading. "But I'll take it. I'm not that interested in money now. I'm more interested in building a fighter, and we're getting a chance to expose Leonard on national TV.

"Take a look at Luis, here," Santoro said. "He's wearing this flimsy leisure suit in the dead of winter. I bet it don't weigh as much as Leonard's gold medal. They've got all the money and a corporation behind them. But all that don't make a difference in the ring.

"Right now, I think Vega is the stronger of the two. I'd bet our whole purse that he could last longer against an animal like Duran than Leonard. Yeah, Leonard's had a lot of amateur fights, but this is different. Vega's used to being waylayed by men, and Sugar Ray is still a boy."

For a moment, Vega found himself with a microphone in his hand and the brief attention of the media. "I didn't come here to praise Sugar Ray," he said. "I came here to beat him." He then quickly disappeared from sight again.

"I was shocked," Leonard deadpanned. "In five years of fighting, I've never had anyone treat me that way. Not even the Russians."

Vega had been one of four names offered to Dundee as a possible opponent for Leonard's debut. Dundee quickly scratched one name from the list.

"The guy was too experienced," Angelo confided, while forgetting the man's name. "You can give away experience or strength, but not both. In a first fight, there are too many question marks. You don't know how Ray will react, especially fighting in his home area. Some guys try too hard before their home fans. But I don't think pressure will bother him, not after the Olympics. He's too level-headed. He doesn't get flustered. He's relaxed, and very teachable. Tell him something once, and that's it."

Leonard, himself, admitted he knew little about his first

pro rival. "All I know is that he's never been knocked down or knocked out. I guess that's why they call him 'The Bull.' "

On the eve of his baptism, Sugar Ray did his best to keep out of sight. He took his girl friend, Juanita, and his two-year-old son, Ray, Jr., to see *Rocky*, the inspiring boxing movie he had already seen several times. Leonard found *Rocky* as suited to his combative mood as the war movies shown by football coaches to their teams on the eve of a game.

After the afternoon movie, he passed up an invitation to a promotional dinner at Jimmy Wu's Chinese Restaurant, preferring to bed down early at the nearby Holiday Inn.

The morning of the fight, there would be a final checkup by the Maryland Athletic Commission. "The only thing I can find wrong with Leonard," quipped Commission Doctor Charles Tommasello, "is that he doesn't like cold hands."

Now it was early afternoon, and the Leonard clan was already encamped in the dressing room, one that had been previously used by Liza Minnelli. All that was missing was the gold star on the door. The room was crammed with CBS cameramen and the assigned commentators—Tom Brooksheier and Jerry Quarry, a one-time "Great White Hope" who never quite got past the "Hope" stage.

"We're going to be all business today," trainer Dave Jacobs advised Quarry. "Ray's going to be a little more serious than he was in the Olympics. The Olympics were all fun."

"Are you afraid?" one of the TV types asked Leonard.

"I'm always afraid," the fighter replied. "Not afraid of fighting, just natural anxiety. I always have the butterflies before a fight. But it goes away once that first bell sounds.

"But I'm glad this is about over with," he sighed, checking his handsome face in the mirror. "It's been a real busy week. But I'm ready now."

By four o'clock, an hour before Leonard would climb

through the ropes, the Civic Center was jammed with over 10,000 fans—more than double the most optimistic forecast by the city fathers. The crowd, composed of a number of boxing neophytes, seemed almost disinterested in the preliminaries, despite the presence of two world-ranked fighters—Ronnie McGarvey and Ralph Palladin. They merely served as warm-up acts for the star attraction.

Now it was 4:45, and Vega, the squat little Puerto Rican, walked down the aisle and entered the ring with hardly a murmur from the crowd. Back in the dressing room, Jacobs looked at Sugar Ray and said, "OK, it's time." And Dundee, trailing the procession, shouted, "Let's go, gang."

A spotlight caught the stage and once more the Olympic theme blared forth as Leonard, resembling a moving American flag, sashayed down the aisle as the crowd unleashed a deafening roar. There would be another roar of approval as he skipped over the ropes and began shadow-boxing, finishing with a blurring combination that made his red tassels stand at attention.

As he stood in mid-ring with Vega, listening to the referee's instructions, Leonard's boyish face suddenly took on the sneer of a well-seasoned pro.

"When he does this," Jacobs would say later, "it's like Jekyll and Hyde. Out of the ring, he's a gentle soul. But inside the ropes, he's a professional killer."

Sugar Ray would spend the next six rounds giving the fans what they had paid to see—a showfull of flash and blinding color, only lacking a final knockout punch.

He beat a steady tattoo on Vega's impassive face with his quick jab, slick combinations, and occasional bolos à la Kid Gavilan. He would taunt his outclassed foe by fighting with his hands dangling at his side and by feigning surprise whenever Vega was fortunate to land a blow. When the crowd noise abated, Leonard would stir them again with an improvised "Ali Shuffle."

"Quit the clowning," Dundee cautioned his protégé between the third and fourth rounds.

Now Leonard was down off his toes, fighting flatfooted to give him more punching leverage in an effort to live up to his prediction of a fourth-round knockout. He opened a two-inch cut over Vega's left eye and bloodied the little Puerto Rican's nose. Just before the bell, a crunching left hook visibly buckled Vega's knees, but survival was his stock in trade.

In the fifth, Dundee was shouting, "Back him up! Back him up!" But Leonard seemed more intent on landing one telling blow. In the sixth, he went all out to provide the coup de grace. By now, Vega's face was a montage of ugly welts and bruises. Leonard tried to finish him with a buzz-saw barrage in the closing thirty seconds, but Vega refused to tumble. In the end, there was no need to await the decision, for Sugar Ray had pitched a six-round shutout on all three officials' cards.

"I hit him with so many combinations, it was just like a rerun of *Rocky*," Leonard laughed at the postfight press conference. "Vega showed the determination of an underdog, just like Rocky Balboa. I remember predicting a fourth-round knockout, but I'm glad it went the distance. It gave me a first-hand feeling of professional boxing."

Dundee admitted that he had reprimanded Leonard several times for showboating and playing to the crowd.

"I reminded Ray that he's in the pros now," Angelo said. "Once I told him, he stopped joking. He's teachable. He listens."

Sugar Ray could also listen to the joyful sound of the Civic Center cash registers that would ring up a record $40,000 for his pro debut. It had been both an artistic and financial success, enabling him to pay off his $21,000 loan after only 18 minutes of fighting.

Luis Vega would leave the Civic Center with little more than bus fare back to Reading and obscurity as a club fighter. His manager, Vic Santoro, was still complaining about "The Bull's" small purse and the favoritism of the officials.

"Leonard kept holding and hitting on the break," Santoro complained, "but the referee wouldn't do anything. That's what happens when you fight a guy like Leonard in his own backyard."

"The hell with it," said Vega, grabbing his patched-up suitcase. "I just thought we should have done better."

★ 7 ★

REFLECTIONS IN A LOOKING GLASS

"It's all happening fast, so fast," said Sugar Ray Leonard, stretching his lithe, young body across a bed in a downtown Baltimore hotel.

Gazing out the window, he could see the immense billboard adorning the side of the Civic Center with the simple message: "SUGAR RAY II." Nothing more needed to be said. As in Leonard's professional debut against Luis Vega, his new opponent, Willie ("Fireball") Rodriguez, of Allentown, Pennsylvania, would be all but ignored by the public and the press. Rodriguez might as well have been an obscure juggler appearing on the same bill with the great Houdini or a fresh comedian trying to break into the business on a show starring Bob Hope.

For fight fans, Sugar Ray possessed that unique charisma that quickly separated him from the faceless crowd of fighters who would spend their frustrating careers training in squalid gyms and serving as cannon fodder for the headlined boxers.

The truly gifted ones—the "naturals" like Joe Gans, Jack

Johnson, Benny Leonard, Willie Pep, Ray Robinson, Joe Louis, and Muhammad Ali—come along about as often as Haley's Comet. They were born to fight, lending a touch of class and artistry to a barbaric sport. Visualizing Ali as a plumber instead of a pugilist is as hard to imagine as Van Gogh painting street signs instead of masterpieces. The world would have suffered the loss of a true artist.

And now the boxing aficionados were ready to annoint the fresh-faced ring prodigy with the same measure of saintliness. Some fighters' psyches are too delicate to endure the pressures of public acclaim. Former heavyweight champion Floyd Patterson was a classic example. After a humiliating first-round knock out by Sonny Liston, Patterson donned a Groucho Marx-like disguise to escape anonymously from the crowd.

But now it was Leonard who sometimes felt himself the focal point of a million eyes, all watching and waiting to see whether he was all spark and showmanship or a fighter of real substance.

As Angelo Dundee, Leonard's wise and witty manager, noted, "There's a time when the public is going to take a bite out of that steak, and it better be good. All the flash and glitter don't mean nothin' if you can't chew it."

Realistically, it was too early in his pro career to determine how well Sugar Ray would withstand the test of time, but, in a period of reflection before his second test against Rodriguez, Leonard admitted things would never quite be the same.

"It's hard to keep your head on straight," he said, "because people just don't see me like they used to. Once they see you on TV, they expect more of you. They expect you to carry yourself a certain way. It's hard just being yourself.

"It creates all kinds of pressure. I try to deal with it, but it's hard. I don't want to change, and I'm not conscious of doing things different now. But my girl friend, Juanita, tells me that I'm already more negative. But I've got to try and protect myself from people who might want to take advantage of me. Dealing with success is something new for me. It's kind of scary."

But his close group of friends and advisors insisted that Leonard was handling the intense pressure like a champion.

"Ray hasn't changed," said Ollie Dunlap, the recreation director at Palmer Park where Leonard first laced on a pair of gloves. "He's the same today as the first time I saw him eight years ago when he began hanging around the gym. He still has time for the people I call 'lunch box Joes.' "

Joe Broddie, his friend and sometime bodyguard added, "None of this Muslim stuff or bragging like Ali for Ray. Ray's his own man, every bit of it. He sets an example for the rest of us—no partying, no drinking, no junk like that."

But things were happening to Leonard fast, so fast. As he confided to the *Washington Star*'s Betty Cuniberti, "I'd just like to walk free, without eyes or cameras constantly clicking.

"One day, I took my son, little Ray, to an amusement park, and this kid recognized me. Then, all of a sudden, there were a couple of hundred people crowding around us. So little Ray said, 'Daddy, we can't enjoy ourselves, can we? People keep messing with you.'

"And these kind of things are happening every day. You walk around, and you're more or less like a shining light bulb in the dark. Everyone sees you and everyone wants your attention. And when you start making decent money, people look at you differently and there's a lot of jealousy involved. They think that any black man who makes good is going to change."

For Leonard, the all-American image fostered by his immense television appeal, proved an extra burden.

"People tend to computerize you," he said. "It's nice that they think you're the all-American kid, but face it, no one's perfect. I know I'm supposed to project a certain image for the kids, but adults should look at me as an adult."

As his fame and bank account grew apace, Leonard found himself beseiged by friends and relatives he hardly knew existed.

"They'd come up to me and say, 'Hey, remember what I did for you? Don't you remember when I lent you a few bucks or bought you lunch?' They're all bringing things up that might have happened when I was just a baby. It's so sad, it's almost funny. When they start seeing dollar signs, that's when they come. I accept it, because it's all a part of growing up."

One aspect of his sudden fame that Leonard found particularly distressing was how his relationship had changed with other fighters who had been less fortunate in pursuing their dream.

"I know I'm lucky," he told Tom Boswell of *The Washington Post*. "People write that it's not fair that I got $40,000 for my first fight while my opponent (Luis Vega) got only $650. But it's not that what I'm getting isn't right, it's what the other guys who are trying to fight their way up from the bottom get that is wrong."

Inside the dressing room, Dundee kept up a casual stream of light banter to relieve the prefight tension while wrapping Leonard's delicate-looking hands with a Kotex pad.

"The first time Angelo did that, I felt real weird," Ray laughed nervously. "I wasn't too sure I liked it. I mean, Kotex. But it worked. It gave me the protection I didn't have when I was fighting amateur, and kept hurting my hands. It's just somethin' less for me to worry about."

Now Leonard was checking his clean-cut features in the full-length mirror. He suddenly unleashed a blinding combination at the grim figure in the looking glass. If looks could kill . . .

His father, Cicero, watches this prefight pantomime and a smile crosses his soft, round face.

"They say Ray spars with the mirror 'cause that's the only man he can find who's as fast as he is."

Now all the laughter is gone from the young fighter. If football players have a "game face" to wear into battle, then, most certainly, Leonard has his "fight face" as the walk to the ring draws near.

"I get all keyed up," he says. "I want to get in and out safely. I can't explain it. It's just something that comes over me. The ring is my domain—my territory. And I don't want anyone invading my face."

Now he was stretched out on the rubbing table and Dave Jacobs, his trainer, was gently massaging his neck muscles.

"I know it's getting close," the fighter says, "but I don't feel anything until it's about five minutes before the fight. Then it hits me. It's like somebody scrapin' your insides. You can't catch your breath."

But once Sugar Ray steps through the ropes, he undergoes an amazing metamorphosis.

"It's a little spooky," says his brother, Roger. "Outside the ring, Ray's as nice as can be. But once he puts the gloves on, his whole personality changes. He's just plain mean."

Roger doesn't volunteer the information, but his nose has been broken three times in sparring sessions with his brother, and they're no longer permitted to work together in the gym.

"Yeah, it's a little frightening," says Jacobs, who trained both brothers. "Ray has a split personality. Away from the ring, he's a sweet, lovely person. Inside, he's a killer."

But this doesn't explain Sugar Ray's compelling hold on the sporting public. Jacobs thinks he knows the answer.

"It's how Ray relates to people," he says. "First of all, the fans love his style of fighting. He combines the flair and showmanship of Ali, Ray Robinson, and Kid Gavilan. But that's only part of it.

"The big thing is that Ray always has time for people. I've seen a lot of name fighters who were too busy to sign autographs or pose for pictures. But this never happens with Muhammad Ali or Ray Leonard. They seem to have time for everyone."

Leonard picks up the thread of the conversation and says, "Look, I don't try to work on my image. If you're a phony, people see right through you. You can't project a certain image if you're not made that way."

He doesn't deny the fact, however, that Ali has had a great influence on his career and style in and out of the ring.

"Ali set the standard," he says. "Boxing is a profession that calls for self-promotion. Before Ali, few fighters even talked for themselves or had agents to help foster their popularity. A lot of people labeled Ali a 'loudmouth,' but he revolutionalized boxing and helped make a lot of other fighters wealthy who might never have gotten a break on their own."

Unfortunately, Ali's munificent ways mostly benefited fellow heavyweights. The charitable flow had hardly engulfed the likes of Willie Rodriguez, a wiry junior welterweight who had won ten of eleven pro fights campaigning in small fight clubs near his home town of Allentown.

But "Fireball" didn't seem depressed by the fact that he would receive only $1,500 for his television debut. Quite simply, he was awed by the prospect of finding himself in the same ring with the ballyhooed Leonard, who would again earn over $40,000 for a six-round effort.

"I'm real nervous about this fight," Rodriguez confided. "My stomach started jumping when I was driving down the expressway and saw a sign that said, 'BALTIMORE, 20 MILES.' Yeah, I've had more pro fights than him, but he's still Sugar Ray.

"I'd love to have tried out for the Olympics in 'Seventy-six, but I needed money real bad just to get by. So I quit the amateurs after fourteen fights 'cause I didn't have any sponsors to support me."

For all his anxiety, Rodriguez would leave an indelible

mark on Leonard. In retrospect, it would prove to be one of his toughest tests on the way to the title.

Deservedly, Sugar Ray would walk off with a unanimous decision, but not before his Puerto Rican rival had convinced both Leonard and his handlers that he was still a long way from maturation.

After shaking his early stage fright, Rodriguez took heart that he had survived the first three rounds and began carrying the fight to his heavily favored opponent. In the fourth round, he delivered two solid hooks that left the former Olympic champ visibly shaken.

But this sudden turn of events seemed to surprise Rodriguez as much as Leonard and he was slow to follow up his advantage. "When you're in there with a fighter as good as Leonard," "Fireball" would later say, "you don't know if he's faking or not. I didn't want to take any chances."

If nothing else, that shaky moment in the fourth round had proved a valuable learning experience for Leonard, making him realize how a single blow could quickly shatter his aura of invincibility.

"I was staggered and my knees buckled," Leonard admitted, "and my mind said, 'Wow, is it all over? Is this what getting knocked out feels like?'

"You can't help thinking about it, even if you survive a scare like that. One lucky punch, or one 'off' night, and it can ruin all your plans and make everything stand still. It's hard for a fighter to admit he's really been hurt or lost a fight. But that's like a man who won't tell a woman that he loves her. It's false pride."

The surprisingly stubborn resistance offered by the underrated Rodriguez had caused Leonard to reappraise his progress as a fighter.

"I'm still in the third grade," he told the postfight press gathering. "I thought I could dictate the fight, but Rodriguez surprised me with his speed. I realized I was in there with a good professional fighter, and I still had a lot to learn."

Dundee was quick to agree. "It's all part of the learning process," he said. "Yeah, he got tagged good a couple of times, but that was carelessness. This kid is still going to school. You start a fighter in kindergarten, and hope that one day, if they've got the ability, heart and desire, they'll graduate with a master's degree—a championship."

It was clear that Sugar Ray Leonard was not yet ready for canonization into boxing's hall of immortals. But, in the next few years, he would quickly outdistance Dundee's "slow-teach" philosophy and, if anything, more than fulfill his manager's great expectations.

☆ 8 ☆

PUSSYCATS AND TIGERS

The ring careers of Sugar Ray Leonard and Howard Davis were running parallel courses. Both had fought in the 1976 Olympic Games at Montreal and returned home with gold medals. Both had captivated worldwide TV audiences with their lightning fists and quick wits. They were bright, articulate, cooperative with the international press and voted the two American fighters "most likely to succeed" in the professional ranks.

The major networks bid eagerly for their talent, Leonard, the welterweight, signing a $320,000 six-fight package with ABC, and Davis, the lightweight, striking a similar bargain with CBS. But both networks were accused of pampering and coddling the former Olympic heroes in a succession of mismatches. Because of their extensive amateur backgrounds, the critics contended that both Leonard and Davis were ready to tackle tougher opposition.

"I think they can both fight just about anybody in their weight class," said Gil Clancy, the veteran trainer-manager who doubles as a TV boxing analyst. "Right now, I feel

Leonard is ready to fight anybody but Carlos Palomino, Pipino Cuevas, or Harold Weston. But if you have a chance to fight a tiger or a pussycat, you're naturally going to take the pussycat."

Despite this gentle needling, Angelo Dundee insisted his protégé was being meticulously groomed, facing either a more experienced foe or a different style in each successive outing, all part of his "thumbscrew principle."

Following his rather sobering experience against Willie ("Fireball") Rodriguez, Leonard had boosted his stock with a third-round knockout of Vinnie DeBarros in Hartford and a fifth-round KO of Frank Santore in Baltimore. Santore marked Sugar Ray's first fight in three months, and snipers in the media blamed his extended lay-off on the "get-rich quick" philosophy of Mike Trainer, his financial adviser. They suggested that Trainer had priced Leonard beyond the means of the independent fight promoter.

"That's a lot of bull," countered Trainer. "We had a fight fall through in Montreal, but not because of money. The real reason was that the promoter got cold feet after a show he built around John Tate and the Spinks brothers really bombed. Then he gave out the story that we were asking for the moon for Leonard to appear there.

"But I've already signed for eight more fights stretching into next year. Everyone wants to see Ray. I could have booked fights all the way through 1979, but we don't want to project too far ahead."

The Santore match figured to be a more serious test of Leonard's stamina. He had moved up from six to eight rounds for the first time. Santore, a veteran of thirty-one fights, had a crowding, aggressive style and the reputation of a dangerous hook in winning all but four of his bouts. But the ex-Marine would never get untracked in this televised fight as Leonard, for the first time as a pro, exhibited the power of a knockout puncher.

In the second round, a lusty left-right-left combination

carried enough force to visibly lift Santore off the floor. In regaining his balance, he twisted his ankle and it would swell appreciably in the next three rounds.

An eight-punch salvo floored Santore in the fourth, and he had to be helped back to his corner. The game Floridian would be dropped again in the fifth, this time falling face forward as referee Tom Kelly went through the formality of counting him out.

But in the flush of victory, Leonard chose to harp at his critics. "First they say, 'Sugar Ray can't hit, he's just fast.' Now I'm sure the same people will be saying, 'Sugar Ray can hit, but he ain't all that fast.' "

The new television darling bristled slightly when someone asked why he had failed to finish Santore sooner after staggering his rival as early as the second round.

"I know I hurt him earlier," he conceded, "but you can't judge a fighter that quickly. Some fighters are crafty and try to sucker you. But you're going to be criticized no matter what you do."

But the television moguls were even more sensitive than Leonard. The ears of ABC sports executives began to burn from accusations that they were intent on fattening Leonard's record by feeding him a procession of "tomato cans" in the argot of the fight mob.

ABC televised Leonard's next match with Augustine Estrada, but widespread media pressure caused the network to cancel the scheduled telecast of Leonard's match a month later against Hector Diaz, a native of the Dominican Republic whose purported record of seventeen victories in twenty-six fights was discovered to be filled with "major discrepancies."

The falsifying of ring records had already caused ABC considerable embarrassment for its involvement in Don King's United States Boxing Championships. Officials from the network made a public apology to a House subcommittee investigating the aborted tournament.

According to both matchmaker Eddie Hrica and Diaz's

manager, Woodrow Larroseaux, the fighter had won his last five bouts prior to his encounter with Leonard. But ABC, mounting an investigation of its own, discovered Diaz hadn't won a single bout during that period. This was substantiated by the president of the Dominican Republic Boxing Commission, who informed ABC that Diaz had not fought in his native land since 1975, refuting the fighter's claim that he had fought there four times since 1976.

Surprisingly, supporters of both fighters castigated ABC and its "supersleuth," Alex Wallau, for ordering the last-minute TV blackout of the fight at the antiquated Washington Armory.

"It's totally unfair," Trainer said. "This leaves a terrible taste in everyone's mouth. It's just awful. ABC is just paranoid after they got burned by the U. S. Boxing Championships. They're breaking their arms patting themselves on the back. ABC sees a chance to show Congress what good boys they are, so they put a cloud of stink over this fight at the last minute.

"They forget Ray is only twenty-one with just five pro fights," Trainer added. "Who's he supposed to fight, the world champ?"

Ironically, only six months earlier, Dundee had rejected a proposed match with Diaz, claiming the Dominican was too experienced for his young fighter.

Hrica, a close confidant of Dundee who helped evaluate and scout Leonard's opposition, accepted the blame for the discrepancies in Diaz's record.

"This hurts my whole career," said the Baltimore native who serves as matchmaker for the Capital Centre. "But when Larroseaux told me that Diaz had five fights in the last nineteen months, I believed it. And I still do. A lot of these fights are fought in bull rings and places where they hold cock fights in the remote parts of the Dominican Republic. You don't find those kind of fights in the record book."

Larroseaux, however, felt he was playing the part of the

"fall guy" and was outraged by the TV blackout. "They grilled Diaz like he was a thief," the angry manager said before his fighter entered the ring against Leonard. "It started when Wallou called me the day before the fight. He told me, 'I'm only a little Indian at ABC.' But he turned out to be a little Indian with a big ax.

"They wouldn't take my word, the promoter's or the *Ring* record book. They had some Spanish-speaking lady call Diaz and ask him a million questions. He couldn't eat or sleep the night before the fight.

"If they were so concerned," Larroseaux added, "why didn't they call it off a month ago? These people always concern themselves with the small fish. What's Diaz getting for this fight—$1,500? They should be worrying about the big-time fighters like Leonard, Howard Davis, and the Spinks brothers, who are all controlled by television. If they are so worried about boxing, let them stay out of the fight game and stick to lily-white sports like baseball and football."

ABC, which elected to show an arm-wrestling tournament in place of the fight on its "Wide World of Sports" show, looked so much the wiser after Leonard disposed of the squat, short-armed Diaz in less than two rounds, following a barrage of blows that started with "a sucker right hand."

Leonard appeared totally unflustered by all the fuss and furor over ABC's decision. "This is my home town," he said, "and I was fighting today for my own people."

The decision-makers at ABC, however, were perfectly willing to bless Leonard's next match against Rocky Ramon, a stubby five-foot-four Texan, who arrived at the press conference in Baltimore wearing a towering Mexican sombrero that all but matched his size. Described by one reporter as a cross between Lou Costello and Lee Trevino, Ramon was built along the same ground-hugging lines of several of Leonard's earlier victims. But his record of 20-11-1 stamped him as superior cannon fodder.

Ramon had gained a small measure of respect from fight critics by staging a close, but losing battle against stylish Philadelphia junior welterweight Mike Everett.

"The promoter in Philadelphia thought I was just another 'tomato can,'" Ramon said, "but I surprised Everett. There was no way I could win, though. It was a charity show. Everett's brother, Tyrone, had been murdered a month earlier. The judges and fans all felt sorry for Mike. I felt sorry, too. But not enough to get robbed of a decision."

A delivery man in San Antonio, Ramon got in shape for Leonard by racing to the top of the 1,062-step Tower of the Americas in his home town. He reached the summit in six minutes and twelve seconds to gain notoriety in the *Guinness Book of World Records*. But trying to climb over Sugar Ray Leonard proved a much tougher hurdle.

If nothing else, Ramon proved he possessed a chin molded out of Mount Rushmore. For eight brutally one-sided rounds, this Latin "Rocky" endured more punishment than Sylvester Stallone's celluloid "Rocky." He was floored in the first and fourth rounds, but bounced back to his feet with the agility of a Chinese acrobat.

With his tremendous advantage in reach, Leonard's pistonlike jab repeatedly sent Ramon's head flying like a puppet on a string. At times, Leonard chose to taunt his diminutive foe by holding him off at length with his left hand while feinting a Gavilan-like bolo with his right. But such hot-dogging tactics only caused the pro-Leonard crowd to sympathize with the outclassed Ramon.

In the final round, Sugar Ray unleashed all his fury in an effort to finish the gritty Texan. But a rubber-legged Ramon was still standing at the final bell and threw kisses to the crowd of 7,000 fans who applauded his gameness, senseless as it might have seemed.

"He said before the fight that he was going to stick to me like chewing gum," Leonard noted, "but he stuck to me like tar. He's the toughest I've fought. He showed me a lot of class."

For Ramon, his face a mass of welts and bruises, mere survival provided unrestrained glee.

"I sure can take a lot of punishment," he said proudly, while gently fingering his new scars. "But my wife says for a little guy with a lot of fights, I'm still pretty handsome. I just want to say I've never been knocked out. Never. And fighting Leonard has been a great experience. His hands are so fast, they're almost invincible. I just thank the Lord I lasted eight rounds."

For all Ramon's gallantry, the critics would continue to question the caliber of Leonard's competition. Howard Cosell, appearing on the "Good Morning, America" show, termed the Leonard-Ramon bout "grotesque." Throughout the fight, a candid Cosell, who earlier in the year had been accused of being a shill for Don King's ill-fated tournament, used such words as "preposterous" and "absurd" to describe the one-sided action.

That same afternoon, CBS was showing another glaring mismatch as Howard Davis toyed with an inept Jose Fernandez. Admitting that such fights did little to enhance boxing's appeal, CBS Vice-President Kevin O'Malley said, "It's a difficult position. We don't want to get in the position of being promoters, yet we want to be informed on who is fighting to make certain we put on decent bouts."

What made the Olympic champions' ties with television even more suspicious was evidence uncovered by a congressional committee that Davis had an option in his contract either to accept $166,000 or $200,000 per fight, with his opponents' purse to be subtracted from the higher figure if Davis chose that. This, in effect, gave Davis the authority to both select his foe and how much he would earn. It was reported that Leonard had a similar arrangement with ABC. But Ray's legal advisor, Mike Trainer, found himself in a "no-win" situation.

"It's getting almost impossible to make matches for Sugar Ray," he confided. "If he knocks somebody out in one round, people say he's fought a bum. If we get him a guy like Ramon with a rock jaw, then the crowd roots for the underdog. We're damned if we do, and damned if we don't."

What followed in the next few months resembled a film clip from that old Hollywood ring classic, *Body and Soul,* in which the mitted hero, John Garfield, marches across the screen, knocking out a procession of Palookas in whirlwind fashion to a background of news headlines interspersed with scenes of a train charging cross-country.

It was much the same for Leonard whose busy itinerary read: Art McKnight, Dayton, KO-7; Javier Muniz, New Haven, KO-1; Bobby Haymon, Landover, Maryland, TKO-3; Randy Milton, Utica, TKO-8, all in the space of eleven weeks.

Only the Haymon fight caused any controversy. The well-seasoned Cleveland campaigner couldn't answer the bell for the fourth round after Leonard had left him draped over the ropes following a savage hook that seemed to find Haymon's chin just a fraction after the bell had ended the third round.

The dazed Haymon had to be dragged back to his corner, but the minute's respite between rounds was hardly sufficient to arouse him and referee Harry Cecchini signaled the fight was over. Leonard then pranced around the ring with arms aloft in a victory salute as the home town crowd of 15,272 fans roared in approval.

But this didn't end the protest. Under the Maryland boxing rules, if Leonard had actually landed his punch before the bell, the referee was compelled to count over the helpless Haymon. "It should be recorded as 'no contest,' " argued Haymon's cornerman, Don Polo. "The referee made a mistake or failed to hear the bell. But he let Leonard hit him after that. I know, though, that protesting won't help. They say it's up to the discretion of the referee."

For the loser, things were still a bit fuzzy. "I heard the bell and started for my corner," said Haymon. "The next thing I remember was a buzzing in my head. I said to myself, 'I'm hit.' Then I found myself sprawled over the ropes."

The videotape of the fight failed to settle the argument. It appeared to show Leonard's crushing hook landing simultaneously with the bell. "I know I hit him before the bell," a solemn Leonard said. "I give the referee credit for trying to guard the safety of an injured fighter."

Someone asked Angelo Dundee if this impressive performance might alter his timetable in preparing Leonard for a title match.

"I know the kid is getting anxious," the manager responded, "but he knows it's not time yet. Too many good prospects have been ruined because they got a championship shot too early."

An eavesdropper recalled how Pete Rademacher, fresh from winning the gold medal in the 1956 Olympics, met heavyweight champion Floyd Patterson in his first professional fight. He dropped the fragile-chinned Patterson in the first round, but Rademacher, himself, was counted out in the fifth round and was never again a serious title contender.

As Dundee told *Washington Star* columnist Moe Siegal, "Rademacher was a great mistake. People remember him only for that Patterson fight. But he was really a good heavyweight, a big moose who could punch. He had no business fighting Patterson, though, and that ended it for him.

"My main man, Ali, could have fought Liston for the title before he did," continued Dundee, "but it was ruled out. My thinking is based on age. Attrition will take over, the champ gets older, and when the young guy is ready, and not before, you step in and, BANG, you've got a new champ. What's the big rush with Leonard? He's a baby still.

"But he's so teachable. He listens, like Ali did when he

Leonard, his mother and father with President Ford at White House reception for Olympic medallists (BALTIMORE SUN).

Sugar Ray works out at the Civic Center (SUNPAPERS PHOTO/WALTER McCARDELL).

Leonard in 1977 bout against Willie (Fireball) Rodriguez (SUNPAPERS PHOTO/WILLIAM HOTZ).

Johnny Gant and Sugar Ray square off before match at the Capital Centre (BALTIMORE SUN).

Dave Jacobs, Ray Jr., Sugar Ray, and Angelo Dundee (BALTIMORE SUN).

Trainer Dave Jacobs, Juanita Leonard, and Sugar Ray leave Olympic Staduim after defeat in first Duran/Leonard match, June 1980 (UPI).

Sugar Ray sparring before Baltimore bout with Willie Rodriguez in 1977 (BALTIMORE SUN).

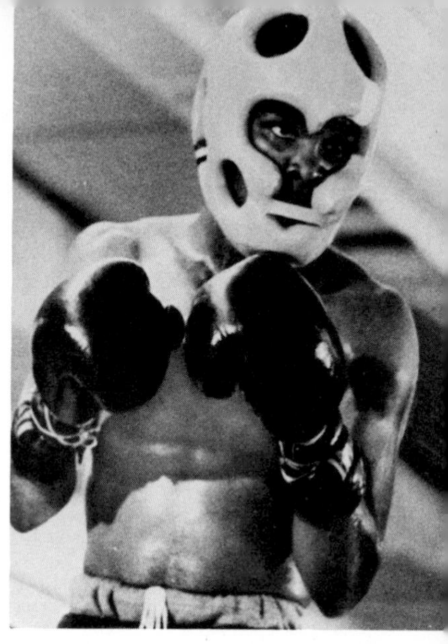

England's Davey "Boy" Green drops to the deck after a barrage of blows from Leonard in March 1980 (UPI).

KO punch in the Green title defense fight (BALTIMORE SUN).

Below: The statistics on Leonard and Duran before their first match in June 1980 (WIDE WORLD PHOTOS).

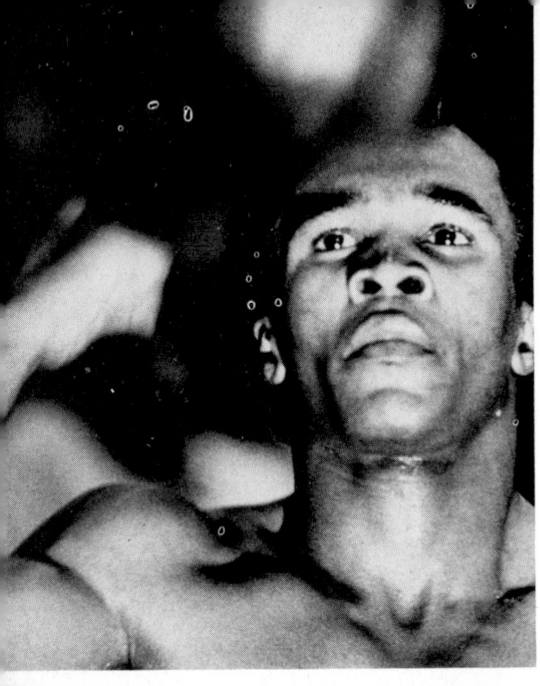

Sugar Ray at the punching bag in training for the first Duran match in Montreal (UPI).

An enthusiastic Roberto Duran at the press conference announcing his match with Leonard (BALTIMORE SUN).

Trainer Dave Jacobs giving encouragement to Leonard as he faces defeat by Duran in their first match (WIDE WORLD PHOTOS).

Below: Roberto Duran jumps for joy as he takes the WBC welterweight crown from Leonard in Montreal (WIDE WORLD PHOTOS).

Sugar Ray lands a hard right to Duran's jaw on his way to regaining his title in New Orleans (WIDE WORLD PHOTOS).

A triumphant Sugar Ray Leonard after regaining his WBC title in November 1980 (WIDE WORLD PHOTOS).

was young, but in a different way. The difference is, I *tell* Sugar Ray. To Ali, I made suggestions.

"With Ali, I'd say, 'Great left-handed uppercut you threw last round. You're the only heavyweight in history who can throw a punch like that.' The truth is, he didn't throw a left-handed uppercut at all, but it was something I wanted to see him do. So, in the next round, he'd go out and throw a couple of real beauts.

"With Ray, it's the same thing. Tell him somethin' once, and he goes out and does it the next time. He's a 'natural,' just like Ali."

Leonard was now deemed ready to go the ten-round distance—the established boxing figure that separates the main-eventers from the preliminary boys. And Dundee was also prepared to test him against fighters whose names were recognizable by more than their next of kin.

Next on Sugar Ray's hit parade would be Rafael ("The Rifle") Rodriguez, regarded in boxing circles as "a stayer" who had won decisions over ex-champions Billy Backus and Denny Moyer and lost close verdicts to Hedgemon Lewis and Harold Weston, two stylish welterweights.

The Rodriguez clan came riding into Baltimore like a band of vigilantes, seeking justice for their brother, Rafael, who would be fighting Leonard in his backyard.

"Coming into another fighter's town," said Rafael, "is like walking into a maze. You expect the worst, and usually get it. Sugar Ray is the big hero here, and he's got the people and the press behind him. It's like fighting two battles at the same time."

Rodriguez's manager, Ron Peterson, insisted that his fighter had repeatedly been fleeced in out-of-town scuffles.

"But, believe it or not," said Peterson, "the worst heist they ever pulled on Rafael was in his own home town of Minneapolis. I should know. I promoted the fight with Hedgemon Lewis.

"This was a rematch everyone wanted to see after Rafael lost a real close decision the first time. This time, though, Rafael knocks him down twice and boxes his ears off for ten rounds. I'd bet a bundle on Rafael, and I'm walking around ringside, getting ready to collect my money when the ring announcer says, 'The winner is Lewis.'

"I went beserk. Here, the poor guy can't even win an honest fight in his own home town. I wouldn't let those officials work another one of my fights.

"I'm hoping these guys in Baltimore got better eyesight. But personally, I think they're nuts. Leonard's a million-dollar property and they're going to get him beat, maybe even knocked out, by my guy."

But no one was more surprised than Peterson when the usually aggressive Rodriguez, who figured to pressure Leonard from the opening bell, fought instead a cautious, defensive battle until the closing rounds when a brief rally fell far short of the mark.

"I don't know what Rafael's problem was," said Alonzo Johnson, the former light-heavyweight contender who served as the loser's trainer. "You can't stand back and let Leonard do his thing. He'll punch you to death. I kept yelling, 'Rafael, take it to him.' But he played right into his hands by waiting."

In his own defense, Rodriguez said he was fooled by Leonard's change in tactics. "Every fight I've seen him on TV," said Rafael, "he took the fight to his opponent. I kept waiting so I could counter. But he fooled me. He stayed back most of the time and did a lot of dancing. I just waited too long."

While Rodriguez waited, Leonard piled up points with a stinging jab and timely combinations that rocked his rival in the second and fifth rounds. Each time, however, he was slow to follow his advantage, electing to play to the partisan crowd with his Ali impersonations.

As they met in mid-ring for the customary touching of the gloves to start the final round, both fighters appeared fatigued. Leonard whispered, "Man, I'm glad it's almost over." Rodriguez smiled and replied, "Yes, sir, so am I."

When the referee raised Leonard's hand, there was almost a collective sigh of relief in his corner.

"The big thing we gained today," said Dundee, "was Ray getting over the psychological barrier of going ten tough rounds. Even if a fighter is in shape, there's always that shadow of a doubt in his mind when he hasn't done it before.

"I'd worked with Rodriguez myself in the past," Dundee noted, "and I knew he had a concrete chin. I'd have been the most surprised guy in the world if Ray had knocked him out."

Buoyed by his first ten-round triumph, Leonard turned from boxer to slugger in his next challenge, flooring Dick Ecklund, a rugged New England club fighter, four times on the way to a lopsided decision before a capacity crowd of 5,000 fans at Hynes Auditorium in Boston. Ecklund was dropped in the second, sixth, ninth, and tenth rounds, but each time, he jumped up quickly and beckoned his tormentor to "come and get me."

In the ninth, the crowd was momentarily stunned to find Leonard on the canvas, but the referee quickly ruled it a slip. "He hit me on the back of the head," Ray explained, "but I was in the process of throwing an uppercut, dipped too low, and slipped to the floor. I'll give Ecklund credit, though. I was throwing good shots all night and he kept taking them."

Dundee's precise "measuring stick" now assessed that Leonard was ready to assume greater risks against ranking fighters. He was no longer the fuzzy-cheeked kid in the "third grade." He had moved up in class much faster than Angelo had calculated. It was time to take Sugar Ray out of his protective cocoon and to see, in fact, if he was ready to fly.

But each step would still be carefully measured. There would be no sudden giant steps that might cause Leonard to stumble and lose his confidence. The threatening presences of the likes of Wilfredo Benitez, Pipino Cuevas, Roberto Duran, and Tommy Hearns were still far off in Dundee's master plan.

"They'll all get their chance one day," Dundee promised. "But I think I know something about bringing along a fighter. You can't keep everybody happy. Hey, there's even some people I know who don't like linguine with white clam sauce."

So while impatient ring critics complained that the obviously talented Leonard was being reigned too tightly, others, like Dundee's old mentor, Ray Arcel, felt he was being nurtured to perfection.

"Sugar Ray's shown tremendous progress in every fight he's fought," said Arcel, who has trained countless champions in a half century devoted to improving "The Sweet Science."

"He is one of the keenest students of boxing I've seen in recent years. He reminds me of another Leonard, one I considered the perfect fighter—Benny Leonard, the greatest of them all.

"Benny was the one guy who could make you do the things you didn't want to do. If you were an aggressive fighter, he'd back you up. If you were a counter-puncher, he'd make you lead. His mind was always working. Well, Ray Leonard is the nearest thing to Benny I've ever seen."

The point Arcel was making was clearly evident in Leonard's next bout against Floyd Mayweather, a slender Detroit boxer whose crowd-pleasing style and unusually quick fists reminded many ringsiders of Sugar Ray. Early appraisals likened the match to Leonard fighting his image in the mirror.

But this would mark a significant step for Leonard since Mayweather, sporting a 15–1 record, would be the first world-ranked foe he would face in his fourteen professional bouts. Mayweather was rated seventeenth by the World

Boxing Council and number four among U. S. welterweights. The prospect of facing a fighter of some stature seemed to fuel Leonard in his prefight training.

"You know," he said, "it's the rough fights that make you. Fighting the top people gives you the pride and you find out a lot about yourself. I don't want to sound cocky, but I really want to be world champion. When I first turned pro, I was just looking for financial security for my family. But now all I think about is being champion. It's my time."

Leonard more than looked the part of a future champion while exposing Mayweather as only a pale imitation. Sugar Ray administered a fearful beating to his highly touted rival before the referee mercifully stopped the slaughter with forty-four seconds remaining in the tenth and final round.

"As a human," Ray said, "I felt the fight should have been stopped in the sixth. A guy shouldn't have to stay in there just to get banged around. That's not what boxing's all about."

But the battered Mayweather, who couldn't remember how many times he had been floored in the eighth round (it was twice), questioned his victor's punching prowess.

"He's no kayo artist," said Mayweather, who insisted he lost his chance of winning when he injured his right wrist in the first round. "A surprise shot might take you out, and he might get you with a flurry. But he can't really punish you if you see it coming. You've got to have a punch in this game. If you ain't got one, you can't keep people off. They keep coming and coming at you. Leonard's a contender all right, but as he moves up the ladder, he's going to meet a lot of fighters he can't intimidate."

Leonard's next challenge would offer a new incentive—revenge. He had fought over one hundred ring wars in the five years since he battled Randy Shields for the National AAU 140-pound title in Boston in 1973, but he still remembered it as if it had happened only yesterday.

"How can I forget it?" he said with a raised eyebrow, after signing to meet his old nemesis in his fifteenth pro bout. "Randy beat me, and that's the last fight I've lost as an amateur or pro. That's why I want this one real bad."

Recalling that long-ago defeat, Ray said, "We just squared off toe-to-toe for three rounds. I figured the decision could have gone either way. But even though I lost, I thought I proved something. Up 'til then, I'd been fighting at 135 pounds, and some people questioned if I was strong enough to compete as a junior welterweight. But I made it all the way to the finals."

After the loss, Leonard's trainer, Dave Jacobs, badgered Shields's handlers for a rematch. "I told 'em we'd fight Randy anytime, anywhere, in the East or in his backyard of Los Angeles," said Jacobs, "but we never got together. Then Randy turned pro the next year while Ray was getting ready for the Olympics."

Understandably, Shields, who had progressed as a pro to a number four ranking in the world, was hardly in awe of the still unbeaten Leonard. For Randy, boxing was one of his less dangerous pursuits. He doubled as a Hollywood stuntman, following in the dangerous footsteps of his father, Sonny, who was a standout lightweight in the Fifties.

"My father was going places as a fighter," Randy said proudly. "He was going to make his debut at Madison Square Garden on November 27, 1955, but that also happens to be the day I was born, and I guess he decided that being home was more important."

Pulp novels and grade "B" movies are filled with tales of ex-pugs reliving their unfulfilled dreams by pushing their offspring into fighting. Just the opposite was true in Randy's case.

"I was the kind of kid who hung around the house a lot," he said. "Most of the families in Los Angeles had swimming pools in their backyards, but we had a ring and light and heavy bags scattered 'round the yard. I'd spend a lot of time watching my father work out.

"He actually tried to discourage me from fighting, but I kept pestering him until one day he took me aside and said, 'If you're determined to be a boxer, I'm going to make sure you learn the right way.' "

Father and son were soon sparring daily, with Randy's mother serving as timekeeper and referee. At first, Randy had to balance himself on five-gallon cans to reach the speed bag, but the handsome youngster, who looks more like a matinee idol than prizefighter, quickly proved he had inherited his father's boxing talents.

He won eighty-eight of ninety-two amateur fights, including his 1973 championship match with Leonard, one Randy recalls quite differently than Sugar Ray. "He tried a lot of that 'hot-dog' stuff with me," Shields said. "I hit him with a solid left hook, his mouthpiece flew out, and his knees buckled. He didn't clown much after that."

The heralded rematch attracted 10,061 fans and a record Baltimore Civic Center gate of $77,434, and when the final bell ended the rousing ten-rounder, Leonard was still unbeaten, but had gained added respect for his clever California rival.

Shields's chin had proved far more durable than that of referee Tom Kelly, who caught a wild right hand by Sugar Ray in the ninth round, and had to be replaced in the ring the final round by judge Harry Cecchini.

"It was a tough fight," an unusually sober Leonard said. "I don't think I was as cocky as I have been. But I learned a few more tricks in this one. It was a matter of wits, and a matter of speed. I wanted this one real bad, much more than any of my other fights."

Dundee shared his fighter's respect for the loser. "Ray had to pull out all the stops to beat him. I knew we were going to have a good fight, but not this good. I've got nothing but the highest admiration for Randy Shields."

To Shields's credit, there was no questioning the wisdom of the Baltimore officials. "When the decision is announced, it's in the books," he said with a slight shrug. "Ray's a slick fighter, and he knows all the tricks, but I can't really say he's the toughest guy I've fought—and I didn't like the way he butted me in the second round.

"A couple of guys came up to me after the fight and said I should tell the reporters that Leonard's a dirty fighter, but he's not. He apologized, and I knew the butt wasn't deliberate. But now we're one and one, and we ought to have a 'rubber match.' "

But Shields was not included in Leonard's future plans. Dundee was already projecting far ahead.

"Sugar will be champion one day, I'm sure of that," said Angelo, momentarily forgetting his customary cautiousness. "Right now, we don't want to rush him, but, at the same time, we aren't slowing him down. From here on out, he fights only contenders."

Small game a thing of the past, Sugar Leonard was now ready to go tiger-hunting.

✯ 9 ✯

THE MONEY MACHINE

The boxing clan gathered in Las Vegas in the fall of 1978 to pay homage to Joe Louis, the former heavyweight king who had suffered another relapse and was now confined to a wheelchair.

On an occasion that brought together so many of boxing's legendary names, most of the conversation was expected to center around great heavyweights—past and present. But surprisingly, most of the night's guests were talking in awed tones about the cartloads of money a precocious twenty-three-year-old fighter—all of five-foot-nine and 147 pounds, with delicate hands (8½) and a petite waist (29 inches)—was delivering bimonthly to his favorite Maryland bank.

"Can you imagine a kid like Sugar Ray Leonard making $40,000 in his first pro fight, and for six rounds?" Billy Conn, the man who had come close to upsetting Louis, asked incredulously.

"I got $2.50 for my first fight," Conn said. "My manager gave me fifty percent of the purse. When I complained, he said, 'Forget it, kid. You lost the fight. And besides, you got somethin' to eat, didn't ya?' "

In retrospect, the record-setting $40,000 purse Leonard received for his pro baptism would resemble a kid's piggy-bank savings compared to the 3 million he would earn in his first thirty-three months of fighting.

Had he been born with the framework of a heavyweight, few eyebrows would have been raised over his prodigious earning powers. For after all, 'way back in 1927, Gene Tunney received $990,445 for his second fight with Jack Dempsey. Tunney would then write promoter Tex Rickard a check for the difference for the right to brag of becoming the first gladiator to earn a flat million.

Some fifty years later, Ali and George Foreman would split 10 million for their celebrated "Rumble in the Jungle." But everyone knew Ali was unique. He had put a capital "I" in inflation long before the Arabs cornered the oil market. And once he removed himself from the ring spotlight, the experts were in agreement that boxing's boom days would be at an end.

As John Condon, Madison Square Garden's vice-president of boxing, predicted following Ali's second "retirement," "Without Ali, everything will return to normal. Today, things are dictated by the TV networks, who pay most of the fighters' purses. TV controls it. They pay for Ali. Without him on the scene, the promoters might get back to paying $150,000 or $200,000 for the big fight the way they used to."

Naturally, Condon was thinking only of the heavyweight ranks. It was utterly inconceivable for a non-heavyweight to command six figures for an appearance. Talented light-heavyweights, such as Conn and Bob Foster, would eat a steady diet of fat-saturated foods, hoping they could compete in the higher tax brackets reserved for heavyweights.

Middleweights, with the possible exception of Ray Robinson, who was as much a master at negotiating as he was at fighting, were considered to be "poor relations" of the heavyweights. And ring earnings would depreciate proportionately with each drop in weight class—the lighter the punch, the smaller the pay envelope. They would fight for crumbs, earning just enough to keep them off the welfare rolls.

But then along came Sugar Ray Leonard, the miniature marvel, who would change all the numbers and conventional thinking in regard to non-heavyweights.

In the words of Sugar Ray Seales, a 1972 Olympic champion who failed to truly capitalize on his gold medal, "Leonard came out of the 1976 Olympics with dollar signs attached to him. And there were people waiting for him, and the dollar signs have been converted into green money."

But why a Sugar Ray Leonard and not a Sugar Ray Seales?

"If I've started a trend away from the heavyweights," Leonard said without false modesty, "then the big thing I had going for me aside from my ability was the exposure I got at the Olympics in Montreal. But I was fortunate to turn pro with the right people behind me. And I'm also fortunate in that I've always been able to relate to people. None of this is something I've had to work at."

"Compared to Leonard," said manager Angelo Dundee, "everyone else is like a funeral parlor."

Dundee had once described Ali as "luminous." A man asked if Leonard possessed that same quality. "Opaque," Dundee replied thoughtfully. "Yes, he's luminous, too. He lights up any room he's in. But opaque is a better word. You can't see through this kid."

Everyone seemed to have their pet theory in explaining Leonard's dazzling charm. "Ali had the controversial dimension," said promoter Bob Arum. "You loved him or hated him. He knew how to stir up people and sell himself. But Leonard is more natural. He's the type you *have* to like. You sit there saying, 'God, I hope he does well.' "

It was this special brand of personal magnetism that made Leonard "prime time" on television in the same context as Ali. But the packaging of the TV darlings was quite different.

"Ray's nothing like Ali," Dundee insisted. "We didn't need any gimmicks to sell him. He didn't have to spout poetry, mug for the cameras, or make bold knockout predictions. The Olympics and TV was all Ray needed. We didn't need to give him an identity."

But that alone did not make Leonard a millionaire at twenty-two. It took the financial wizardry of Mike Trainer, the Silver Spring attorney, to convert Leonard's career-launching $21,000 kitty into a quick fortune that would make the corporate giants green with envy.

Each month, Sugar Ray, the president and lone stockholder of his corporation, would receive a Xeroxed printout of the substantial dividends accrued from his investments in real estate, U. S. treasury bills, tax-free bonds, and high-quality stocks. He could afford to jet cross-country on impulse to rub elbows with Hollywood celebrities or drive to his dentist in a chauffer-driven limousine. In time, he would build an $850,000 mansion (with a swimming pool and tennis court) in the Washington suburbs not far from the lower middle-class black enclave where he had lived most of his life.

It was an empire built on Trainer's clever manipulating of the television networks, but the straight-talking attorney would be the first to admit that he could never have anticipated such opulent living for his young client the day Leonard's closest friend, Janks Morton, first proposed the idea of converting an Olympic gold medal into legal tender.

"Truthfully," Trainer said, "I had no idea what Ray's boxing talent was worth."

Recalling his conversation with Morton that fateful day, Trainer asked, "Do you think he can earn as much as $20,000 a year?"

"More like $100,000," said Morton, who would also prove ultra-conservative.

"You must be kidding?" Trainer replied. "Is this kid that good?"

"Good enough to be the biggest thing in boxing when his career ends," said Morton.

But Trainer, although a newcomer to the cutthroat fight game, had an innate feel for knowing where all the gold was hidden. With the skill of a master juggler, he had the spokesmen for the three major networks playing into his hands in their eagerness to gain exclusive rights to this charismatic fighter who was made for the living room.

At first, Trainer negotiated a $350,000 six-fight contract with ABC. Overjoyed with the ratings from Leonard's appearances, ABC would up the ante to $1 million for the privilege of showcasing him in five prime-time fights beginning in 1979.

In addition to having ABC, CBS, and NBC engage in a mighty tug-of-war, Trainer would strike separate cash deals with arena promoters who would not benefit from the TV negotiations for Leonard's services.

The greening of Sugar Ray Leonard would resurrect once forgotten fight towns like Hartford; Dayton; Springfield, Massachusetts; Portland, Maine; and Tucson. In time, it would make Leonard the most lucrative road show since Bing Crosby and Bob Hope chased a sarong-clad Dorothy Lamour around the world.

The mere mention of Leonard's name would cause fight promoters across the country to start salivating like Pavlov's dogs. The name of the opponent, or more precisely, victim, mattered little. But Leonard's name up on the marquee, and a sellout was all but guaranteed.

"Selling Leonard isn't like booking a normal event. He's a 'happening,' just like Muhammad Ali," said Arizona promoter Steve Eisner, who would reap a handsome profit from Sugar Ray's stunning first-round knockout of Daniel Gonzalez at the Tucson Convention Center. Leonard took home $200,000 for less than three minutes' work, but Eisner wasn't about to quibble.

"Look," he said, pointing to the capacity crowd of 9,000 fans. "This kid's drawn more people in this building than even Elvis Presley. He's truly remarkable. He's got what people in Detroit call 'composture.' That's half composure and half posture.

"When I booked this fight, I didn't even know who Leonard's opponent would be and, frankly, I didn't care. I left that to his advisors. But the first day I announced that Leonard was coming to town, I sold $50,000 worth of tickets.

"One big gambler from Las Vegas called and tells me in a real rough voice, 'You better save me $5,000 worth of good ringside seats or I'm putting you on my blacklist.' I tell you, with this kid, it's a real circus."

Asked if he could explain Leonard's unique box-office appeal, Eisner said, "This kid is America's new sweetheart. He's like a black Shirley Temple. Everybody loves him. And, you know, like little Shirley, we watched him grow up before our eyes. Even Ali didn't get the exposure this kid has received. We've watched him mature from the time he was in the Olympic Trials, to winning the gold medal in Montreal, and now we're seeing him really blossom as a great professional fighter.

"Originally, I wanted to book Leonard into the Arizona State University fieldhouse. I was sure I could sell the joint out. But the college administrators were afraid I'd give their place a black eye by bringing in professional boxing.

"But I can't complain. I drew over 9,000 people to see Leonard fight some Argentinian nobody could find in the record book. Just amazing."

A few folks south of the border had actually heard of Gonzalez, who was ranked number four in the world, thanks to a gaudy record compiled against obscure pugs in South American villages and a reputation for never having been knocked off his feet in sixty-eight scuffles. The squat-sized Argentinian was accompanied to the arena by a seranading bank of mariachi musicians, but the festive air would soon turn into a wake.

Before the fight, Eisner had presented Leonard with a set of Everlast gloves. But Dundee made the promoter shop around for a pair of Reyes gloves, a Mexican brand that is preferred by punchers. Eisner seemed surprised, reminding Dundee that his protégé was not regarded as a knockout artist. "We might surprise you," Dundee smiled.

Known for doing the "little things" that help win fights for his large boxing stable, Dundee had paid a call on Gonzalez minutes before the call to the ring, ostensibly to check the Argentinian's hand wraps. He was greeted by a dressing room full of Gonzalez's cronies, who kept their hero from engaging in the usual prefight shadow-boxing ritual that gets a boxer unlimbered for real combat.

Returning to Leonard's dressing room, he advised Ray, "Nail him right away. This guy is cold as ice."

Leonard followed Dundee's orders to the letter. A picture-perfect right cross deposited Gonzalez on the seat of his pants before Howard Cosell could warm his tonsils. By sheer willpower, Gonzalez staggered back to his feet and then surprisingly spit out his mouthpiece as Leonard moved in for the kill.

For a split second, Sugar Ray eyed his rival suspiciously. "I thought he might be trying to sucker me," he said, "but when I saw his eyes spinning around in his head, I knew he was really hurt. I wanted the referee to stop it, but he wouldn't. So I nailed him with another right."

Before Gonzalez landed a second time, his manager, Amilcar Brusa, had jumped into the ring, waving a white towel in a show of surrender.

While Leonard cavorted gleefully around the ring with a Mexican sombrero borrowed from a ringside customer, his mother, Getha, complained, "I wasted a tranquilizer. I never thought it would be over this fast. And I know Grandpa Leonard back home won't like it, either. It takes him awhile to get comfortable in his rocking chair."

A man with little compassion asked a still fuzzy-headed Gonzalez if he now considered Leonard the best fighter he had faced in his sixty-nine-bout career.

"I don't know," the little welterweight said wearily. "I wasn't around long enough to find out."

The fight had ended before the mariachi band had played its first encore. But no one seemed to complain about its brevity, least of all Leonard and Eisner, the promoter, who had both profited handsomely.

For some, however, Leonard's sudden wealth was a source of irritation, particularly a veteran campaigner like Johnny Gant, a product of the same mean streets of Washington that had spawned Sugar Ray.

On January 11, 1979, Gant, who was fighting professionally long before Sugar Ray had laced on his first pair of gloves, challenged Leonard for the Maryland state title. They would be fighting for something far more meaningful than the purse—the bragging rights to the title of the toughest guy in the neighborhood.

At the prefight conference at the Capital Centre in Landover, Maryland, a brief jog from both fighters' homes, a reporter asked Gant, "Suppose Leonard had all this talent, but not the recognition he's gotten? What would he be doing now?"

"Struggling, just like me," said the poker-faced Gant.

One could expect a touch of bitterness on Gant's part. He was the "dues payer" finally getting a decent break while Leonard, "the new kid on the block," had it made from day one.

Gant, however, maintained his composure; in the years since a nineteen-month prison term at age sixteen he had become quite a stoic and had learned to hide his anger well.

"I don't mind Leonard making the money," he said. "I'm

actually glad for him. He's handled himself well and looked out for his family. But I resent fighters who don't have half my ability making big bucks. I've waited a long time for my time to come."

With his standoffish defensive-style of fighting, punctuated by a lightning jab and crisp counters, Gant had always been considered a "spoiler" in boxing parlance. Mention his name in a roomful of fight managers, and they'd exit in the panic of a Chinese fire drill.

It led to long periods of unemployment for the slender Washington welterweight and always elicited the same response from Jimmy Dudley, his long-time advisor, when someone inquired about his fighter:

"When's Gant going to fight again?" a man would ask.

"The first," Dudley would reply.

"First of February?"

"Naw, the first chance he gets."

Although he remained in the Top Ten welter rankings for close to six years, Gant never gained any measure of popularity by fighting in the Baltimore-Washington area he considered home turf.

"I've fought in London, Honolulu, Puerto Rico, and Paris, and they all cheered me as a classic boxer," Gant said with a touch of pride. "They love me everywhere. Everywhere but back home."

But winning on the road is more difficult in boxing than any sport, a fact of life Gant would painfully learn time and again.

Dudley had kept a diary of itinerant horrors in his memory box for deliverance whenever a reporter hovered into view.

"Like the time we're fighting Eddie Marcel in Trinidad," Dudley said. "I didn't start worrying about Johnny getting a fair shake until I see all the judges get up and applaud when Marcel climbs into the ring. And they were all drinking rum before the fight. By the time it started, I don't think they could tell the two fighters apart.

"But that didn't help us," Dudley added. "Now I'm trying to get into the ring to work Gant's corner. I discover there's no steps on my side, and I'm too old to jump that high. So I ask the promoter, 'How'm I supposed to work with my fighter, by Morse code?' And he says, 'Don't you remember? You flipped a coin and lost, so Marcel got the side with the steps.' I was learning fast.

"Well, Gant wins nine out of ten rounds, but the officials give it to Marcel. Now the crowd goes wild. At least, they've got a sense of justice. But they start pelting the ring with rum bottles and I get clipped behind the ear. And that's how I spent my last night in Trinidad, picking glass out of my head."

The litany of hard luck tales goes on and on as Gant nods his head silently in agreement.

"I've thought of quitting the ring a dozen times," the fighter said. "It just gets too frustrating. I had one shot at the title—against Angel Espada in 1976. I had to take the fight on thirteen-days' notice. It was take it or leave it. They offered me $12,000—more than I ever made before, so I took it. But I wasn't close to being ready, and he beat me. A month in the gym, I would've beat him, and I'd be champion today and making big money."

Gant now cast a jaundiced eye toward Leonard, who was surrounded by a small army of media types fighting for attention.

"I've known him since he first started fighting," Gant said. "My younger brother, André, and Ray started at the same time and fought in a lot of amateur tournaments together. I always thought Ray was 'a comer,' but I was surprised he went on to win a gold medal. There's been great Olympic fighters like Ali, Joe Frazier, and Sugar Ray Seales, but they didn't get half the exposure Ray got. His timing was perfect.

"The previous Olympics in Munich had all that ugliness with the terrorists killing the Israeli athletes. America was looking for new heroes. Sugar Ray came along and jumped right over the moon."

Leonard, likewise, had early memories of Gant, the fighter.

"I first saw Johnny when I was fourteen," he recalled. "He was fighting a main event at the Kalorama Roller Rink, where they used to hold fights occasionally. He won big, and I said to myself, 'This guy has class and style. He can really fight.' But I never pictured myself being in the ring with him one day. You don't think that way.

"Honestly, I wish Johnny had made as much money as I have, but you can't fault anyone. I just happened to come along at the right time. But people forget that I paid my dues like everyone else. I was an amateur for eight years, fighting the best amateurs in the world, and, believe me, a lot of those European fighters are better than our professional fighters in the States."

The Gant-Leonard contest was one of those rare matches created by public demand, an old-fashioned neighborhood battle pitting the crafty veteran, just cresting the hill, against the young upstart who could boast of doing everything just a little bit better.

It was also a match that forced Angelo Dundee to choose sides. For close to a year, Dundee had been booking both fighters, working in Gant's behalf to achieve another title shot. But pushed into a corner, Dundee elected to cut his ties with the older fighter.

"It's a bridge Johnny has to cross," Dundee said. "It wasn't a fight I was anxious to make. In fact, I talked the people out of making it three months earlier. But now I can't stand in Johnny's way. The public wants him to fight Leonard. They almost demand it. And when you get in that kind of a situation, it's time to step aside for the good of the fighter."

Obviously, it was also a sound business decision for Dundee, who didn't need anyone to remind him of Leonard's vastly superior earning powers and still unrealized boxing potential.

Once before, Dundee had been forced to choose sides. That time, he sided with Jimmy Ellis when Ali was mounting one of his comebacks in 1971, following his political exile for refusing induction into the army. Dundee would help carry Ellis back to his corner in the eleventh round, but, in time, he was back in Muhammad's good graces and would pad his bank account substantially as the once and future heavyweight king's chief trainer.

Dundee's instincts were again right on the money. The ground swell from the interminable barroom debates quickly snowballed until a rockin' and rollin' capacity crowd of over 19,000 screaming fans jammed into the Capital Centre to witness the showdown between Gant and Leonard.

From the opening minutes, it was apparent that Gant could neither match the firepower nor the all-around boxing talent of his aggressive young rival. In the first round, a head-spinning combination by Leonard made Gant's knees tremble.

The "old man" would make one gallant attempt to turn the fight in his favor when he suddenly turned bold in the fifth round and caught Leonard with five solid right hands. But Sugar Ray refused to give ground, and staged a stirring rally in the closing minute of the round to catch the judges' eyes.

Leonard would seize upon a small opening in the eighth round to overwhelm Gant and end the veteran's hopes of springing a major upset that would catapult him back into title contention.

A sharp jab, followed by a series of jolting uppercuts and finally capped by a shattering left hook, sent Gant's mouthpiece flying across the ring. Another booming hook deposited Gant in mid-ring. Glassy-eyed and rubber-legged, he beat the count with only twenty seconds left in the round. But there was no escaping Leonard, one of the great finish-ers in boxing history. Another blinding barrage left Gant swaying helplessly on the ropes and referee Joe Bunsa moved in quickly to throw a protective shield around him.

Amid the bedlam of the postfight press conference, Leonard said he had become enraged after the first round when Gant had called him "a boy." "I guess he found out that the boy had become a man," Leonard laughed. "This was like my dream come true. I knew I was too strong for him.

"Tonight," he added with emphasis, "I made all the people realize that an experienced, classy fighter like Gant doesn't mean all that much when he is fighting someone who is as dedicated as I am to winning the championship. I'm going to bring the welterweight title back to Maryland where it belongs."

It was a night Sugar Ray had clearly established himself as the toughest kid on the block. And after a few more tomorrows, he would rule the world.

☆ 10 ☆

WEIGHING RAY'S FUTURE

Back in the winter of 1977, following his effortless conquest of Hector ("Chinto") Diaz, Sugar Ray Leonard held a press conference in a dingy backroom at the Washington Starplex Armory.

A young lady with a tape recorder, grown weary of all the technical questions about jabs, hooks, and counterpunches, asked in exasperation, "Mr. Leonard, are you going to be heavyweight champion one day?"

While veteran sportswriters bit their lips to stem their laughter, Sugar Ray, with that dead earnest look he gives to all questions, ludicrous or otherwise, replied, "No, Ma'am. Maybe one day I'll grow into a middleweight and win that title, but I don't think I'll ever be another Ali."

Even the thought of the baby-faced Leonard one day developing into a full-fledged middleweight seemed a bit preposterous at the time. He had dazzled the boxing world in 1976 by winning an Olympic gold medal as a junior welterweight (140 pounds). But it was his lightning hands and feet and blinding combinations, not his punching power or musculature that had impressed the critics.

However, after Leonard had scored successive TKO's over a pair of former title contenders in Armando Muniz and Johnny Gant, picturing the twenty-two-year-old Marylander as a prospective middleweight was no longer a farfetched notion. For Sugar Ray now seemed capable of outboxing or outpunching his rivals by simply changing gears as the strategy dictated.

After watching another of his victims being dragged back to his corner, Leonard observed, "As an amateur, I was content to win on points. I relied strictly on speed because my hands were so fragile from fighting so often. But fighting as a pro is more dangerous. I want to get the fight over as quickly as I can."

But Leonard's sudden surge of punching power went beyond mere practicality. While he did not quite fit the "before" and "after" parts of the classic Charles Atlas character who undergoes a lightning metamorphosis from a scarecrow to a musclebound brute, his once-lanky frame had shown amazing development since his amateur days.

"I can't believe the difference," said Angelo Dundee. "I look at those old Olympic films of Ray when it looked like the gold medal weighed more than he did. Then I look at films of his recent fights, you can see how his upper body and arms have developed. That's where he gets the added power. It's no secret."

The fact that Leonard could now flex Popeye-like biceps did not alter his well-charted course to the welterweight title. But it allowed Dundee to test his fast-rising protégé against established junior middleweights in future bouts.

"Don't worry," said Dundee, "we're not going to make Ray 'blow up' for this fight," he assured the press after Leonard had signed to fight Canadian middleweight champion Fernand Marcotte. "He'll come in around 148 to 150 pounds. Instead of drying out to make 147, he'll come in his natural weight.

"But the real purpose of fighting a middleweight," Dundee explained, "is to see how Ray might fare against a welterweight with punching power—someone like Pipino Cuevas or Thomas Hearns."

Marcotte, a rugged French-Canadian with a 36–9–2 record at the time, was best known for his durable chin and his history of never having been knocked off his feet. He was trained by his father, Fernand, Sr., who also acted as interpreter for the French-speaking fighter. But the father-son relationship ended once Fernand, Jr., put on the gloves. Poppa Marcotte would then start barking orders like a top sergeant training a raw recruit.

"I speak to him very rough, like you sometimes should to a fighter," he said. "Like yesterday, he wants to only jump rope for two rounds. I say, 'No, man, you go five rounds with that rope, and then you exercise just like yesterday. You've got to keep it up.'

"Yeah, he was mad, but he did it. If he wasn't my son, I might have said, 'Oh, hell, skip the two rounds, and get the hell out of here.' "

To Poppa Marcotte, the prospect of Leonard whipping his finely tuned son was as likely as a sudden snowstorm in Miami Beach, where the fight was being waged. "Leonard can never knock out my son, and he has to be extremely lucky to beat him, by a cut or something, that is the only way. But if it goes past the seventh round, Fernand will knock him out, because he is much the stronger. I can tell you that for sure."

All the brash talk from Poppa Marcotte encouraged only a polite yawn from Sugar Ray, who was waiting his turn to step on the scales at the prefight weigh-in at the Miami Beach Convention Center. It had attracted the usual collection of back-slappers, sychophants and well-wishers, who all clucked admirably in the background as to how composed the youthful Leonard appeared on the eve of battle.

Only the owl-eyed Dundee seemed wide awake, for Miami Beach was his old stomping ground. He knew both the territory and his audience. He had witnessed thousands of these prefight clambakes in the company of champions, contenders, club fighters, and Palookas who never graduated from the preliminary ranks. And, of course, each of them approached a fight in his own, unique style. With only light prodding, Dundee launched into an hour-long dissertation on the subject, beginning with an appropriate Muhammad Ali story.

"It happened right here in Miami Beach in 1964," the veteran trainer said. "That was when Ali was getting ready for his first fight with Sonny Liston. Ali had Liston convinced that he was scared out of his wits when he staged that prefight tantrum.

"Muhammad was ranting and raving like a lunatic, screaming, 'Let me at that big, ugly bear, Liston.' It was really convincing. His blood pressure soared, and I remember the commission doctor saying, 'He's in mortal fear. We'll have to call the fight off if he doesn't calm down.'

"A few minutes later, I was alone with Ali, and he started laughing. He told me, 'Liston's been bragging that he's afraid of no man alive. But Liston means a sane man. He's got to be afraid of a crazy man like me.' "

The psychological warfare had as much effect on the malevolent-looking champion as the physical punishment Ali doled out the following night when Liston relinquished his crown while sitting on his stool with a sore shoulder.

"Now let me tell you about a heavyweight I had named Johnny Holman, back in the Fifties," said Dundee, getting a second wind.

"Holman was just about ready for the scrap heap when he came to see me in Miami. The first thing I did was to make him feel like a human being. I gave him a new nickname, 'Big Jawn.' Everytime he walked in the gym, I yelled, 'Hey, Big Jawn, you're lookin' great.' I got everybody to say it until he started to believe it.

"Well, surprisingly, Holman started winning and gaining new confidence every fight. And now he started talking about this dream house he always wanted to buy. I finally got him a good payday for fighting Ezzard Charles, the ex-champion, in 1955. Charles still figured to beat Holman easy. They made him eight-to-one. And ol' Ezzard was giving him a boxing lesson early in the fight and I could see Holman's ready to toss in the towel.

"I almost have to prop him up in the corner, but now I'm yelling in his ear, 'You're letting that old man steal your dream house. He's already taken the shutters and the doors.' Well, 'Big Jawn' got the message. He goes out that next round like a tiger, and damned if he didn't knock out Charles in the ninth round."

By now, everyone in the gathering was dusting off his favorite yarn in a story session that began to resemble "Can You Top This?"

"If you guys want to talk about fighters getting themselves messed up," said a man from Baltimore, "let me tell you what happened to Ray Robinson, when he was trying to win the middleweight title back for the ninth or tenth time. He was getting a return match with Paul Pender, the Boston fireman, but he needed a good tune-up to get him in top shape.

"A Baltimore promoter named Al Flora convinces Robinson that he's got the perfect guy for him—a tough truck-driver named Tony Baldoni, who looked like he was carved out of granite. Flora tells Robinson, 'You can drop a safe on this guy's head and it wouldn't make a dent.' Robinson checks the record. He sees Baldoni's a club fighter who always stays ten rounds, and he says OK.

"So they book the fight for the old Baltimore Coliseum. But the night before, they hold a big press party and Sugar Ray, of course, is the main attraction. They ask him to make a little speech, and he gets up and tells 'em about the night before he fought Jimmy Doyle in Cleveland, he had this awful premonition that he was going to kill him. And just like he dreams it, he hits Doyle on the chin the next night, and he never gets up.

"Well, Baldoni's eyes are getting bigger and bigger while Robinson is telling this story. Finally, he begs Robinson, 'Whatever you do, Ray, don't have any dreams tonight.'

"The night of the fight, they play 'The National Anthem,' and Baldoni is standing so stiff in his corner, it looks like rigor mortis has already set in. He looked whiter than a ghost. The opening bell rings, Robinson comes out slow, prepared for a long night. He tests Baldoni with a shot in the ribs, but tough Tony crumbles like a sack of potatoes. And now you see somethin' real funny happen. Robinson's trying to prop him up, but a derrick couldn't have got Baldoni back on his feet that night.

"The joint was sold out, and now the crowd is throwing bottles and fruit in the ring, but Baldoni's afraid to get up. And you know who's the maddest guy of all? Yeah, Ray Robinson, the guy who wins by a first-round knockout."

"Yeah," said a guy in the crowd around Dundee, "sometimes even the winners are losers."

But Sugar Ray Leonard was still strictly a winner, in the ring and at the box office. His fight with Marcotte had attracted a crowd of 8,000 fans, proving a greater draw than the heavyweight championship matches in the same ring between Floyd Patterson and Ingemar Johansson in 1961 and Ali versus Liston three years later.

The enthusiastic mob saw Leonard survive his first "over-the-weight" test while hardly breaking a sweat before the lopsided brawl was stopped at 2:33 of the eighth round. Marcotte had found himself on the floor for the first time in his forty-seven-bout career earlier in the round after catching a perfectly timed uppercut by Leonard flush on the jaw. The Canadian champion rolled over on his side like a wounded whale, but amazingly regained his feet at the count of eight. However, referee Jay Edson took one look at the state of Marcotte's bloody face and rubbery legs, and quickly raised Leonard's hand in triumph.

"Fighting a middleweight was no different than fighting a welterweight," Leonard contended. "It's all a matter of confidence. I never allowed Marcotte to use his weight advantage (155½ to 149½). I took away his punching power by moving from side-to-side. But the more I hit him, the more he fought back.

"I'd catch him with a real good shot, and he'd half-smile and say, 'That was good.' So I'd hit him a little harder the next time and tell him, 'Try that one for size. That's real nice, too.' "

Leonard dominated the fight from start to finish, winning every round on the officials' cards before the lopsided match was halted in the eighth. As early as the third round, Marcotte was in obvious trouble, bleeding from an ugly gash along his right eye that required twelve stitches after the game Canadian wobbled back to his dressing room.

"Too fast, too strong," Marcotte muttered through his puffy lips. His father, applying an ice bag to his son's swollen face, was in complete agreement.

"Leonard will be welterweight champion by the end of the year," the elder Marcotte predicted with rare insight. "I don't care who he fights—Benitez or Cuevas. It doesn't matter.

"He's too strong for Benitez and too fast for Cuevas, who will get tired chasing him after a few rounds. Cuevas is like my son. He will look for that one big opening, but it may never come against a Leonard, who is a true master just like the original Sugar Ray—Ray Robinson."

In a postscript, Dundee reminded reporters that Marcotte had arrived at the prefight press conference without a pair of sneakers. He had graciously equipped his rival with a pair of shoes belonging to Leonard.

"Marcotte tried them on," Dundee laughed, "but they were too fast for his feet."

As had become the custom of late, a reporter asked

Sugar Ray if he could project himself into a title fight by late fall. Before he could respond, Dundee began shaking his head negatively. His fighter picked up the unspoken message and, with his usual diplomacy, said, "We're one big family. When we decide I'm ready, that's when I'll fight for the title."

But it wouldn't end there. The issue of exactly when Leonard would be ready to challenge for the title became a point of contention between Dundee and Leonard's attorney, Mike Trainer, who was already busy negotiating with the two leading promoters, Bob Arum and Don King, for a possible November showdown with Benitez. Ultimately, Trainer would have the final word and Dundee's role in the "inner family" would diminish considerably. At the time, however, Dundee insisted there were "too many variables" to consider.

"How can you predict what will happen in October or November?" he said. "Maybe both Benitez and Cuevas will have lost their titles by then. After all, who could figure that Leon Spinks, with only a handful of fights, could whip a Muhammad Ali?

"And just maybe," Dundee added, "I'd rather have Ray fight Roberto Duran first. That could be the most attractive fight of all. But we're not going to rush into anything. Ray's an ideal fighter to manage. He never questions my judgment."

Dundee then offered another interesting possibility: having Leonard jump right into the junior middleweight division after so easily overpowering Marcotte. "I'm not going to sacrifice Ray's strength to keep him a welterweight if he's a natural 150-pounder. If that's the case, we'll go after the junior middleweight crown right now. Whatever division Ray is fighting in will be the most popular one. He's the hottest name in boxing today."

But for all practical purposes, it seemed best for Dundee to keep Leonard fighting in the welterweight class where his potential rivals were far better known and attractive at the box office than the rather obscure fighters toiling in the next weight class.

Leonard did, in fact, return to the welterweights for his next scuffle—a startingly brief encounter with Daniel Gonzalez at the Tucson Community Center on March 25, 1979.

"You think ABC is mad at me for ending it so quickly?" Ray kidded after his 123-second performance had left scant time for commercial breaks. "I don't think Gonzalez figured I could punch that hard. He came boring in right from the start. I caught him with a left that put his chin in perfect position for the right that dropped him. I've never thrown a better right than that one."

The abrupt ending caused the cynics to seriously question Gonzalez's gaudy record of 64–2–2, including his boast of never having been caught in a horizontal position.

"It has to be legitimate," Trainer insisted. "Gonzalez had to bring a fight-by-fight record along with his passport."

"Listen," Dundee chimed in, "with a record like that, I don't care if he was fighting his sisters. He had to beat a lot of good fighters along the way."

Ray's mother, however, registered a mild complaint. "I don't think Grandpa Leonard liked it one bit," she surmised. "I don't even think he was settled in his rocking chair back home before the fight was over."

Grandpa Leonard had enough time to take a brief nap and make several trips to the icebox between rounds when his favorite grandson next appeared on television from the Dunes Hotel in Las Vegas.

Dundee would pose a new challenge for his fast-stepping protégé who was continually outstripping the curriculum imposed by his teacher. This time the test would come in the shape of a durable southpaw named Adolpho Viruet, whose awkward style and concrete chin had made him *persona non grata* among rival managers.

Adolpho, however, was far less celebrated than his brother, Edwin, a classy lightweight who could boast of being one of the few fighters to have survived ten rounds against the "stone fists" of Roberto Duran. But, as an amateur, Adolpho was considered the brighter prospect and might have accomplished more as a professional had it not been that he enjoyed training about as much as a kid likes spinach.

Joe DeMaria, who served as manager, trainer, and surrogate father to the fighting Viruet brothers, once warned Adolpho, "Either get in the gym or don't waste my time. I have to keep reminding him, 'When you've got money in your hand, you've got power.' But Adolpho is hard to convince."

Adolpho believed in making the most of every day. After registering an upset over hard-punching Bruce Curry, who had lost to Leonard in the finals of the 1976 Olympic Trials, Viruet treated all his neighborhood friends to a night on the town. The next morning, DeMaria searched throughout Spanish Harlem for his missing fighter. Finally, he discovered Adolpho sleeping off his night's merrymaking in a pigeon coop atop a ghetto tenement.

"I've drained my bank account on these two boys," DeMaria said. "I even had to buy Adolpho an overcoat for Christmas so he could get through the winter. I'm not in great shape myself. But when I'm in the gym with Adolpho and Edwin, I feel like I'm a sixteen-year-old kid again. I'm happy all the time."

There were reports emanating from New York that Leonard was being set up like one of Adolpho's pigeons. As one knowledgeable boxing man advised, "Dundee could be making a mistake this time. Teddy Brenner (former Madison Square Garden matchmaker) is co-promoting this fight in Las Vegas, and he's been in the gym with Viruet every day. Brenner wants to make a name in Vegas, and if this fight is close, Leonard could be in trouble."

It was all idle gossip. After spending two rounds getting to know Viruet's unorthodox style, Leonard took charge of the fight, flooring the stocky southpaw for the first time in his career with a right hand in the fourth round. It only seemed to enrage the Puerto Rican, who quickly bounced up and engaged his tormentor in a furious toe-to-toe exchange for the final minute of the round.

In the closing rounds, Viruet resorted to roughhousing and was subsequently warned for hitting low, elbowing, and holding. But the bullying tactics were all in vain. In the final tally, Adolpho had earned only the ninth round on all three scorecards.

"When you make a great fight against a southpaw, you've got to be talented," Dundee gushed.

The locker room would be much more subdued following Leonard's next test, and, for the first time, Dave Jacobs, Sugar Ray's every day trainer and "five A.M. conscience," would openly criticize Dundee's selection process.

Dundee had matched Leonard against Marcos Geraldo at the modern Centroplex in Baton Rouge, Louisiana. Geraldo, a native of Mexico, had the same kind of untraceable record as fellow Latin, Daniel Gonzalez, who had lasted less than a round against Sugar Ray only months earlier. But there were two major differences. First, Geraldo could fight. And second, he was a bonafide middleweight—160 pounds of muscle and sinew.

Leonard, of course, would win the fight, but not before being hit several times harder than he could ever remember. In the third round, Geraldo nailed his slender rival, whom he outweighed by seven pounds, with a booming hook. Leonard would later insist it was a butt, but it had the same paralyzing effect.

"Suddenly, I saw three of him," Ray confided. "I was trying to distinguish who was who when BAM, he caught me with a real good shot. Lucky for me, the bell sounded a few seconds later."

A dazed Leonard wobbled back to his corner and complained to Dundee of his triple vision. As ever, the wily trainer had the perfect solution. "Hit the one in the middle," Angelo ordered.

In time, the three Geraldos dissolved into one tough Mexican, but still not quite strong enough to overcome Leonard's superior speed and effective punching. Sugar Ray would win six rounds on two cards and seven on the third. Still, it had been a sobering experience for the unbeaten welterweight, who was forced to give ground more than once in the closing rounds.

"He hits as hard as I thought he would," the winner said, "but I was never in any real trouble. I know a lot of people said, 'This guy's too big for you.' But I learned how to move on a guy this way and keep out of trouble when I have to."

For Dave Jacobs, the trouble was hardly necessary. "There's no doubt in my mind that Ray is the best welterweight in the world," said the man who had brought Leonard from a novice to an Olympic champion. "And I believe he can beat a Cuevas, Palomino, or Duran if he has to. But these guys are all welterweights, too.

"Ray's no middleweight, and he's got no business fighting them as far as I'm concerned. This Geraldo was a real tough monkey. He had to sweat it out to get down to 160 pounds. By fight night, he must have ballooned back to 165. Ray weighed only 153 with all his clothes on. It just doesn't make sense to have overgrown middleweights beating on him.

"Yeah, Ray won," Jacobs added with a shrug, "because he outsmarted Geraldo. He stayed on his bicycle for ten rounds and outboxed him. But if it had been power against power, who knows what might have happened?

"Remember when Ray Robinson tried to step up in class and beat Joey Maxim for the light-heavy title? They said the heat that night at Yankee Stadium beat Robinson, not Maxim. But Maxim conserved his strength and used his extra weight to wear Robinson down.

"Same with Leonard," Jacobs concluded. "If he was meant to be a middleweight, he would have been one by now. But he's a natural welterweight, and that's where I'd like to keep him fighting if I had my way. I don't want to see any more 'experiments' against middleweights."

Jacobs's warning, however, went unheeded. Leonard's next opponent would again be a junior middleweight—Tony Chiaverini, a former college linebacker who was rated number four in his weight class. But this time, he would give a virtuoso performance before forcing his well-regarded rival to quit on his stool after the fourth round of their match at Caesar's Palace.

Known as a strong combination puncher, Chiaverini, a left-hander, tried mystifyingly to outbox Leonard, whose hands were flying faster than a blackjack dealer.

When the stocky Kansas City boxer tried to use his weight advantage by moving inside, he was quickly discouraged by a hailstorm of blows. By the third round, Chiaverini's right eye was all but closed and his face looked as if it had been caught in a sewing machine. There was no need to continue the one-sided battle after the fourth round, when a towel was waved as a sign of surrender from Tony's manager, Dave Conchola.

"His speed?" Chiaverini said in reply to a question. "I could see every one of his jabs. I watched all of them fly from his shoulder right into my face," the loser said in a feeble attempt at humor.

Now 23–0, Leonard returned to the welterweight ranks for his final two shakedown cruises before challenging Benitez for the World Boxing Council title—the match Trainer had been plotting for so long.

Pete Ranzany was next on Sugar Ray's "hit" list. The craggy-faced Californian had an impressive 45–3–1 record, including a knockout victory over Randy Shields, Leonard's one-time tormentor.

It catapulted Ranzany into a championship match with WBA titleholder Pipino Cuevas in September, 1978.

Fighting in his hometown of Sacramento, Ranzany figured, at least, to have the fans in his corner. But when a patented Cuevas hook left him twitching on the canvas and they carted him back to his stool after less than two rounds of fighting, he could hear the 17,000 fans feverishly chanting, "Mexico, Mexico."

Now Ranzany was being challenged by Leonard for the North American welterweight crown, and the former migrant worker would receive 75,000 for his effort—more than double the money he earned for his brief encounter with Cuevas.

"It's funny," Ranzany said following a prefight workout, "but all of a sudden I'm hearing from a lot of 'old friends.' As a kid, I was strictly a loner. I never had more than one or two close friends. I was shy and I stuttered a lot. No one wanted me in their high school crowd. Now they all seem to want me, but I don't want them."

After becoming an outstanding amateur fighter in the Army, Ranzany competed in the 1972 Olympic Trials, but lost in the semifinals to Sugar Ray Seales, the eventual gold medal winner. A year later, he would lose a split decision to a young fighter from the East by the name of Ray Leonard, but Ranzany's memory remains fuzzy on the details.

"I discovered there was a lot of politics involved in amateur fighting," he said, with a touch of bitterness. "A lot of times, the fighter with the right connections could win while half trying. It can really disillusion you."

Ranzany gave up fighting for several years. It took a group of ten Sacramento businessmen to rekindle his interest. They formed a corporation called "Ran-Sac, Inc." that provided Ranzany with a living allowance while he devoted all his energy to fighting.

He quickly developed a strong following in the Sacramento area and moved quickly through the welterweight ranks to obtain the number one ranking that earned him his shortlived match with the heavy-fisted Cuevas. Ranzany rebounded from this staggering loss to win his next four fights and entice a lucrative television date with Leonard.

"As soon as I heard Leonard's name," he said, "I dug my old combat boots out of the closet and started running. I know he's getting the fay end of the purse ($225,000), but he's TV's darling. Everyone thinks I'm the underdog, but I don't think so."

Ranzany would feel quite differently the next day after licking his wounds in his plush Las Vegas hotel suite. But he should have expected the worst. All the omens were against him. Before the Cuevas fight, he awoke to the sound of a rare Sacramento thunderstorm. And, on the eve of the Leonard fight, Las Vegas would be hit by its hardest rainstorm in months.

A few hours later in the Sports Pavilion, Ranzany would be engulfed by a shower of jabs, hooks, and uppercuts. Early in the fourth round, Leonard forced the gritty Californian against the ropes with a series of hard jabs. He followed this with a seemingly endless volley of blows. Ranzany dropped to his knees, made a gallant effort to regain his balance, but slumped again to the floor to take an eight count.

He clambered back to his feet and shook off concerned referee Joey Curtis, but another head-rocking hook by Leonard ended matters for good at 2:44 of the fourth round.

"I'm getting sharper as I go along," said an "unmussed" Leonard. "What people don't realize is that I can punch. I think Ranzany realized my hands are quick. As long as I get the big bucks, I don't care if they say I can't punch."

Ranzany wasn't about to argue the point. "Before the fight, I didn't think Leonard was as good as he is. I don't remember much about what happened, but I never thought he could drop me. He knocked me down, so I guess he punches pretty good. But with Cuevas, I didn't know where I was at. Now, I'm just a little fuzzy-headed and Leonard must have hit me with a million shots."

But Leonard had hit Ranzany hard enough to make the California brawler contemplate a new career. "I'm not going to keep fighting to become a punching bag," he said, packing it in for the night.

There would be one last tune-up for Leonard against Andy Price before his million-dollar match with Benitez. But already Sugar Ray's clique of advisors were eyeing Roberto Duran for a fight that would make boxing history. The grand hype was about to begin.

☆ 11 ☆

WAITING FOR ROBERTO

Sugar Ray Leonard and Roberto Duran were playing an intriguing game of cat and mouse in among the gambling tables at Caesar's Palace in Las Vegas. Without an angry word passed between them, they provided almost as much diversion for the high rollers as backing a crap shooter on a hot streak.

Inevitably, the denouement would come when Duran would trap Leonard in a corner and force him into a showdown of wits and courage. But for now, they were still in the preliminary stages of their war of nerves.

The two popular welterweights were appearing in separate ten-rounders at the gambling casino on a nationally televised show featuring a heavyweight title match between champion Larry Holmes and Earnie Shavers, the baldheaded dreadnought.

In the halcyon days of Muhammad Ali, the mere suggestion that the heavyweight king needed such a strong supporting cast to carry the show was unthinkable. But Holmes was still desperately trying to escape Ali's giant shadow, and, because of their similarity in style, he had always been put down as a cheap imitation of the former champion.

And so it took the addition of the charismatic Leonard to attract a prime-time television audience, even though he was scheduled to fight a rather obscure California welterweight named Andy Price. The indomitable Duran would provide a tasty appetizer in his match against a youthful Mexican beanpole named Zerferino ("Speedy") Gonzalez.

"Face it," said a boxing promoter, pointing a finger toward Leonard, "this guy does big ratings, second only to Ali. He's show biz, a real performer. If it was between a Holmes-whoever fight and a Leonard-Joe Blow match, you'd want Leonard."

This was all too evident the week before the fight as Leonard attracted large galleries to his workouts, while Holmes had trouble drawing more than a handful of curious onlookers to his public sparring sessions in the Sports Pavilion. In fact, Holmes was running a poor third behind Duran.

"Duran creates the excitement and I create the money," quipped Sugar Ray one day, while catching some sun at the outdoor pool. "I've already told [promoter] Don King that a fight with Duran should be worth a minimum of 5 million."

"Is that for both of you?" asked a startled listener.

"No, just for me," Leonard replied.

Sugar Ray seemed almost disinterested about his upcoming encounter with Price. Instead, he had spent most of his time in Las Vegas dogging the footsteps of Duran. He could be spotted daily among the crowd at the Panamanian's workouts, taking mental notes for future reference.

"I wasn't spying on Duran," he laughed when questioned about his detective work. A spy would be more discreet. I'm really as much a boxing fan as a fighter, and I like to observe how different fighters train.

"I was quite impressed by Duran's training procedure,"

he confided. "It's unique. He hits the speed bag with his head and really works on the skip rope. He makes that rope sing. But I understand all the kids in Panama skip rope in the streets."

"Does Duran respect you?" a man in the crowd asked.

"I don't know," Ray said, "I can't understand Spanish."

"Do you respect Duran?" the same guy persisted.

"People who don't even fight fear Duran," Leonard said with a sly grin.

No one had bothered to ask his opinion of Price, who was regarded in boxing circles as a "spoiler." He was an unpredictable fighter, who, on his best nights, had scored stunning upsets over a youthful Pepino Cuevas and former welterweight champion Carlos Palomino.

"After I beat Cuevas in 1976," Price said in the coffee shop one morning, "I thought I was in for a title shot against Angel Espada. But Espada passed me up to fight Cuevas and lost his title. I knew Cuevas wouldn't risk fighting me again, so that left me in limbo."

The Californian's ring career took a serious nosedive at that point. He was finally rescued by actor Burt Reynolds, who employed Price's mother as a cook and took an active interest in her fighting son. Acting as his "angel," Reynolds put Price on a regular salary and also paid his college tuition, which led to a job as a parole officer in the tough Watts section of Los Angeles.

Price remained loyal to Reynolds, but the relationship failed to produce any fights in the California area.

"I was always fighting guys in their own backyard," he complained. "I lost to Harold Weston in New York and dropped a decision to Davey Boy Green in London, even though I beat him to death."

In frustration, Price broke his ties with Reynolds and signed a contract with singer Marvin Gaye, who had more success finding his fighter competition on his home turf, a move that improved his record and led to his TV date with Leonard.

With his $40,000 purse, Price was earning more from this one fight than he had totaled in forty previous bouts. Leonard, of course, was pocketing the lion's share of $300,000, but Price displayed no envy for his millionaire rival.

"He's a brother like me," Andy said matter-of-factly. "He's made it the easy way. I wish I could have made it the easy way. In the end, it'll be the same. We'll both be rich," he added confidently.

Knowing Price's reputation as a "spoiler," a few boxing insiders voiced surprise that Leonard, with the promise of a $1 million title match with Benitez only two months off, would even take a small risk by fighting the cagy Californian.

"I want people to realize now that I'm trying to dominate the ring," Ray explained. "I want people to see that what I've been saying the past two years isn't a lot of hogwash. I know some people accuse me of being a 'hot dog' or trying to impersonate Ali. But there's only one of him. I've combined the talents of Ali, Ray Robinson, and Joe Louis and made myself."

Although it was considered such an "out" fight that the Las Vegas betting parlors refused to post odds, Sugar Ray did his best to hype interest in his match with Price.

"There's a rumor going 'round New York that I might be ripe for an upset," he said in a stage whisper, knowing that he had planted the rumor himself.

Uncharacteristically, Angelo Dundee was predicting a quick knockout for his unbeaten protégé. "Price is a cutie who likes to counter-punch, and he could outslick Ray for a round or two. But I can only see him ending up on the floor."

To be sure, Dundee had again done his "homework." He coyly showed a group of reporters a piece of notepaper on which he had scribbled his scouting report on Price:

"Swings right hand in wide arc. Keeps feet close together. Can be pushed off-balance. Strictly left-hooker. Heavy-legged. Has trouble backing up. Feint jab, wait for left, then counter. Everything works!"

But even the optimistic Dundee couldn't have expected it to work so well, and so quickly. A head-snapping jab, followed by an overhand right, sent Price flying against the ropes late in the first round. Leonard quickly pounced on his dazed rival and raked Price's body with a dozen punches, capped by another booming right hand that left the Californian sprawled on the canvas.

Price tried desperately to regain his balance, but then collapsed in a frightening heap. The ring doctor was summoned and Leonard looked on with great concern as it took more than a minute before the loser could be propped up and carried back to his stool.

"All week," said a relieved Leonard, "Price kept talking about an upset. But the only upset was that he got up at all."

Some ten minutes after, Price still remembered little about his brief encounter. "Everything went so fast," he said, trying to remove the clinging cobwebs from his brain. "It's weird, but I didn't think he could punch that hard. But I guess he does. I'll have to check the films to see what happened."

Leonard, of course, didn't have to wait that long. "I figure by now people realize I can punch," he said. "But it's always better to be underestimated. I hope it continues that way throughout my career."

Asked how many punches he had unleashed in his knockout salvo, Leonard flashed his boyish grin and said, "When I start throwing punches, I hate to count. It's like counting money."

It would take him considerably longer to count the money—$300,000 for two minutes and fifty-four seconds of work.

For those keeping tabs, Duran was forced to work a great

deal harder for his $100,000 the same night. He had to endure the stinging jabs and elusive footwork of Zeferino Gonzalez, who lived up to his nickname "Speedy" by managing to avoid the frustrated Panamanian tiger over the ten-round distance. Gonzalez, in fact, was brash enough later to suggest that he had deserved the decision.

In any case, ringsiders making comparisons were now ready to concede that Leonard was ready to challenge the man with "Fists of Stone."

But Leonard managed to keep his priorities in order. "First, he said, "I must worry about Wilfredo Benitez and winning the welterweight title. Then I'll be thinking about Mr. Duran."

☆ 12 ☆

"WAR OF THE WUNDERKINDS"

A "DO NOT DISTURB" sign hung on the door of Sugar Ray Leonard's suite at Caesar's Palace on the Las Vegas strip. It was ten P.M., Pacific Coast Time, just the hour when the high rollers prepared to test their luck at blackjack, roulette, and baccarat at the casino tables.

At a plush ballroom adjoining the casino, family, friends, and freeloaders were toasting the new welterweight king, who, several hours earlier, had lifted the crown from twenty-one-year-old Wilfredo Benitez.

The knockout had come only six seconds short of the final bell. Despite the loud protests of the gamblers tempted by the four-to-one odds favoring Leonard, referee Carlos Padilla had moved in quickly to throw a protective blanket around Benitez. Prompted by the fate of middleweight Willie Classen, who lay unconscious in a New York hospital that same night after absorbing a brutal beating at the hands of Wilford Scypion, Padilla would take no chances.

But Classen, who would die a few days later, was not on

the minds of the celebrants at Las Vegas. They laughed, drank, and danced to the throbbing disco beat until Charles Brotman, Leonard's personal publicity man, silenced the band and asked for a moment's attention.

"Ray sincerely regrets that he can't be with you to share this great moment," said Brotman, "but, quite frankly, he's feeling very drained. He's tired and slightly dehydrated, and just wants to rest and be by himself for awhile."

Upstairs, Sugar Ray eased his aching body into a king-sized tub of hot water. "I need a rest, a long rest," he said between his bruised lips. "Do you know that in the last ten years, there's probably been only three months when I wasn't either training for a fight or in one?

"Just think of all those thousands of miles I must have run at four in the morning, all those push-ups and calisthenics, all that sparring, and then the actual fighting. I've been going almost nonstop except for that short time after the 'Seventy-six Olympics. But either you do or you don't. Time don't wait."

Grimacing slightly, he stretched out full-length in the soothing water. "I feel a lot like 'Rocky,' " he said. My whole body aches. It even hurts to smile. This was my ultimate test. Pressure. All that pressure."

Mike Trainer, the Maryland attorney who had helped launch Sugar Ray's professional career with a $21,000 kitty from local businessmen and well-wishers, leaned over his fatigued friend and gave him a playful pat on the back.

"Doesn't it make you feel good to know you don't have to do this anymore if you don't want to?" Trainer said.

Leonard laughed ruefully. He knew full well that, downstairs, promoter Bob Arum was already making plans for his next multimillion dollar match. The menacing shadows of Roberto Duran, Pepino Cuevas, and Tommy Hearns already loomed on the horizon.

Gingerly, the fighter climbed out of the tub and carefully scrutinized himself in the full-length mirror. Like his life-long idol, Muhammad Ali, Leonard makes no effort to hide vanity. He believes the condition of a fighter's face reveals his true worth as a practitioner of "the Sweet Science."

"I hate to get hit," he had said passionately. "I'm not in this game to show I can take a punch. That's crazy. Why that guy in Louisiana (middleweight Marcos Geraldo) hit me so hard, I wanted to quit. When a guy tags me with a shot that could put a scar on my face, I get real angry. A change takes place in me that I can't explain. I want to make his head go flying off his shoulders."

But the mirror on the wall had no need to say he was still the fairest of them all, the all-American boy with the radiant Pepsodent smile and winning personality. That could be left to his fans and admiring friends. "Luminiscent" is the way his manager, Angelo Dundee, had described him.

The face in the mirror looked considerably older than twenty-three, and somehow wiser bearing the scars of battle. The cheekbones were swollen, the corner of his right eye gashed, ugly welts under both eyes, and a growing "mouse" on his forehead. It was like Dorian Gray viewing the first signs of decay in his portrait.

"Is that me?" Sugar Ray questioned the mirror. Knowing the answer, he turned off the bedroom light and excused himself. He would sleep fitfully, both his mind and body feverish from the dramatic events that had led to his coronation as the World Boxing Council welterweight champion.

An hour before in the press tent, before a crowd of reporters and squealing female fans, he had tried to describe what the war of the wunderkinds had been like. Listening to Leonard's story, one could think back to Ali's second encounter with Leon Spinks in New Orleans when Muhammad, in a stage whisper, had vowed to never again subject his aging body to such physical torture.

"They say you have to go through windmills to be a champion, and what did I do?" Leonard asked the crowd surging around him, and heard a chorus of "Right on!" in response.

"In that fifteenth round, I looked across the ring and said to myself, 'Oh God, he's still standing.' In those last few minutes, I felt close to death. We were both near exhaustion, but I think my conditioning really paid off. I had to bring out everything that was inside me.

"I've taken my dream and made it a reality. I said a long time ago that I would become a champion. But the critics said I was a Hollywood actor. They said I could never go fifteen tough rounds. I took so much abuse and criticism and been through so much. Now I think the people will have to accept me as the champion."

Benitez wouldn't argue the point. "He won the fight. I have no questions," said the little Latin.

"Wilfredo means he has no alibis," said a man acting as interpreter. But Benitez needed no help.

"I've never lost before," he said, "but I lost tonight. But I will not cry, because I know we will have another great champion in Sugar Ray."

Benitez, who had won two world titles by the time he was eighteen, had not been so quick in his praise of Leonard in the prefight buildup. The proud Puerto Rican had taken umbrage at the four-to-one odds favoring the challenger. The betting had been lively, although many of the gamblers viewed the odds as prohibitive. The cynics questioned Sugar Ray's substance, believing that he had benefited from the same type of media hype that had made light-punching Chuck Davey the short-lived darling of television in the early Fifties.

"Leonard has a style that is terribly pleasing to the eye," offered Benitez's manager, Jim Jacobs, over cream cheese and bagels in the hotel coffee shop.

"I liken Sugar Ray to a painfully exquisite woman. He has all that dazzle and charm, but when he enters that ring against Benitez, we are going to discover whether beyond all that outward beauty is a truly professional fighter.

"In Leonard," Jacobs continued, "you see a fighter with tremendous speed—a fighter in the grand style of Ray Robinson who can throw four- and five- punch combinations. He can miss you with the first two, but knock you out with the third, which is terribly impressive. And in all his fights, he seldom gets hit a telling blow. That's because he chooses when and where he wants to fight. But some painfully beautiful women hide behind that beauty. We will find out quite soon if that is the case with Sugar Ray."

No one has a greater appreciation for the savage beauty of the boxing ring than Jim Jacobs, who boasts of owning ninety-five percent of the fight films in existence, including the only copy of Bob Fitzsimmons's knockout of Gentleman Jim Corbett in 1897.

"I started collecting films in 1944 when I was fourteen," he recalled. "You could buy up films cheaply then. I don't mean the films alone. I mean the commercial rights to the films. I was using my father's money, of course, at the start. But I never believed what began as a hobby could be so lucrative."

Through his exclusive copyrights, Jacobs parlayed his fight film monopoly into a king's ransom. But most of all, Jacobs, who recently began collecting fighters, too, is a boxing aficionado who studies and critiques the ring styles with as discerning an eye as Pauline Kael reviewing Hollywood films.

Consequently, no one is considered a greater authority than the fifty-year-old New Yorker when it comes to comparing the relative merits of fighters. For he had committed to memory the unique moves of every noteworthy fighter from the bareknuckle days to the modern era—from A (Ali) to Z (Zale).

Under pressure, Jacobs will insist that beauty is in the eye of the beholder, and that nothing can cause a greater polarity of opinion than the merits of boxers from different eras, a situation that fosters the endless barroom debates over whether the unchained fury of a Rocky Marciano could offset the mesmerizing skill of a Muhammad Ali.

"I just completed a film of Sugar Ray Robinson," Jacobs noted. "It's called *Pound For Pound* and gives convincing evidence that he was probably the greatest fighter of all time—lightweight, welterweight, or heavyweight.

"But I learned a long time ago," he added after a pregnant pause, "never to judge a fighter until you have closed the final page on his career. Had I judged Sonny Liston after his first-round knockouts of Floyd Patterson, he would have been the greatest heavyweight of all time. But Ali exposed Liston.

"Leonard has the possibility of being the greatest of all time. At this point, he has no visible flaws."

But now the erudite Mr. Jacobs was being asked to judge a beauty contest between Benitez, the master of "cool" and understatement and the flamboyant, charismatic Leonard, who possessed all the legerdemain of Ali.

Jacobs could have withdrawn from the argument on prejudicial grounds after acquiring the contract of the precocious Benitez, whom he considers one of the true modern ring treasures. But Jacobs, the fan, could not duck a heated debate without interjecting his expertise. He insisted that only the most knowledgeable observers fully appreciate Benitez's subtle ring gifts, while the casual fight fans were blinded by Leonard's lightning hands and feet and Ali-like mannerisms.

"Leonard is that rare combination of a fighter and entertainer," he said. "And through the great assistance of Howard Cosell, who has been singing his praises since the 1976 Olympics, Leonard has become an American institution.

"That's why in the United States they treat Benitez as just an opponent. Wilfredo's a magnificent boxer and punches hard enough to get your attention. Only in the Latin countries do they fully appreciate Wilfredo's talent.

"What you must remember about this young man is that he responds best to pressure. When Wilfredo fights ordinary fighters, he is ordinary. He prepares for these matches with great indifference. He only fights great fights against great fighters. He needs the challenge to motivate him."

Benitez's two biggest tests prior to the Leonard match came against Antonio Cervantes, from whom he won the junior welterweight title before his eighteenth birthday, and Carlos Palomino, from whom he captured the welterweight crown two years later.

"Both of those fights went fifteen rounds," Jacobs noted, "but after almost an hour in the ring, Wilfredo toweled off his face and there was nothing to reveal that he had been in a fight, let alone a championship match."

Because he had acquired his boxing skill at such an early age, Wilfredo had a disturbing habit of regarding his rivals as willing foils, a supreme confidence bordering on boredom. Jacobs, therefore, spent the weeks before the fight repeatedly reminding his fighter that Leonard was not an overachieving preliminary boy.

"I keep telling Wilfredo, 'Leonard is magnificent. Leonard is the greatest. Leonard is in a class by himself.' Why? So that when Wilfredo beats him, he will get full credit."

Jacobs, a champion in his own right (he was world handball champion from 1959 through 1971), feels that no one looks for more excuses than a man who has lost backing a heavy favorite.

"The thing we want to avoid," he said, "is that when everyone picks Leonard to win, they won't say later, 'We overrated him, and he disappointed us.' By giving Leonard credit now, they will later be forced to admit that Benitez is better."

Benitez seemed outwardly amused by his underdog role. When a reporter confronted him with Leonard's prediction of a tenth-round knockout, the champion made his knees quiver in mock fright and said dolefully, "I realize I am in grave danger."

Another man with a microphone asked in a somber tone, "Here you are, the champion of the world, and yet you are a four-to-one underdog to Leonard. How does that make you react?"

"My object is to salvage some dignity Friday night," Benitez said soberly while Jacobs smirked in the background like the Cheshire cat. There was a sneaking suspicion that Jacobs, the cinematographer, was also writing the script.

Later, out of earshot of Jacobs, Benitez told reporters, "I don't care if he is favored. I will knock him out. He can't take my punch. He's just a boxer. He may even be a great boxer, but this time he's fighting with a champion."

"Who is faster than Leonard?" a man asked.

"I think the champion," said the champion.

Benitez's bold talk did not influence the oddsmakers. Explaining the strong support for Leonard, Bob Martin, who establishes the accepted betting line in Las Vegas, said, "Before his last three fights, Sugar Ray might have been only six-to-five to whip Benitez. But he looked so devastating in beating Tony Chiaverini, Pete Ranzany, and Andy Price, everyone figures he can't lose.

"When I sat down to make a line on this fight, I asked myself, 'What does Benitez have that can beat Leonard? He's not as quick, he's not as good a boxer, and he can't stop anyone with his punch.' Benitez's greatest asset is his defensive ability. But being defensive can't beat Leonard. It just means that Benitez might survive the fifteen rounds to lose the decision."

Faith in Benitez was hardly enhanced by an article that appeared in *The Ring* magazine shortly before the fight. It was entitled, "*Why Benitez Will Lose His Title.*" Hardly startling in itself except for the fact that the author of the piece was Wilfredo's father and trainer, Gregorio Benitez.

"If I say he is going to win," Papa Benitez explained to a curious press, "then he no work."

Papa Benitez simply would not abide a profligate son. There was that night in New York when he clowned and mocked Harold Weston, a clearly inferior foe, and was forced to settle for a draw by the unimpressed judges. He returned to his corner to be greeted by a loud parental slap and a grim reminder from Papa that Ali confined all his hijinx to after-business hours.

Papa Benitez always knew best. In 1962, he had moved his family back to his native Puerto Rico from a bleak Bronx ghetto where he had worked for seventeen years as an auto mechanic. "Too much dope, too much trouble," he said. "I told my four boys, 'We go home where it is not so bad.' "

They returned to St. Just, a farming community outside San Juan, where Gregorio erected an all-metal gymnasium for his four offspring, who would all become professional fighters—Gregorio, Jr., Alphonso, Frankie, and Wilfredo, the youngest.

Gregorio was too bowlegged to suit his father's boxing tastes. Alphonso was too bright, and shipped off to school to study electrical engineering. Frankie loved the ladies and hated the gym. Papa Benitez showed him the door.

That left Wilfredo, who, at age seven and sixty-two pounds, made his debut in the Puerto Rican Golden Gloves, battling to a draw against a boy three years his senior. At age fifteen, he won his first pro scuffle, flattening one Hiram Santiago in the first round for a fifty-dollar purse.

Two years later, his father gave his blessing to the match with then junior welterweight king Antonio ("Kid Pambele") Cervantes, a wily veteran of eighty-four pro bouts. His Puerto Rican kinfolk were aghast. They accused Papa Benitez of excessive greed in throwing his promising, but untested son to the wolves.

Even after Wilfredo boxed Cervantes's ears off to claim his first title at age seventeen, acceptance from his countrymen came slow.

"Before," said a baffled Wilfredo, "when I was just a

contender, they all admired me. Now I win a championship, and they look at me as if I'm a freak."

Hard as it may be to imagine, Benitez was already a world champion while Leonard was still priming himself for an Olympic gold medal. Even the politicians who rule the boxing organizations found it hard to accept. They stripped young Benitez of his 140-pound title when they deemed he took too long recovering from an auto accident that damaged his fists.

"After that," Gregorio said, "Wilfredo lost his enthusiasm, his fire for fighting."

It was then that Papa Benitez elected to sell his son's contract for $150,000, ten percent of his future earnings, and two tickets for each fight. "I want to be like Pontius Pilate and wash my hands of the whole thing," he said.

Don King was the first to enter the auction, but the flamboyant King was more interested in promoting Wilfredo than managing his ring affairs. "Don is always in a hurry," said Gregorio. "I don't do business with people in a hurry."

Gregorio then approached Garden matchmaker Teddy Brenner for help. But Brenner cut the conversation short. "If you find a taker," said Brenner, "and he wants to match your son with a fighter, and you disapprove, who will Wilfredo listen to? Just forget it."

Papa Benitez finally found his "angel" in Jacobs, who was willing to put up his money and remain in the background while the father continued his Svengali act.

"Wilfredo will now be in position to get big-money fights," Gregorio said happily. "Now we will both make money."

Jacobs tried to remove some of the parental pressure from his fighter by adding former welterweight and middleweight champion Emile Griffith as co-trainer in time for Wilfredo's title challenge against Carlos Palomino. But the arguing in the corner between Griffith and Gregorio was more heated than the championship battle, which Wilfredo won with surprising ease.

The "love-hate" relationship between father and son continued when Benitez defended his newly won crown against Harold Weston. "You're not training hard, so I won't be with you," said the elder Benitez, admonishing his son for expending more energy in pursuit of the opposite sex than in his prefight conditioning. Gregorio knew that even a playful Wilfredo could whip Weston without benefit of his learned counsel.

The constant prodding of Papa Benitez had a salutary effect on Wilfredo. He was a demon in training for the Leonard match. Witnesses shook their heads in disbelief at his daily regimen, in particular his rapid-fire push-ups, each one performed with one less finger until, for the grand finale, a one-handed, one-finger push-up, like Charles Atlas holding up the world with his index finger. This new seriousness impressed Jacobs to no end.

"He has that touch of fear, that same fear a great actor feels opening night on Broadway," Jacobs said, "the same fear a surgeon feels when he is about to open your head."

Cus D'Amato nodded silently in agreement. D'Amato, the foxy old manager who deftly guided Floyd Patterson through a succession of over-the-hill fighters and canvasbacks to the heavyweight crown and who later brought Jose Torres to the threshold of the light-heavyweight title, was back on the scene as an "advisor" to the Benitez camp, but mostly as a confidant of Jacobs.

D'Amato is ageless. He looked the same and had lost none of the intensity he had had twenty-five years ago when he was the Don Quixote of boxing. Those were the days when he had fought against the monolithic International Boxing Club and Madison Square Garden, both controlled by the late Jim Norris, whose fortune was estimated at $300 million.

Patterson would earn over $8 million in his association

with D'Amato, while effortlessly defeating such harmless challengers as "Hurricane" Jackson, Brian London, and Pete Rademacher. D'Amato's share would be spent in his endless court battles against the boxing octopus. It was a strange twist. Instead of the standard Hollywood script of the fast-talking manager leaving his battered fighter penniless, it was D'Amato who was forced to declare bankruptcy while Patterson left him, after growing weary of Cus searching under his bed for enemies, imagined or otherwise.

"I never cared much for money," D'Amato would later say. "I was more interested in the sport. I lived from fight to fight and used my own money to fight the IBC. I never asked Patterson for a nickel."

Torres would also kiss D'Amato good-bye after languishing through long periods of unemployment.

He had imported Torres from Puerto Rico after spotting him as an outstanding amateur. D'Amato also sent a round-trip ticket for Jose's father, "because I feel your son needs parental advice." He had also told the young fighter: "You're not to sign a contract with me. I want you to feel free to leave if you are not happy with our arrangement."

Jose took him at his word when Cain Young, a wealthy real estate man, promised to hasten his march to the title. "I'll give you your release," said D'Amato. "I want you to be champion even if I'm forced to leave you. But we will still be friends."

D'Amato soon became a pariah on the boxing scene, although he vowed, "I'll be back. Enough people in the game are aware of what I can do. Then I will pay those people to whom I owe a proper debt."

And now he was back to lend his wisdom to young Wilfredo and serve as a buffer between the fighter and his domineering father.

"Listen," said Cus, in a confidential tone. "I don't want to get Wilfredo's old man in trouble. But I know for a fact that the boy was all of twelve when he won the National AAU lightweight title. I really couldn't fault his father. He had seen Wilfredo beat grown men on the streets of Puerto Rico. He knew he was good enough to beat the best amateurs. But only twelve—that must be the most extraordinary record in boxing history," added D'Amato, arching his bushy white eyebrows. "Then, five years later, he was good enough to win a professional title. Remarkable, just remarkable."

But even while lauding Benitez, D'Amato's piercing eyes were centered on Leonard, who was busy administering a painful beating to his cousin, O'Dell Leonard, a junior middleweight who served as a sparring partner.

"That young man," he said, "is the best finisher in boxing today. In fact, the best since Joe Louis. You know," he continued, "Leonard really hasn't learned much as a professional. By that I mean he already had considerable skills after completing his amateur career. The big difference now is that he does things intuitively. He has supreme confidence that when he delivers a particular punch, it will do exactly what he meant it to accomplish, be it a jab, hook, or uppercut. That only comes with a relaxed state of mind, and some fighters never attain that perfect chemistry of mind and body."

Sensing that his listener was beginning to believe D'Amato was working the wrong side of the street, the crafty Cus quickly changed direction.

"Leonard will face the moment of truth when he catches Benitez with a solid punch and discovers that he's not there to be hit with five or six more punches," he advised. "Benitez is a superior defensive fighter. He won't be standing in front of Leonard like a punching bag. And Benitez won't be intimidated by Leonard's actions or reputation. He is arrogant enough to believe that there is not a welterweight alive who can beat him.

"That's why this will be a most revealing fight for Leonard," D'Amato concluded. "If he beats Benitez, then we may be able to mention him in the same company with people like Sugar Ray Robinson."

When D'Amato's evaluation reached Leonard's ears, he emitted a deep-throated laugh. For Sugar Ray had been fighting Benitez in the recesses of his mind ever since the match was first announced five months earlier. And the outcome was always the same: Sugar Ray standing in center ring with his gloved hand raised in triumph.

"It's like a cartoon," Sugar Ray told *Washington Post* columnist Ken Denlinger. "I know exactly what's going to happen, punch by punch, round by round.

"I've got great respect for Benitez, and I give him tremendous credit for winning two titles at such an early age. But Friday night it will be like a giant chess game. Benitez and I are going to be student-teacher. Whenever he makes a mistake, I am going to show him why he is not supposed to do that."

Leonard spent long hours studying Benitez in films of past fights. "He doesn't like people dictating the fight to him," Sugar Ray noted. "I saw that in his first fight with Bruce Curry when he was knocked down three times. He got rattled and became cautious. He loses his confidence when he misses a few punches and can't do what he wants to do. He shakes his head and loses his courage."

Someone interrupted the monologue and asked Sugar Ray if he ever felt fear himself before entering the ring.

"Yes," he said. "Sometimes, I get butterflies. I get scared about what can happen. No, not about losing. About other things. Like what happened to Willie Classen. You think about that before you walk to the ring, but I never carry it into the ring with me. I don't worry about myself as much as what I might do to my opponent. But for this fight, I've been completely relaxed. It's come at just the perfect time for me.

"I started with the drive and natural ability," he said. "Now when I step in the ring, I'm at the stage where I feel totally in control of the situation, like Frank Sinatra stepping before a microphone. I know I'm the dominant one.

"I've prepared my whole life for this fight. It's been a long, tough road—ten years of my life devoted to fighting and living in the ring. Now I'm going to finish the job."

Owl-eyed Angelo Dundee, trainer to ten world champions, including Ali, toweled off his new protégé while offering his own analysis of the fight.

"It's a mistake to sell Benitez short," said Angelo, who was responsible for choosing all of Leonard's opponents on his way to the title encounter. "I think Benitez has suffered from the same communications problem as Roberto Duran and Carlos Monzon. They never got their due as true champions because they spoke Spanish and didn't get the same publicity as the American fighters. But all I keep remembering is that Benitez already owned two world titles at twenty-one. What other fighter ever did that?"

Dundee, while leaving the everyday training to Dave Jacobs, who had been Sugar Ray's tutor since he first laced on a pair of gloves at fourteen, was always around to provide the finishing touches.

"Drudgery. That's the thing that licks a lot of fighters," Angelo advised. "But this kid loves the gym. You don't have to go looking for him in the morning. He's out on the road at five A.M., waiting for you."

Sugar Ray helped to relieve the daily drudgery by enrolling in dance classes. "Cha-cha, disco, ballroom, you name it, and I've tried it," he said. "It's just to break up the monotony of the gym."

As the Benitez fight drew closer, he would spend more time dissecting films of Wilfredo's past battles.

"You want to know something about the other guy when you're getting ready for a fight," he told Phil Jackman of the *Baltimore Evening Sun*. "You want to find out what he does best—a hook or something. But once you're in the ring, it's a whole new ball game."

But that didn't stop the nightly "movies" in Leonard's Las Vegas suite as Sugar Ray and Dundee critiqued all of

Benitez's moves. Dundee, as usual, had done his homework well. He dipped into his pocket and showed a reporter his latest scouting report scribbled on a piece of wrinkled note paper:

> "Lots of hand waving.
> Throws slip jab.
> Left jab always works.
> R/foot in bucket.
> Straight R/H best punch to land with.
> Benitez always leads with right.
> Motion—must slide over in clinches.
> Can outpunch him—uppercut will work."

When the projector clicked off, Dundee said, "My man will win because he's a better puncher and he can dictate the fight. He's got an awkward, but effective style. He doesn't do a lot of dancing, but he's got great body movement. He bobs and weaves and makes you miss, then BAM-BAM-BAM, he's nailed you with those quick counter-punches. That's how he suckered Palomino.

"But Ray won't walk straight at Benitez," Dundee added. "He'll attack him from all angles. Benitez has never fought a complete fighter like Leonard, especially with Ray's left hand. He can double up with the hook and change speeds. Benitez can give you a shoeshine with his quick combinations, but Ray's jab will throw him off kilter.

"That's the great thing about this kid. He's multifaceted," said Dundee, without missing a beat. "He can box you, fight you, and gamble with you. But after all this talk, it still boils down to the guy on the stool. One-on-one."

While the fighters and trainers plotted last-minute strategy, the moneymen were busy in the counting house, happily contemplating their rewards from the richest non-heavyweight match in boxing history.

The two precocious welterweights were dividing $2.2 million, with Benitez getting the extra $200,000 for owning the title. No fighter save for a heavyweight had ever approached these astronomical figures—not a Ray Robinson, Rocky Graziano, Willie Pep, or any of the legendary fighters of the past.

The plotting for the multimillion dollar contest began in the spring of 1979 when Leonard's lawyer, Mike Trainer, first approached Jim Jacobs with an offer he couldn't refuse—an opportunity for Benitez to get rich.

Jacobs fully realized Sugar Ray's box-office magic, unmatched by any modern fighter with the exception of the incomparable Ali. In less than three years of professional scuffling, Leonard had already surpassed the $3 million mark in ring earnings. Benitez, on the other hand, had never earned more than $150,000 in a match.

And the champion was a relative stranger compared to Leonard, whose animated face had graced the TV screen in twenty of his first twenty-five bouts. He received a staggering $40,000 for his pro debut at the Baltimore Civic Center in February, 1977, toying with one Luis ("The Bull") Vega for six rounds. Benitez settled for $50 in his pro baptism and a line of agate in the San Juan dailies.

Trainer had all the financial figures on his side. "Ray is providing nearly eight times the money that Wilfredo ever made on a fight," he argued.

"But Wilfredo is not just another opponent," Jacobs countered. "He is the champion."

The debate raged for four hours in Jacobs's apartment until Trainer offered Benitez the extra $200,000 on the condition that the match be held on a neutral site, meaning anywhere but Puerto Rico where the champion would have strong vocal support. They settled on Las Vegas, which was hardly neutral considering the fact that Leonard had waged five fights in 1979 in the gambling capital, becoming almost as much of a fixture as the one-armed bandits. But Jacobs had coaxed the most money out of the pot. Now he would let Benitez do the fighting.

They now took their package to promoter Bob Arum,

who dealt regularly in multimillion dollar heavyweight extravaganzas. But a $2.2 million price tag on a non-heavyweight bout even tested Arum's credulity.

"I thought they were both crazy," Arum said in retrospect. But, surprisingly, Arum found a ready buyer in ABC, which had already spent so much time and money in fostering Leonard's pro career. "Frankly," Arum said, "I didn't think NBC or CBS would go for the price, but I had to give ABC the impression that there was fierce competition to air this match."

ABC agreed to contribute $1.9 million. Arum, in turn, sold the fight to Caesar's Palace for $500,000 and picked up an additional $150,000 for foreign rights. That added up to $2.55 million, assuring Arum of a tidy $250,000 profit.

Now the money was in the bank and the prefight ballyhoo had spent its course. The talking was over. It was time to fight.

Leonard, as usual, was "prime time." Because of his tremendous appeal, his match with Benitez would be viewed at ten P.M. back East, following the middleweight match between champion Vito Antuofermo and Marvin Hagler.

Antuofermo, a native of Bari, Italy, who would later hone his boxing skills fighting in the alleys of Brooklyn, was a fighter in the truest sense. The street brawler excited the Las Vegas crowd with his raw courage, carrying the battle by walking head-on into Hagler's thundering fists. At the final bell, Antuofermo's face had been transformed into a grotesque red mask, but he had endured the pain to gain a crowd-pleasing draw, enabling him to retain his middleweight crown a little longer.

The unrelenting savagery of the middleweight match offered a stark contrast to the exquisite boxing match that would follow between the two wunderkinds.

Benitez and Leonard stood in mid-ring, their finely tuned bodies glistening under the bright klieg lights as referee Carlos Padilla muttered the code of ring etiquette.

For close to a minute, they stood eyeball-to-eyeball, reminiscent of the days when malevolent Sonny Liston would try to wither his opponent with an evil stare.

For Benitez, the fixed expression was easy to attain. His face always wore a look of indifference, as if to say that he would get this tedious job over as quickly as possible and get on with more meaningful pursuits.

For Leonard, with all the boyish charm that made him America's media darling, the staring match was entirely out of character, a mindless charade performed for the TV cameras.

The opening bell ended this silent pantomime and Leonard moved quickly to the attack. He bounced several jarring hooks and combinations off Benitez's chin.

In the third round, Leonard stunned the crowd by dropping Benitez with a lightning jab, a feat that seemed worthy of only Joe Louis. But Benitez, more embarrassed than hurt, regained his feet at the count of two and, surprisingly, Leonard appeared reluctant to follow up his advantage.

Sugar Ray would show his first signs of frustration in the fourth round. He was measuring Benitez's jaw with right hands, but time and again, Wilfredo, with an almost imperceptible shrug of the shoulders or darting of his head, would have the punch go whistling harmlessly by his ear.

"It was as though I was looking into the mirror," Leonard would say later. "I've never been exposed to a fighter who could slide punches like this. No one. I mean *no one* can make me miss punches like that."

Dundee had warned his fighter of Benitez's extraordinary defensive skill, but Leonard persisted in throwing the right hand in an effort to end the match quickly.

"Go to the body. To the body. And keep that jab in his face," Dundee constantly shouted from the corner.

A familiar face then suddenly loomed over press row. It was massive Bundini Brown, Ali's personal "witch doctor," who had stood beside Dundee so often in Muhammad's corner.

"Angie, he's gotta go for broke," bellowed Bundini, making himself, as usual, a vociferous participant in the proceedings.

The fight had now become a battle of wits and mutual respect for each other's ability. The sneers that marked the prefight confrontation had been replaced by nodding appreciation when either fighter landed a telling blow.

It clearly lacked the blood and thunder of the Antuofermo-Hagler war. But this was as much a test of the mind as brute strength, a fight to be relished by the connoisseurs of the ancient sport.

The first blood-letting occurred in the sixth round when Leonard missed a right hand and his momentum carried him on a collision course with Benitez's head. Blood spurted out of the wound high on Wilfredo's forehead and trickled into his eyes, momentarily blurring his vision.

The bleeding continued to hinder the champion into the seventh round when Benitez was presented with a new handicap. He damaged his left wrist, and for the better part of the round, his left hand hung limply on his side.

To discourage his rival's growing confidence, Benitez left his corner at the start of the eighth round with a beatific smile on his face and mocked Leonard by sticking out his tongue, an insolence he paid for quickly as Sugar Ray delivered a stinging combination to the champion's chin.

Again, to start the ninth round, Benitez bowed politely from the waist and then launched a highly effective counter-attack. For a few minutes, Leonard appeared baffled by the sudden turn of events and fought with uncharacteristic caution. It caused a leather-lunged fan to shout, "Sugar, you sure don't look like Sugar Ray."

The pace slackened noticeably in the tenth round and scattered boos were heard from the crowd lusting for a resumption of the bloodbath that had preceded this scientific squabble. Leonard responded to the hooting by unleashing a blinding series of blows that forced the champion to seek asylum on the ropes.

Benitez was now growing visibly weary, a condition perhaps brought about by an eight-month lay-off between fights. Leonard was gaining confidence with each new round. His booming rights were now penetrating Wilfredo's defenses. Before the fourteenth round, Dundee spotted a friend on press row and asked for a quick computation of the fight to date. He got a thumbs-up sign in reply and nodded approvingly.

But the Leonard corner would take no chances with a close decision, and Sugar Ray was sent out for the kill in the final round. And Benitez, sensing his crown was now in peril, met his challenger in mid-ring for the violent showdown.

Now both fighters were winging knockout punches, but Leonard landed the first damaging blow, a straight right flush on the chin. With D'Amato's praise of being a great finisher echoing in his brain, Sugar Ray unleashed all his fury. Punch after punch. Punches too quick to count. Three brutal hooks in succession that buckled Benitez's knees.

The champion instinctively moved inside, hoping to tie up Leonard's flying pistons and buy some time. But he walked straight into a head-spinning left hook that sent him sprawling to the canvas.

By dint of will, he regained his balance, but his gloves were now resting on the ropes, an open target for the advancing Leonard, who scored with three more damaging blows before referee Padilla rushed in to signal an end to the fight.

Spectators who had backed the underdog howled in protest at Padilla's action, coming only six seconds before the final bell. But it mattered little since Leonard had been ahead on all three judges' scorecards.

As Padilla protected Benitez's quivering body, Leonard

sprinted across the ring and leaped onto the second strand of ropes, thrusting his arms skyward in a rapturous sign of victory.

Sugar Ray was now on top of the world, a lofty exhilarating perch from where he could look back and see how far he had come in such a short time.

☆ 13 ☆

LOVE: LOST AND FOUND

It should have been the best of times, but the twenty-three-year-old man-child was going through another difficult passage in life—the transition from a gangly amateur champion with a shiny gold medal dangling around his neck to a world figure with growing responsibilities to his family and the public at large.

Two months after winning the title, he would marry his childhood sweetheart, Juanita Wilkinson, who had given birth out of wedlock to their son, Ray, Jr., in 1974. Getting married would be one of the few major decisions he would make without first consulting his "family" of advisors.

"I wasn't ready before," he would explain when asked why the wedding date had been delayed for so long. "I wasn't settled in my mind. I was always on the go. But now I feel I'm finally ready to face some serious commitments."

A more serious demeanor would now greet Sugar Ray in the looking glass. He would turn inward, hoping to find his true self, not the fanciful figure found on the TV screen and in the media hype. He felt prepared to assume added responsibilities in governing his life in and out of the ring.

Juanita's love for Ray had survived the trauma of the nationally publicized paternity suit, long and painful separations while he prepared for another fight, and the petty gossip and jealousy of friends and neighbors.

Even after they had taken the marriage vows, the idle tattling continued. Juanita recalled standing in a supermarket check-out line one day and hearing another customer discuss her wedding. "She said it was ridiculous," Juanita told Judy Mann of *The Washington Post*. "She said the whole wedding was a 'put-on' and that it was ridiculous to have a six-year-old son as the ringbearer.

"At first, I was in shock. I never heard anyone talk about our situation that way. So I stood there, thinking I should say something, but then if I do, I could end up in an ugly fight. So I said nothing. And when I came home to Ray and told him what had happened, he said he was really proud of me."

Despite her husband's fame and fortune, Juanita, who was employed as a gas station attendant when they first met ("I'd be greasy and smelly and he'd be so clean"), managed to keep her independence and sense of value.

"I'm not a celebrity, but a celebrity's wife," she said, "and for that reason I have to put up with a lot of foolish things. Ray knows, however, that I don't like the limelight, and he doesn't push me out in front with him.

"Of course, it's been a big change, coming from nothing to everything," Juanita added, "but I'm not used to splurging. People look at me and say, 'You don't look like Sugar Ray's wife.' Why? Because I don't wear ten gold rings and I'm not flashy?

"I tell these people, 'I don't have a penny. Ray's rich. He's the one who takes all the risks. I have it if he gives it to me, but I'm not rich.' Keeping that attitude has helped, but, of course, what's his is mine.

"But I don't want to be totally dependent on him. I don't

want to lose my identity. I want to be in on everything. I don't want to be an object."

Juanita is fully aware that her husband's celebrity puts him in contact with beautiful women famous in their own right, and others simply seeking to share some intimacy with Sugar Ray.

"Lola Falana, Jayne Kennedy, and Diana Ross are all friends of Ray," she acknowledged. "But that's it, they're just friends. But I can't have too many girl friends my age who are single. They might say, 'Hey, regardless of who Juanita is, I like this man.'

"If I weren't sure about this relationship, it would be harder. Before we were married, I used to be insecure. I wasn't sure he wouldn't go out with someone else. But as time went on, and we got closer, I started feeling, if he hasn't changed this far, he's not going to change any time soon."

Sugar Ray admires the "fighter" in his petite wife. "For a long time, Juanita felt like an outcast," he told Betty Cuniberti of *The Washington Star*. "But now she's my little manager. She's a big part of my boxing life.

"I love her because of her nature. She's sensible and she doesn't lose her perspective on life, going from rags to riches. She still likes everyday things and respects everyone.

"When I was a bachelor, I was caught up in material things. I could get whatever I wanted. Fancy cars. Women. You name it. Simple things didn't mean anything anymore. But it was a big put-on. I didn't know what was legitimate anymore. But Juanita gives me a sense of direction, a sense of faith, a sense of feeling."

As he confided to Tom Boswell of *The Washington Post*, "People still see me as that kid with the medal hanging around his neck and a handful of play money. They mistake my kindness for weakness. But my kiddie days are over. I'm as grown a man as I'm ever going to be. If I could do, say, and go like I did when I had nothing, I'd be the happiest man in the world. But I can't.

"Frankly," he added, "I don't like doing the things I used to. If the little things that made you laugh don't make you laugh anymore, that doesn't mean you've 'changed.' It means you're older, more mature.

"The one thing I hate is when friends start asking me about my fame and money. And they get that look, just like the people in a shopping center when they're all waiting for the first person to ask for an autograph so they can all stampede. When the conversation turns like that, I get discouraged. That person has destroyed every bit of confidence and respect I had in him. He has put out the fire."

Despite this show of independence, outsiders would continue to strongly influence his life. His "inner family" that had once served as a model of togetherness and camaraderie was now showing its first serious signs of disharmony.

For the sake of efficiency, Sugar Ray would see fit to reduce his board of consultants. Mike Trainer, the attorney with the Midas touch, and Janks Morton, Leonard's most trusted chancellor, would now step front and center while the other "family" members began to fade in the background.

"Mike, Janks, and me make all the decisions now," Leonard said succinctly. And Trainer would add, "This show has only one star, and that's Ray."

Some of the shunted "family" members accepted their demotions philosophically. Dundee, who had skillfully navigated Sugar Ray through the welterweight ranks to the world title while hardly getting his hair messed, would continue to receive fifteen percent of the purses in his role as "manager." But his decision-making was now minimal. "I'm a lesser character in this play," acknowledged Dundee. But one of the "outcasts" did not accept his lesser role in the new scenario without a public outcry. While Ray and Juanita were honeymooning in California and Las Vegas, Dave Jacobs, who had been Leonard's everyday trainer from his first days as a fighter, decided to take on Trainer, the exchequer of "Sugar Ray Leonard, Inc."

Jacobs had maintained his silence throughout Ray's rapid rise through the ranks. But he had watched uncomfortably his once-influential position with Leonard deteriorate ever since Dundee was invited to join the "family" as Ray's principal matchmaker.

Although Jacobs still supervised Leonard's training as a pro, Dundee, because of his easily recognizable face and his great rapport with the press, would receive the accolades for honing Sugar Ray's abundant ring skills. Dundee made a conscious effort to duly acknowledge Jacobs's part in the fighter's success, but when the TV cameras panned Leonard's corner, it was always Angelo's smiling visage that appeared on the screen.

If he could not have his share of glory, Jacobs, at least, wanted his share of the profits. He would request a new contract calling for ten percent of Leonard's future earnings, a standard figure for trainers of established fighters.

Trainer interpreted the action as a sign of pure greed and excommunicated Jacobs from the "family" by posting a letter to his attorney, Spencer H. Boyer.

"It's better to be on the outside looking in than on the inside and treated like a dog," Jacobs reacted bitterly. "I don't think this was Ray's doing or that Angelo had anything to do with the decision. But these people act as if I never did anything for the boy.

"They forget I was there from the beginning," he continued. "When Ray wasn't earning a penny, I built him into an Olympic champion. Now that he's making millions, they figure I'm not worth the customary ten percent a professional trainer gets."

Jacobs contended that he had not signed a formal agreement with Leonard at the time he turned professional in

1977. There was no need for one, he insisted, because of their close "father-and-son" relationship.

"I've been making as little as one percent of his earnings from all these $250,000 fights," he noted, "but I didn't want to rock the boat while Ray was chasing after the title. But after he beat Benitez, I felt it was time to ask for my fair share."

Before confronting Trainer head-on, Jacobs first met with Leonard to discuss his future role in the family. "Ray offered me a fat salary," he said, "but it really wasn't enough to make me quit my job as boxing instructor at the Oakcrest Recreation Center.

Ironically, it was Jacobs who helped convince Leonard that he could not forsake his God-given talents as a fighter after winning the Olympic gold medal.

"We were coming home from Montreal," he recalled, "and Ray kept telling everyone he was finished fighting, that he'd accomplished his goal winning in the Olympics. He kept giving away his ring equipment to friends and fans. Finally, I told him, 'Ray, you'd better hang on to some of that stuff. You might just change your mind in a month or so.' "

For a moment, the conversation ended. There was a long, pregnant pause. But Jacobs now regained his composure. "I still love Ray Leonard," he said with a catch in his throat. "I only wish him Godspeed. I have no regrets. If I had to, I'd do it all over again."

The fact that Jacobs had made his contract hassle a public matter disturbed Trainer, who mounted a quick counter-attack in the press. The attorney insisted that he had offered the trainer a new contract "that was more than fair under the circumstances—a flat fee of $25,000 per fight.

"I don't like anything that indicates that David Jacobs has not been treated fairly," Trainer said emphatically. "I'd like to find a fight trainer who gets paid more. What we offered him was far in excess of what he has made in previous fights, and many times more than he earns working full-time at the recreation center.

"We've had an arrangement with Jacobs since Ray turned pro, and we were led to believe that he was quite happy with it. Then Ray became a champion, and now he wants a percentage of what Ray earns. We don't want to fire him. Ray loves him. But if he won't work for Ray, well then, he can quit."

When news of Jacobs's "dismissal" reached Leonard's ears in Las Vegas where the honeymooners were making a final stop, the fighter, at first, voiced surprise.

"It must be a rumor," he said. "I wish somebody had told me." But when a reporter relayed Jacobs's remarks, Ray sighed audibly and added, "It's really a matter of percentages. I really haven't been home long enough to talk things out with Jake. But we've always worked as a team. I hope we can still work it out."

A few days later, Leonard and Jacobs would confer privately and temporarily settle their differences. Jake would continue to serve as his everyday trainer, but their once close relationship would never quite be the same again. As Janks Morton reflected, "Dave just couldn't stop thinking of Ray as his little-boy son."

After the troubles had been aired in the area papers, Leonard's second family was no longer regarded by outsiders as passengers on the *Good Ship Lollipop* enjoying a million-dollar pleasure cruise through life. It wasn't *Mutiny on the Bounty* either, but the chain of command was now clearly evident.

"A couple of people had to realize who was working for whom," said Morton, who was now closest to the king's ear. "They're working for Ray, not he for them."

The once-bubbly family atmosphere surrounding Sugar Ray had now been replaced by a coldly efficient business mood. Yes, the kiddie days were over for Leonard. He was now a full-fledged corporate giant with a fortune waiting at the touch of a glove.

☆ 14 ☆

THE EMPIRE IS FALLING

"Let us honor if we can
The vertical man
Though he honor none
But the horizontal one."
—W. H. Auden, "Epigraph for Poems," 1930

Over and over again, the two fighters flailed at each other on the videotape. It was reminiscent of those seemingly endless brawls staged between two robot boxers in a penny arcade.

A voice with a thick British accent intoned excitedly, "Davey Boy is beating him to the punch. Palomino just blinked."

Davey Boy Green's one big round would be shown again and again during the two-hour press conference at the Capital Centre. Subliminal is what the hucksters from Madison Avenue call the technique. Show something often enough, it will slowly sink into the subconscious, and, inevitably, the target of the sales pitch will become a believer. "Big Brother" never had it so good.

Somehow, the reporters present never got to see Davey Boy carted back to his corner in the eleventh round after blindly walking into a vicious left hook by Carlos Palomino. On the strength of one good round against the former welterweight champion, Davey Boy Green would be sold as a legitimate challenger for Sugar Ray Leonard's newly won crown.

No matter that the stocky Britisher's 33–2 record was padded with victories against such clawless tigers as Barton McAllister and Angus McMillan, who seemed more suited for the stage of the Old Vic than the boxing ring. When Green ran out of native "tomato cans," promoters obligingly imported canvasbacks from America, including several fighters still under suspension in the States for having been knocked out in the last few months.

And no matter that in his only other venture outside the British Isles, the root farmer from Chatteris lasted less than three rounds against a thirty-six-year-old melancholy Dane named Jorgen Hansen. There was always a ready explanation.

"Everybody loses," said Green's trainer-manager Andy Smith, in his East Anglian brogue. "The great Joe Louis was knocked out by Max Schmeling, the incomparable Ray Robinson lost more than a dozen fights, and Willie Pep lost a few, too. Davey just made a mistake against Hansen. He staggered him in the third round and got careless. Hansen nailed him a good shot, and the referee, who was Danish, jumped right in and stopped it."

And no matter that Davey Boy was ranked no better than number ten by *Ring* magazine. There would be time enough to build a new bold image for the challenger whose craggy face looked like it belonged to a catcher who had forgotten his mask while handling Nolan Ryan.

In a matter of a few weeks, Davey Boy would be passed off to the press as a combination of Rocky Graziano, Carmen Basilio, Fritzie Zivic, and Jake LaMotta—a man of a thousand faces, but all resembling what's known in the venerable boxing trade as a "face fighter."

"Does this look like a face that has taken a beating," Green would argue earnestly. "I'm a box-fighter. I can box a little, and fight a lot. I don't take punches. You have to miss the right ones. After all, you can't take a bath without getting wet, now can you?"

And Smith would add in his fighter's defense, "Davey's real strength as a fighter is just that. That's fighting. He likes to have a fight or a brawl, as you Americans say, when he climbs in the ring. He doesn't lead with his face like Vito Antuofermo. But he's a totally committed fist-fighter.

"He's a throwback to Graziano. The American public will love him. Everything Davey does with one hundred and twenty percent effort. And it would be a great feather in his cap to beat Leonard in his backyard."

To heighten Green's image as one tough hombre, Davey Boy paraded around press headquarters in New Carrollton, Maryland, wearing cowboy boots and an oversized Stetson, a gift from heavyweight John Tate. But it only made him look more like a little boy dressing up for a game of "Cowboys and Indians."

And so the hype continued. The public might be fooled, but not Leonard. In a moment of candor, Sugar Ray said, "A lot of people are asking, 'What's a Davey Boy Green?' and, I guess, I'm one of them."

Instead, the people should have been asking, "Why a Davey Boy Green?" The answer was a simple matter of dollars and cents. Promoter Bob Arum, who had helped arrange Leonard's title fight with Wilfredo Benitez, was rewarded with an option on Sugar Ray's first title defense. But for a mere $1.4 million, Leonard was not about to risk his good looks against such formidable foes as Roberto Duran or Thomas Hearns. Nor would he accept the challenge of Pepino Cuevas, who at the time, owned the half of the crown recognized by the World Boxing Association, a less powerful affiliation of ring organizations.

But in staging the Leonard-Green match in Sugar Ray's backyard, Arum was also practicing "one-upmanship" on arch-rival Don King. Originally, the bout had been ticketed for Las Vegas, where WBC heavyweight king Larry Holmes was defending his share of the title against butterball Leroy Jones in what King advertised as the "feature bout" in a four-hour TV extravaganza that included WBA heavyweight champ John Tate's match with Mike Weaver and a light-heavyweight title bout between Marvin Johnson and challenger Eddie Gregory. The last two fights would be waged in Knoxville, Tennessee.

But neither Arum nor Leonard's tough-minded attorney Mike Trainer were willing to accept the idea that Leonard would appear on the "undercard" to Holmes, or even King Kong, for that matter.

"Leonard's the superstar, not Holmes," Arum insisted. "Sugar Ray demands a larger audience than Holmes. If ABC elects to put Holmes on after Leonard, they might find a lot of people flicking off their television sets."

The television moguls could argue that Holmes's lopsided match with Jones was the main attraction, but old-time boxing buffs knew better. As Angelo Dundee noted, "The main event has always been ten P.M., prime-time. And that's when Leonard is fighting."

Arum then turned altruistic in explaining why Sugar Ray was staging a "homecoming" after having fought five of his six previous battles in Las Vegas.

"In order to have boxing flourish, you can't keep bringing big fights to the gambling casinos," he said. "They can't be put in a position where they can monopolize the action. Sooner or later, the people will get the wrong impression—boxing, TV, and gambling. You have to take the fights to the people. And this is a 'people's fight' at 'people's prices.' "

A goodly number of the 19,000 Capital Centre seats,

however, were priced at fifty and one hundred dollars, making one wonder what kind of "people" Arum had in mind. It was a rather steep price to pay to see a rather obscure British fighter, considering England's long and horrendous history of producing horizontal fighters for export.

Britain's international boxing record had been consistently dismal ever since Professor Jim Figg gave up his heavyweight title around 1720. Even London's political cartoonists couldn't avoid lampooning their fallen brethren. In one memorable sketch, a boxing writer was depicted stretched out flat with a "DO NOT TILT" sign at his feet. And the caption read: "This way I can get a better slant on British boxing."

The most recent victim in this succession of horizontal heavies from England had, of course, been Henry Cooper—the walking "Bloodmobile"—who gained ignominity among his countrymen at the hands of Muhammad Ali. After flooring Ali early in the match, he had more than paid for the insult by losing five pints of blood before the referee mercifully stopped the bloodbath.

Hearing this brief recounting of Britain's nebulous boxing past, Davey Green's manager snapped, "Very funny, very funny, but let's talk about recent history. Have you looked at the record lately?" he challenged a writer. "If you did your homework, you'd discover that England presently has three world champions—Jamie Watt, the lightweight; Maurice Hope, the junior middleweight; and Alan Minter, who just won the middleweight title from Antuofermo."

Now Smith was clearly gathering steam. "Our fighters are restoring the roar of the British lion for the first time since Winston Churchill, and this is no lend-lease program. We intend to keep these titles," the little Scotsman vowed.

"The truth is, that despite our reputation," added Smith, "we've always had some pretty fair fighters. People like

Freddie Mills, Tommy Farr, Randy Turpin, Kenny Buchanan, and Terry Downes. When people come up to me and say, 'British guys can't fight,' I always tell them, 'I wonder what a fellow named Adolf Hitler thought after he tangled with our blokes.'

"What people seem to forget is that our whole island is about the size of Florida. And, if you compare the two populations, we've probably produced as many good fighters as America. You must keep everything in perspective."

That was the problem. Putting Davey Boy Green in perspective caused only yawns in the Leonard camp. About the only concern of the oddsmakers, who had made the champion a six-to-one favorite, was whether Sugar Ray would take the root farmer from the fens too lightly. Having attained the status of a champion, Leonard, shrewd observers speculated, had lost the drive and burning ambition to make every match count.

Once again, Angelo Dundee, who had managed or trained nine world champions, was consulted as an expert on the subject.

"The only guy I can think of was Jimmy Ellis," said Dundee. "Now, Jimmy was one beautiful kid, a choirboy from Louisville who started out the same time as Ali. They even fought each other in the amateurs. When I first met Jimmy, he was a stylish middleweight, but he had a lot of medical problems—carbuncles, tonsils, you name it.

"I knew that the kid was really suffering making the 160-pound limit. So one day I told him, 'Put the gloves away until you get yourself together and feel healthy again. Then we'll talk about fighting.' The next time I saw Jimmy, he was a full-fledged heavyweight, rarin' to go."

Ellis's timing couldn't have been better. His blossoming coincided with Ali's political exile from the heavyweight throne for his antiwar stand in 1967. Ellis proceeded to whip Leotis Martin, Oscar Bonavena, and Jerry Quarry in an elimination tournament to claim the vacant title in 1968.

"Jimmy was only twenty-eight at the time," Dundee recalled, "but he got his belly full after he won the title. He made only one defense against Floyd Patterson, but then he wanted to rest on his laurels.

"The money back then wasn't anything like what it is today with the TV revenue, but we had an offer to fight this guy Dave Zygliewicz in Houston for an easy $75,000. But Jimmy's sparring partner, Joe Shelton, takes him aside one day and says, 'You don't want to go down to Texas and fight a white boy. If you win, they'll blow your brains out.'

"Then Shelton starts telling Ellis about the time Bobby Baker went to Texas to fight Roy ("Cut-'n'-Shoot") Harris. Baker won the first few rounds, but then someone waved a gun in his corner, and Baker lost heart.

"So Jimmy comes back to me," Dundee continued, "and says he wants no part of Texas. Joe Frazier goes down there instead and knocks Zygliewicz stiff in one round for an easy $75,000. A year later, Frazier whips Ellis for the uncontested title, and I'm thinking of all the money Jimmy threw away. He could have added another million to his bankroll without breaking a sweat."

Dundee, however, had no fear that Leonard would turn soft and lazy after winning the title. "Ray wants to fight every couple of months," he said. "He'll go nuts if he doesn't fight. Besides, having the money is a good feeling. Ray's looking to the future, to buy a nice house [Leonard was already making plans to purchase an $850,000 manse], and enjoy the fruits of his labor."

When someone mentioned to Sugar Ray that he had already gained financial security with $4 million in ring earnings, the fighter shook his head. "It's just not the money," he said. "I've always got to set new goals for myself. I felt let down after winning the Olympic title, and

I had that same empty feeling after I beat Benitez for the welter crown. I needed a new incentive to keep my fighting edge.

"In my own mind, I believe I'm a great fighter," he said, without false modesty. "You earn that respect by winning a championship. But the public always finds new challenges for you. They won't recognize me as a great champion until I clean up the whole welterweight division. That means I have to beat Duran, Hearns, and Cuevas before I gain acceptance.

"I'm twenty-three now, and I'd like to quit by the time I'm twenty-seven. But I'm not setting a specific timetable. That's unrealistic. I just want to get out of this game financially independent and able to take care of my family and close friends."

He had invested most of his earnings in blue-chip bonds and real estate, only occasionally splurging on luxury items. "After the Benitez fight, I sported myself to a Mercedes," he said. "It helps ease the pain."

Introducing his parents to "*la dolce vita*" has been far more difficult.

"My mother and father are real dollar-conscious," he said. "They know value. If I buy them plane tickets for a vacation trip, they'll give them back and hop in a car to save a buck. If Ralph Nader had my parents on his side, he'd solve all his consumer problems in a few days," Leonard laughed.

But Davey Boy Green was still wearing a sneer to match his cowboy hat at the prefight weigh-in. Public relations man Charley Brotman tried to induce a laugh when he announced, "Green, ten stone, nine [149 pounds]?" But the taciturn fighter refused to smile.

"I've tried talking to him," said Leonard, "but he says he doesn't want to get to like me before the fight. He wants to hate me."

"He can't say anything that will get me mad," Davey Boy

responded with a snarl. "I know he wants to make me angry, but I won't oblige."

There was a strong contingent of British press on hand. They had been to Las Vegas to see their countryman, Alan Minter, upset Vito Antuofermo to claim the middleweight crown. Next, they traveled to Atlantic City to watch Liverpool's John Conteh take a fourth-round swoon against Matthew Saad Muhammad, a.k.a. Matt Franklin, and then in a drunken revelry, go dashing through the hotel corridors in his birthday suit, scaring chambermaids half to death.

But not a single British writer thought there was anything about Davey Boy Green that might put the fear of God in Leonard. The consensus of opinion was that Green was incontestably out of his league, and that the six-to-one odds favoring the champion were really quite modest after assessing the comparative merits of the two fighters.

Their fear for Davey Boy's safety was well founded in the aftermath of the brief, but frightening battle. Green entered the Capital Centre ring wearing an oversized tiger-pelt robe that was intended to enhance his tough guy image. But it only drew jibes of ridicule from ringsiders. "Is this guy an Englishman or an Eskimo?" one wag shouted.

The now customary eyeball-to-eyeball confrontation followed as referee Arthur Mercante spelled out the code of boxing etiquette. But it would provide the only comic relief in an otherwise appalling mismatch.

From the early moments of the opening round, it was painfully evident that the plodding Green was in over his head. Leonard, looking totally relaxed, found his squat British rival as easy to hit as a heavy bag, peppering him with a dazzling variety of jabs, hooks, and combinations while bringing blood from Davey Boy's flat nose.

It was more of the same in the second and third rounds as Green continued to walk headlong into Sugar Ray's pistonlike fists. He was punishing his foe with such ridiculous ease that it seemed he could very well decide the exact time and place in the ring where the accident would happen.

Before the fourth round, Dundee instructed his fighter, "Green's swinging wildly, baby. Take your time. Wait for an opening and just pop him."

It was more than a pop. More like an explosion. A thundering left hook that Leonard would later call "the hardest punch I've ever thrown" left Green twitching convulsively on the canvas at 2:24 of the fourth round.

Seeing Davey Boy's desperate state, referee Mercante stopped counting at six and waved two doctors into the ring. And Andy Smith had rushed to his stricken fighter's side almost at the instant his head hit the floor with a sickening thud. It would take several minutes before Green regained his senses and was carried back to his corner, where he would question his handlers, "What happened?" like the victim of a hit-and-run accident.

"That was the first time I was frightened by a punch I threw," Sugar Ray said. "Everything was just on time. It was short, straight from the body, and hit him flush on the chin. When he lay there so still and I saw his eyes roll back into his head, I was scared.

"I kept saying to myself, 'Get up, Davey, get up!' I had a strange and sensitive feeling."

"Sensitive?" inquired a British writer.

"Yes, sensitive," Leonard assured him, "because I had no animosity toward him. It's just part of being a fighter. But when will people start to realize that speed dominates experience; speed dominates power, speed dominates everything. Speed will always do the job."

No one agreed more than Andy Smith after he had made certain Davey Boy could now negotiate under his own power.

"Gentlemen," he said to the press, "you have just witnessed a young man who may be the greatest welterweight champion ever."

Letting that definitive statement sink in, Smith added, "Davey fought a good fight. Going in, I thought we had a chance, otherwise we wouldn't have come all this way. But Davey just wasn't in the league to fight this man Leonard. He is just too good. He is awesome."

This time, Smith's counterpart, Angelo Dundee, was not available to provide his post-fight commentary. Dundee, in fact, had also been rendered unconscious, a victim of a sneak punch by a Leonard camp follower on the short walk from the ring to the interview room.

The assailant was identified as Joe ("Pepe") Saunders, who had volunteered to serve as Leonard's personal chauffeur the week of the Green fight. Saunders's association with Sugar Ray went back to his earliest days as an amateur fighter, but he now seemed anxious to reestablish his presence in the champion's growing entourage.

"This guy was trying to get by Ray's side when we left the ring," said Dundee, who was now suffering a severe backache and headache. "The security cops asked me if I wanted him thrown out, and I told them, 'No.' And the next thing I remember, I was waking up on the floor."

Several eyewitnesses contended that Dundee and Saunders exchanged angry words during the procession from the ring and it resulted in the surprising knockout. In any case, Dundee refused to press charges.

"I can't start hurting people now," the manager said. "Putting him in handcuffs was probably enough to scare him."

A tearful Davey Boy Green silently wished he had brought a pair of handcuffs for Leonard. "I let all my people down," he said sorrowfully. "They came all this way to see me and I let them down."

A month later, the British Boxing Board of Control was urging Green to put both his tiger-skin robe and gloves into permanent mothballs. By this time, Leonard was already tracking bigger game.

As the crowd thinned in his dressing room, Sugar Ray

shouted to a retreating reporter, "Isn't it obvious now that I would knock Duran out?"

In three months time, he would get a chance to fulfill his prophecy.

☆ 15 ☆

THE UNHOLY ALLIANCE

Sugar Ray Leonard and Roberto Duran stood toe-to-toe, menacing each other with pillow-sized gold gloves amid the opulent surroundings of the Waldorf Astoria ballroom. It was a fitting setting for the official kick-off to what veteran boxing publicist Irving Rudd modestly proclaimed, "The Event of a Lifetime."

Judging by the crowd of media types it had attracted, Rudd didn't seem far off the mark. It was a day for speaking only in superlatives—big, Bigger, BIGGEST!—a welterweight showdown that promised to break every existing record for a non-heavyweight fight.

Multimillion dollar figures were being tossed about as carelessly as a couple of kids pitching pennies. Gate receipts for the title match at Montreal's mammoth Olympic Stadium, plus revenue from closed-circuit television outlets were projected as high as $30 million, a staggering sum that would easily eclipse the record $18 million jackpot that Muhammad Ali and Joe Frazier attracted for their first encounter at Madison Square Garden, March 8, 1971.

To herald their wildly anticipated confrontation, the two combatants had dressed to fit their sharply contrasting images.

As befitting the chairman of the board and sole stockholder in a million-dollar corporation, Leonard, the meticulous boxer, was conservatively attired in a dark blue suit with muted stripes, especially purchased for the occasion at Sak's Fifth Avenue.

Duran, on the other hand, was a picture of sartorial splendor. To match his reckless style, the one-time street brawler wore an eye-catching beige silk suit he had custom-tailored at "a special price" of $450. It was set off by a beige-on-beige shirt, a beige-and-brown tie, and, of course, beige-colored shoes.

But the clothes adorning the former lightweight champion were quite modest compared to the dazzling collection of jewelry that completed his colorful ensemble.

Hanging around Roberto's olive-skinned head was a monstrous ten-ounce gold medallion with a large "R" as its centerpiece surrounded by clusters of diamond and sapphire chips. It was valued at $25,000. He also sported a rock-sized gold-and-pearl ring on his left hand that carried a $15,000 price tag, and a smaller diamond ring on his left hand worth $6,000. And, for a finishing touch, a $1,000 diamond was embedded in his right earlobe.

And where had Duran purchased all these glittering gems? a man politely inquired.

"At a place in midtown called 'The Bargain Bench,' " the interpreter replied.

Standing together, the two immaculately groomed fighters looked far too civilized to consider practicing mayhem on one another. For the time being, their anger, feigned or otherwise, would be restricted to verbal jousting.

Eyeing the crowded room of reporters and cameramen, Leonard unleashed the first blast of venom when he said, "I don't want to just beat Duran, I want to kill him."

Questioned later about this uncharacteristic threat, Sugar Ray confessed, "That was ninety-nine percent hype. I had to speak to Duran in his own language. I couldn't just say I wanted to whip him. 'Kill' is a word I knew he'd understand."

There was more, of course. "All the reporters keep writing about his 'dangerous eyes,' " added Leonard. "But eyes don't do the punching. I admit he was a great lightweight champion, but he's a welterweight now, and the guys he's beaten to date aren't even in my class. That's why I'm going to destroy him as I destroyed all the others."

If Leonard had hoped to enrage Duran's Latin temper with his tough talk, he was to be greatly disappointed.

"I don't have any speeches," Roberto said, fixing his rival with an evil stare. "I am here only to fight. I don't like talking. Leonard does all the talking, but he talks mostly garbage. He says he is this, and he is that. But he's nobody. When I get in the ring, I fight. I don't jump or dance around. And that is why Leonard's days are numbered. I don't care about the money. Today, I'm a rat . . . a very hungry rat."

Expectedly, both fighters claimed victories in the psychological warfare following their first face-to-face confrontation.

"Did you see how badly Duran was perspiring?" Leonard asked several reporters. "I thought he was wearing a sweatsuit. He must be worried about something, don't you think? He called me a clown, but I'm twenty-seven and oh. Maybe they don't have any television in Panama."

To onlookers, Duran seemed as frightened of Leonard as King Kong of Fay Wray. The swarthy Panamanian wore a knowing smile like the Cheshire cat as he left the press conference accompanied by his foxy, eighty-two-year-old trainer Ray Arcel. Slapping his fighter on the back, Arcel chirped, "We won it right there. Leonard is full of bleep. He's scared to death of you."

The war of nerves had started. Battle lines were already

being drawn for the classic battle still two months away. The "people's fight" had become a surprising reality long before even the most wildly optimistic fight fan might have anticipated.

To most insiders the prospect of a Leonard-Duran match had seemed unlikely before 1981. Leonard's lawyer, Mike Trainer, and Duran's advisors strongly counseled by Don King, had not been able to resolve their differences, and so the Leonard camp began to look elsewhere for Sugar Ray's next opponent. Only a few weeks earlier, in fact, a match had been tentatively arranged that would pit Leonard against Pepino Cuevas for the undisputed welterweight title.

But that, of course, was before World Boxing Council President Jose Sulaiman convinced Cuevas that it was best for all concerned to step aside in favor of Duran.

All the backroom plotting and Machiavellian intrigue led to the improbable merger of Bob Arum and Don King into "BADK, Inc." To those aware of their past grievances, it was as unlikely a happening as the Ayatollah Khomeini inviting the Shah of Iran to a tea party.

As a man well-acquainted with both parties testified, "They really hate each other's guts. It's no 'put-on' to get their names in the paper. But Arum and King are still basically businessmen. They don't have to talk to each other to do business and make tons of money."

Over the past decade, Arum had seen fit to call King "another Idi Amin." King, on the other hand, has depicted his arch-rival as "a Jewish Hitler." Snake, liar, cheat, and crook have been other terms of endearment they've exchanged in and out of print.

They are truly boxing's *Odd Couple*. Together, however, they grew to control all the important ring titles and fighters in the world today with the exception of Leonard, who, for the most part, had been able to dictate his own terms.

Arum, a rather ordinary-looking man with a sheepish

grin, is the son of an Orthodox Jewish accountant, who raised his family in the crowded Crown Heights section of Brooklyn.

King, a hulking black man with hair like an exploding artichoke, was the product of the Cleveland ghetto. He was forced to fend for himself as an adolescent after his father died in a steel mill accident and left behind six sons.

Arum earned straight As at New York University and then graduated *cum laude* from Harvard Law School. But his real strength was with figures. At thirty, he was hired as a tax expert for the U.S. Attorney's office in Manhattan and successfully tackled such giants as Stavros Niarchos, First City National Bank, and Macy's.

King's great strength also lay in numbers—the kind that could be found on little slips of paper in a street lottery. As a teenage "runner," he showed great aptitude for his job and before he was old enough to vote, he had "graduated" to the title of "numbers baron" in Cleveland.

"I have a Ph.D. from the ghetto," he would boast good-naturedly. "I majored in numbers, garbage, rats, and roaches. Hell, it's nothing to be ashamed of. A lot of numbers guys put their kids through school and helped make them doctors and lawyers. I got a lot of pressure from the syndicate guys, and they tried to blow me away a couple of times. I've still got some shrapnel in my neck. But I guess I was lucky."

One time, though, Don King wasn't so lucky. He hired an ex-con to run numbers for him, but when a big pay-off took place in the new man's neighborhood under suspicious circumstances, a street confrontation took place that led to the runner's "head meeting the concrete."

"Much to my deep contrition," said King, "he expired seven days after our fight." It resulted in a four-year manslaughter rap, but King turned the prison sentence into a valuable learning experience.

Reflecting on his "matriculation" at the Marion (Ohio) Correctional Institute (class of '71), he said, "That was the best thing that ever happened to me. While I was in the slammer, I earned honors taking correspondence courses from Ohio University. I also read every book in the prison library—Voltaire, Shakespeare, Aristotle, Tolstoy, you name it. In the matter of education, I went in with a popgun and came out with the atom bomb."

While King was building his font of knowledge and vocabulary, Arum was busy on the outside building a power base and padding his bank account while circling the globe with Muhammad Ali. From 1966 to 1974, he served as Ali's personal promoter and attorney. Even when Ali was exiled for his antiwar stand, the whiz kid from Brooklyn created a new champion by staging an elimination heavyweight tournament. And Arum would be waiting with open arms to welcome Ali back when he resumed his ring wars in 1974.

But the golden goose would suddenly disappear following "Ali-Frazier II" in 1974 when an upstart named Don King formed an alliance with the once and future heavyweight champion.

"I sponsored a benefit for a black hospital in Cleveland," he recalled, "and I got Ali to fight an exhibition. We made a lot of money for the charity, but I also got my foot in the door with Ali's people."

From this brief encounter with Muhammad, King began formulating grandiose plans. While boxing's hardcore dismissed him as a loose-tongued braggart with empty pockets, he set the establishment on its ear by somehow inducing the government of Zaire to risk $10 million in the promotion of Ali's most memorable "Rumble in the Jungle" with George Foreman.

In a few short years, Don King had done the impossible. The one-time street hustler had graduated from a tiny, rent-free jail cell to a $73,000-a-year penthouse in Rockefeller Center. And he had bucked heads with the powerful Arum to establish himself as an equal in the cutthroat boxing jungle.

"There's only been two promoters in my class—P. T. Barnum and Mike Todd," King crowed from time to time. "But they were both white dudes. I'm black and a full-blooded egotist. I pay attention to what all the big people do around me, and then I act twice as bright."

In 1975, Arum and King first acknowledged that they needed each other in order to stage "Ali-Frazier III," a.k.a. "The Thrilla in Manila." It was both an artistic and financial success, but when the co-promoters met in the counting house, each accused the other of juggling the books.

"He handles receipts the way he handled the numbers game," charged Arum.

King, a master of circumlocution, dusted off one of his favorite parables to describe his feelings for Arum.

"Arum reminds me of the asp who asks the alligator to carry him across the rising river to the safety of the high ground," King said.

" 'You know you're going to bite me,' the alligator said.

" 'That wouldn't make any sense,' the asp protested. 'If I bite you, we'll both drown.'

"But as soon as they reached the deep water, the asp bit the alligator and they began to sink.

" 'Why did you have to do that?' the alligator asked, as his lungs filled with water.

" 'I can't help it,' said the asp. 'I'm a snake.' "

But as Duran and Leonard exchanged angry words, dirty looks, and vows of violence in the Waldorf ballroom, Arum and King were caught embracing each other like long-lost brothers.

"I'm thrilled to be co-promoting this great fight with my friend Don King," Arum said with a forced smile. "And my good friend and I believe that, if handled properly, we can gross over $30 million.

"I anticipate that Leonard can earn more than the $6.5 million Ali received for fighting Ken Norton at Yankee Stadium in 1976. If Leonard doesn't make more than that, than King and I aren't doing our jobs as promoters."

King nodded animatedly from under his giant Afro. "This is 's.k.d.'—something kind of different," he said.

Later, away from the microphones and flashing cameras, he confided to a few reporters, "It's only a moratorium. See me when it's all over."

Despite King's self-imposed silence, several key questions still begged to be answered: Why did Cuevas step aside without a whimper of protest? Why did Mike Trainer decide to deal with King, for whom he held about as much affection as Arum did? And just who was Colonel Ruben Paredes, the mystery figure who reportedly made World Boxing Association President Rodrigo Sanchez see the wisdom of a Duran-Leonard match?

Unraveling these riddles requires that the characters in the rival camps be clearly drawn.

On Leonard's side, we would find Trainer allied with Arum. They were easily outnumbered by the Duran forces that included King, WBC chief Jose Sulaiman, and Colonel Paredes, who served as security chief for General Omar Torrijos, the president of Panama.

Sulaiman fired the first shot by issuing an ultimatum to Trainer, threatening to strip Leonard of his WBC crown unless he bypassed Cuevas and "was ready to bargain in good faith with Duran's people."

Accused by Trainer of strongarm tactics, Sulaiman explained, "We (the WBC) can not allow Leonard to fight whoever he wants in defense of his title. He must fight the number one contender, who happens to be Roberto Duran in the WBC rankings. Not the likes of a Davey Boy Green."

Still, Trainer insisted he would not buckle under the threats of Sulaiman or the coercion of his "pet promoter," Don King.

"We never received a letter from Sulaiman telling us what we can and can't do with Ray's title," the attorney said. "So how could we have done anything wrong by agreeing to fight Cuevas? But I can't see the WBC taking Leonard's title away. I know Sulaiman's not dumb."

Trainer also figured he had won his showdown with King. "He thought I couldn't buck him," Trainer told *The Washington Post*'s Tom Boswell. "Or he thought he could mesmerize me with all those ridiculous parables about tigers eating lions. Or he thought we'd buckle when he started slinging mud, accusing me of paying Duran $500,000 under the table to buy his contract away from King.

"The real truth," Trainer added, "is that King's little empire is shrinking and he's in a panic. Out of frustration, he's acting ridiculous and immature about the Leonard fight. He's probably promised Duran $2 million and counted on plenty for himself, too. It was a heckuva shock for him to come to me and be told we didn't need or want him, but that we'd give him a cut just to be friendly. We told him he could have the foreign TV rights and handle the under-card. That could gross him as much as $600,000.

"We've discovered, in working with these people, if you don't have options, you're cooked. If they know they're the only game in town, then they've got you. But we're not going to crack. It's against every sound business principle we've had to work with."

But King and Sulaiman still hadn't played their trump card in their high stakes game with Trainer and Arum. They would enlist the aid of Colonel Paredes, whose persuasive powers were well-known to the Panamanian populace.

Actually, Colonel Paredes had no need to lecture Cuevas, a Mexican, on the benefits to Latin American unity his bowing out of the Leonard match would bring. He could, instead, have saved considerable travel expenses by first consulting World Boxing Association chief Rodrigo Sanchez, who just happened to reside in Panama. It didn't take long for Sanchez to realize the wisdom of Colonel Paredes's appeal. In fact, not a word was uttered in protest when the Cuevas-Leonard fight suddenly evaporated in thin air.

The party line was that Cuevas had suffered an eye injury weeks earlier while knocking out South Africa's Harold Volbrecht. The cut hardly seemed serious at the time, but it became a convenient way of temporarily removing the Mexican from the picture.

Even the usually infallible Howard Cosell admitted he was totally perplexed by the sudden change of characters, a note of utter candor that merited a historic asterisk. "I don't know why Cuevas was ditched," Cosell confessed, "and that's the boxing business for you."

Sports columnist Dick Young of *The New York Daily News* was hardly as naive. He was the first to insinuate that Sanchez, the WBA chief, had been less than gently persuaded by Colonel Paredes before endorsing the Leonard-Duran match.

"We never pressured anyone," said Luis Henriquez, an honorary vice-counsel in Panama, who also served as a first lieutenant in the Duran camp. "Despite what you might have read in the New York papers, we simply asked Mr. Sanchez and the WBA to do what they considered was right for the sport of boxing and Panama."

To which Dick Young responded, "On behalf of *The New York Daily News*, I would like to say one word, 'Bullshit!' "

In the aftermath of all the political maneuvering, Trainer insisted that it had all worked out in the best interests of "Sugar Ray Leonard, Inc."

"First," he said, "I have to say that there were some very influential people who wanted the Duran-Leonard fight to happen before Cuevas got his chance. It became rather complicated.

"But the Duran fight was the one we wanted anyway. It was just that for the longest time, we couldn't get his people off dead center in our negotiations. They had threatened to strip Ray of his title if he didn't fight Duran on his terms, and then we heard we couldn't get the WBA to sanction a Leonard-Cuevas fight. But when we announced we'd fight Cuevas on TV without sanctioning, that scared the hell out of Duran's advisors.

"That got us over the hump," Trainer noted. "Now they were afraid that Duran might have to wait another year before getting a shot at Leonard. I wouldn't want to say that we used Cuevas to get Duran, but that's the way it worked out, didn't it?"

Trainer also insisted that he had not sacrificed any of his principles in inviting King to join in the action.

"King helped bring in Duran," he said, "but it didn't cost me anymore. I told him. 'If both of you can live off Arum's share, I'd rather have two instead of one,' and they worked it out."

Oh, if it were so easy. According to one source, Arum and Trainer tried up to the last minute to remove King from the picture, hoping to deal independently with Duran's millionaire "godfather," Carlos Eleta.

"Trainer and Arum were in Braniff's VIP Lounge at Kennedy Airport, waiting for their flight to Panama," the source said. "But the flight was delayed for several hours, and who should catch up with them, but King? I guess they knew then that their little game was up. They had to finally agree to give King a piece of the cake."

Of course, Trainer remembers the incident quite differently. As he later recounted, "It got real uncomfortable in that lounge. I was sitting between Arum and King, trying to make polite conversation. But they refused to talk to each other. Finally, I said, 'This is silly. Either you guys settle this thing or I'm going to Panama by myself. It's a shame, because this is a great promotion, and there's enough in it for both of you.' "

Trainer's voice of reason ended the prolonged silence and created an uneasy detente between the arch-rivals that Arum would sardonically christen the "Panama Pax."

To Trainer's credit, Leonard still retained the lion's share of the projected income. Duran, supremely confident he could wrest the title away, settled for a guaranteed $1.5 million as his end of the purse. Trainer conservatively estimated that his boxer-client would earn a minimum of $6 million, and possibly as much as $10 million after selling the site rights to Quebec's Olympic Installation Board for $3.5 million in U.S. currency. The bulk of Leonard's money would come from eighty percent of the closed-circuit TV revenue, with Arum and King dividing the remaining twenty percent after the first $2.5 million had been creamed off the top, including Duran's share.

Even before the fight was officially announced to the Canadian press, Jean-Yves Perron, director of the Olympic Stadium complex, conducted a brisk ticket sale. In a matter of weeks, all 1,500 ringside seats at an inflationary $500-a-copy, had been spoken for.

"Duran is very popular in Canada," Perron said, "but not nearly as popular as Leonard."

Yes, with an odd sort of justice, Ray Leonard was returning to Montreal where his "journey had ended" four years earlier with the winning of an Olympic gold medal. But now he was at an even bigger crossroads in his life, coming face-to-face with the man with "Hands of Stone."

☆ 16 ☆

"MANOS DE PIEDRA— HANDS OF STONE"

"Cholo's coming. Cholo's coming." The word spreads like a brushfire through the cramped streets of New York's garment center. Pushcarts are temporarily abandoned by their Spanish-speaking navigators who have learned Roberto ("Cholo") Duran is back in town.

"Cholo" is the nickname for their favorite fighter. The name is derived from the wild mane of black hair that in Indian style frames Duran's swarthy, handsome face set off by his penetrating leopardlike eyes.

Yes, "Cholo" was back in town, if only briefly, to begin training for his heralded title fight with Sugar Ray Leonard in Montreal. To the Latins, Leonard is a pretty boy, a matinee idol not truly suited for the macho sport of boxing. But "Cholo" is one of them. He is "family." "Cholo" is something special because he fought his way out of the same mean streets that form the boundary lines of their meager surroundings.

For "Cholo," it was a matter of surviving on his wits and stonelike fists and the relentless fury that burns inside his small compact body. The slums of Chorillo, Panama, near the Canal Zone were his training ground, but it might as well have been Spanish Harlem. By his shining example, he had given them all a dream to live with, the faint hope that somehow a miracle would suddenly transform their pushcarts into winged chariots that would transport them from their ghetto existence.

It was now approaching one o'clock. Lunch hour had passed, but the men with their carts seemed untroubled by the thought of being docked an hour's pay or losing their jobs. For this would be their last opportunity to see Duran in the flesh before he left for the fresh air and relative seclusion of a Catskill mountain resort to resume his training.

They crowded into Gleason's Gym, a hole in the wall on West 30th Street, close to one thousand of them paying one dollar to Sammy Morgan, the aged caretaker with the face of a bloodhound. Gleason's is strictly a blue-collar gym. There are no East-side types being gently massaged. No weekend athletes flexing their flabby muscles on Nautilus machines. No whirlpools, saunas, or jacuzzis to ease tired bodies. Gleason's is strictly functional. Leonard, with his clean-cut features and Pepsodent smile, would look as much out of place in these grim surroundings as a Hollywood star.

There has been no attempt to cover the stain-blotched walls with colorful fight posters. No paintbrush has been raised in anger since the bareknuckle days. The lights over the blood-stained ring aren't strong enough to attract a moth. A flight of creaky stairs leads to an overhanging balcony, indicating this might have once served as a dance hall. But the only music now came from the rat-a-tat-tat of muscular, young men hitting a speed bag or the grunts and groans of sparring partners dancing between the ropes.

Only a one-time brawler like Duran could feel at home here. Suddenly, there is a shout from the doorway. "He's here!" they scream in Spanish. And a spontaneous chant begins: "Cholo, Cholo, Cholo."

Duran heads a platoon of trainers, advisors, and hangers-on. He has a baseball bat flung over his right shoulder like a soldier marching to the front. It's a gift from Reggie Jackson.

A man in the entourage explains, "Roberto loves baseball. He was a shortstop—a good one on the sandlots back in Panama. Even now, when he's home, he sneaks off to play with the kids. But Carlos [Duran's manager, Carlos Eleta] makes him stop. He tells Roberto, 'You have stone hands. They're good for fighting, bad for baseball.' "

Duran is now sitting in a packed dressing room barely big enough for himself. He undresses near two battered lockers bearing the names of "Sugar Bee" Carter and Johnny ("Boy Boy") Gallo, two obscure pugs long forgotten.

While Duran chatters animatedly in Spanish, a reporter asks Freddie Brown, a seventy-two-year-old with a face like an old boxing glove, whether the fire still burns inside Duran—a Duran who had been fighting professionally for over a decade, winning all but one of his seventy-two bouts.

"Everyone wants to know, 'Is he still hungry?' " said the ancient trainer, who still had a cigar clenched between his teeth. "They think because a Zeferino Gonzalez or a Jimmy Heair goes ten rounds with him, that Roberto is slipping. But Roberto won't push himself against guys he knows he can lick. He needs a challenge. This is something different. He's wanted Leonard for some time, and he'd fight him for nothin'. But his pride's been hurt because Leonard is getting most of the money. That will only make him more mean."

Duran, who understands English but prefers speaking in his native tongue, said through his interpreter, "I'm very happy now. Before Leonard came along, I was very sad. I'm not happy for the money. But I am happy for the fight."

At one time, Duran fought merely to survive. It was a way of life in the rat-infested barrios of Panama.

"As a kid, Roberto fought in the streets just to have enough to eat," said Ray Arcel, the eighty-two-year-old trainer of countless world champions who has been in Duran's corner since he lifted his lightweight title from Kenny Buchanan in 1972.

"His parents split, and he was sleeping on the streets before he was ten. Sometimes, he'd swim to the Canal Zone to pick fruit off the mango trees. He'd stuff his trousers with mangoes to eat and to sell later. One time, he took so many, he almost drowned on the swim back.

"Stealing fruit," added Arcel, "was also how Roberto got to meet Carlos Eleta, who is one of the wealthiest men in Panama. At one time, he owned Air Panama, TV stations, a baseball team, and the country's biggest racing stable. He lives on this big estate where Roberto and his older brother, Domingo, used to go to climb the trees and steal coconuts. Carlos caught him one day, but he thought so much of this little kid's courage, that he all but adopted him.

"Roberto was already fighting professionally when he was sixteen. Alfredo Vasquez, the jockey, was his first manager. Mr. Eleta went to see him fight and fell in love with him, and his *corazón*, or heart, as we say in the States. He said Roberto's heart was as big as his body. So he offered Vasquez three hundred dollars for his contract. And can you believe that Vasquez accepted?"

Long before the millionaire Eleta came into his life and helped make Roberto almost as wealthy as himself, Duran had earned a reputation as a ferocious street fighter. So legion are the tales about his boyhood brawls that it is difficult separating the man from the myth.

There was the time Roberto took a girl to a dance. He was only fifteen. Three men began flirting with his girl. They mocked him when he asked them to move on. In a matter of minutes, they were all stretched out cold on the dance floor. The paddy wagon later carted the three victims and Roberto to the police station for questioning. They all pointed to Roberto as the aggressor, but the police sergeant laughed at the notion that this little gutter snipe could have wreaked such destruction on three grown men.

Years later, Duran would accept an even sterner challenge when his macho image was questioned. "We were walking down a street in Panama," recalled Arcel, "when some guys began taunting him. They said he couldn't punch as hard as Antonio Cervantes, who was then the junior welterweight champion. Roberto doesn't say a word. He walks across the street to where a big carthorse was standing. He slams a right fist into the horse's side, and the horse fell over like it had been shot."

Duran nods in agreement as the Bunyanesque tales are told. "From the time I was a kid," he said, "I felt nobody could beat me. I first learned to fight while I was selling papers and shining shoes, and somebody would try to take away my territory. I fought all the kids, big and small. I am still the same street brawler. No trainer has changed me. My best teacher is a hit in the head."

Story hour is over. It's time to work. Duran is now in the ring at Gleason's, surrounded by his fanatical supporters who hang over the sagging ropes like spectators attending a cockfight. They shout words of encouragement in Spanish and Duran is visibly amused, waving his gloved fist at the crowd.

"It's crazy here," Brown complains later. "How can a fighter do his work? They won't let him breath. They idolize the guy. But he loves all the attention. These are his people, and he wants to give them a good show. But he needs some breathin' room. That's why we're taking him to the mountains. The man needs to work and rest."

Now Brown yelled, "Time!" and the man called "Cholo" begins to systematically dissect a sparring partner named Simon Smith. That familiar killer look is back in his piercing eyes. It matters little that this is only a sparring session, some three weeks before his date with Leonard. Duran wants to destroy the man in front of him.

"He don't want to know from nothin' when he gets in the ring," Brown advises. "He doesn't care who's standing in front of him. It could be a midget or King Kong. He wants to kill 'em all."

The crowd is quickly caught up in the fury and begins to chant feverishly, "Cholo, Cholo, Cholo!" as Duran doubles Smith in half with a vicious hook to the body. Brown feels the fighter has had enough after four hard rounds, but Duran now has his rhythm and persists in fighting another round with a beanpole named Don Morgan. In the final minute, he chases Morgan all over the ring like a tiger tracking a wounded prey. Morgan seems as relieved as a convicted killer getting a last-minute pardon when Brown finally screams, "That's it!"

"When my people come to see me," Duran said, while wiping the sweat from his glistening beard, "I want them to see a great champion. I don't play. I fight. I don't worry what people say about me. What matters is that I perform better than anyone in the ring. I don't want to make myself famous. That's up to the people. But when my people come to see me, they see a real fighter, not a clown."

A man asks Duran if he respects Leonard. "He is good," he said, "but he's fighting someone who is better."

Another man with a notepad wonders if Roberto dreams about the upcoming fight.

"Every night," he said, flashing his brilliant white teeth. "And it always ends the same way," Duran smiled, now performing a pantomine of a man standing over his vanquished foe. "I don't hate him. I just want him . . . I want to knock him out."

"How do you think Leonard will fight you?" asks a voice in the crowded dressing room.

Duran wiggles his hips girlishly in response, drawing raucous laughter. "But he can't beat me by running and dancing, and all that clowning won't help him, either. I think I know how he will fight me, but that is my secret. But if he chooses to fight like a man, I will kick his butt."

Did Duran feel that Leonard's worth as a fighter was greatly inflated by the hucksters of television and Madison Avenue who fought to showcase his "boy next door" looks and charm?

"I don't know if this is true," Roberto said seriously. "But I know he has fought only dead people. But when he signed to fight me, he signed his own death sentence."

Had he not seen Leonard outslick Wilfredo Benitez for the welterweight title?

"What I see is chicken [Benitez] fighting Leonard. Me no chicken."

"Leonard's a fine fighter," interrupts Arcel. "I'm not underestimating him. But he can't beat my guy. When Roberto is inspired, he's relentless.

"The thing with Roberto," the wizened trainer continued, "is that he gets stronger the longer the fight goes. By the time the seventh round comes, Leonard won't believe the pressure. If it goes past ten, you'll see the greatest fight of all time."

Now Duran is back in his blue overalls. He now has a Yankee hat—a gift from then-Yankee pitcher Ed Figueroa—to go with his Reggie Jackson bat. Figueroa asks to have his picture taken with his favorite Latin fighter, but Arcel shrieks in the background, "Who needs these guys? Roberto's a fighter, not some fancy ballplayer. Let 'em stay where they belong."

Duran laughs at the unexpected outrage. He is now weaving his way through the crowd of admirers, pausing to stop for autographs and candid pictures with an adoring fan. He climbs inside the courtesy van that will carry him back to his swanky Fifth Avenue hotel, but for an hour, he has rekindled the dream of an army of down-in-the-heel admirers.

Back in his plush hotel suite, Roberto soon grows restless watching the afternoon soap operas.

"What's your favorite TV show?" someone asks.

"Whatever's on," he said with a sad shrug.

He rises from his bed and informs Freddie Brown he is going to spend some time walking in Central Park and watching the kids at play.

A newsman asks if he is afraid to visit the park at night for fear of being mugged.

Roberto Duran throws back his darkly handsome head and laughs and laughs and laughs.

✯ 17 ✯

"LE FACE-A-FACE HISTORIQUE"

"Sixty seconds make a minute, but one good 'second' in a fighter's corner can make a champion."
—Ray Arcel

"The Fight" . . . the inevitable fight. Like two shooting stars flashing through the heavens, Sugar Ray Leonard and Roberto Duran moved on an unalterable collision course until, bigger than life, they would collide head-on at Montreal's Olympic Stadium for the welterweight title.

There would be no need for gimmicks, hyperbole, or fanciful slogans. No "Rumble in the Jungle" or "Thrilla in Manila."Just "The Fight." Leonard vs. Duran, enough to stimulate the salivary glands of every red-blooded boxing buff in anticipation of the world's two best gladiators battling to be king of the hill.

Indeed, the multitude of press agents worked overtime to earn their keep in beating the promotional drums. And so we were offered "Beauty and the Beast," "Fast hands and Stone Hands," and "The Matador and the Bull," enough beguiling titles for a modern edition of *Aesop's Fables*.

"Forget all the bull," Leonard growled at one point. "This is reality. This is no fairy tale."

Still, a surrealistic cloud hung over the dream fight—one of those once-in-a-lifetime happenings like Woodstock that only the participants could truly experience. In professional boxing's all-too-personal jungle, only the first Ali-Frazier match at Madison Square Garden in 1971 had inflamed the imagination like this wildly anticipated showdown between the fight game's two mighty mites.

"The first Ali-Frazier fight was truly unique," noted Jim Jacobs, the man whose film collection includes some of the century's greatest fights. "You had a match between two unbeaten heavyweight champions. The only way that could have happened was to have put one of them in exile, as was the case with Ali."

But, of course, Ali vs. Frazier was more than an historic accident. It was a classic matchup of a consummate boxer and a bristling war machine—a promoter and fight fan's ultimate fantasy.

And now, on June 20, 1980, in Montreal, the same magical ingredients were being offered in miniature by two welterweights whose combined record boasted ninety-eight victories and one defeat (Duran suffered his only setback in seventy-two bouts to Esteban DeJesus in 1972).

Again, like Muhammad Ali's past extravaganzas, this would take on the aura of a holy war between Leonard, the creature of television, the media's "Mr. Perfect" versus Roberto Duran, the creature of the ramshackled slums of Panama, the devil incarnate of the Barrio. Sides were as clearly drawn as the Israelis and PLOs. Everyone was ready to offer his unassailable opinion on the outcome of the fight.

"The boxer is Leonard, the speed is Leonard, the puncher is Leonard," said Jacobs, who dissected fight films with the meticulous care of a coroner examining a murder victim. "To think that Duran can punch harder than Leonard is a grievous miscalculation.

"Duran terrorized the lightweights, but he has not threatened too many welterweights," Jacobs continued his analysis. "He was a great lightweight. He is a good welterweight, but hardly a great one. The mere fact that he added some blubber to his frame doesn't necessarily mean that he has increased his punching power proportionately.

"And to equate the Duran of, say, 1975 with the Duran of today is to suffer a serious fixation of the mind. Duran has never been a one-punch knockout artist. He wears his opponent down by the accumulative effect of his punches. But Leonard, on the other hand, is quite capable of stopping a man with a single punch."

Realizing he was building an airtight case for Leonard, Jacobs said, "There is one area in which Duran holds a convincing edge. He has been involved in over a dozen championship fights and has withstood tremendous pressure. Leonard has been tested only once—against Benitez. I can't seriously count the Davey Boy Green fight as a title defense. It was a tragic mismatch. Going against Duran will be Leonard's true test of greatness."

In the opposite corner was Cus D'Amato, boxing's ageless Svengali, who molded world champions out of the introspective Floyd Patterson and the literary-bent Jose Torres.

"Most of what goes on in a fight is psychological," D'Amato proposed. "Boxing is more brains than brawn. The uneducated fight fan perceives Duran as a pure savage who walks in blindly in the hope of delivering a crushing blow. But this is a gross injustice. For Duran is an extremely cagey fighter who is quite unpredictable. And the more unpredictable he becomes to Leonard, the more frustrated the young champion will become."

Asked for an example of Duran's unpredictability, D'Amato said, "He has mastered several moves that made Rocky Marciano so dangerous. He feints a right hand to sucker his opponent and then delivers an overhand left. Marciano knocked out a lot of guys that way, and Duran does the same thing.

"Firepower?" D'Amato said, in response to another question. "Oh, Leonard has sufficient firepower to hold off Duran. But it is more a question of whether he has the psychological maturity.

"I detected this in his fight against the Mexican middleweight, Marcos Geraldo. Leonard displayed moments of indecision after being hit with a solid punch. He became defensive. He can't afford to do this against a man of Duran's tenacity. Pressure inhibits Leonard's performance. The logical thing would be for Leonard to sidestep the charging Duran. But I've never seen Leonard employ this tactic, and I've observed him quite a bit."

Questions and theories. The essence of a great fight. Psyches would be probed as thoroughly as bosoms at a "Miss America" pageant. Everyone searched for meaningful clues that one of the fighters might unconsciously offer during the excrutiatingly long training periods.

Leonard did most of his serious training at the Sheraton Hotel off the Capital Beltway in New Carrollton, Maryland, only a Sunday punch from his neighborhood haunts in Palmer Park. For one dollar a head, close to five hundred fans a day packed the exhibition hall draped with golden tinsel to watch Sugar Ray's daily regimen. Like bobbysoxers from another era, they swooned and screamed encouragement.

"Do it, Sugar!" "You're lookin' real sweet!" "Right on!" they screeched as Leonard pursued and battered Mike James, an apprentice pro, as easily as punching a heavy bag.

James was wearing a T-shirt with "DURAN" stenciled across his chest. In fighting style, the young novice bears as much resemblance to the indomitable Duran as Sylvester Stallone to Rocky Marciano. But Leonard is practicing psychological warfare.

"I've got a tendency to loaf sometimes in training," he confides, "but when I see 'DURAN' in front of me, I want to tear the other guy's head off."

Of course, it does little for James's well being. During his first public workout, Leonard tags his inexperienced sparring partner with a short hook under the heart. Seemingly falling in separate parts, James drops to the canvas in the same sickening manner as Davey Boy Green's swoon several months earlier. After a few anxious moments, James recovers his breath and balance and Leonard is by his side to provide both comfort and encouragement while the crowd shouts its approval.

"They told me to keep throwing right hands," said James, still slightly breathless. "I'm supposed to be Duran, but Sugar knows I'm going to throw the right and keeps beating me to the punch," the novice adds with a sad shrug.

It is a painful scenario that will be repeated on an almost daily basis, with James playing the fall guy at 150-per-beating. Reporters soon begin questioning the wisdom of Leonard engaging in such child's play while preparing to tangle with a man-eater like Duran.

"The perfect sparring partner would be a carbon copy of Duran," said Angelo Dundee, appearing on the scene a few weeks prior to the fight. "But there's no such animal. Duran is Duran."

A man who only recently visited the challenger's camp brings the news that Duran has engaged a Leonard look-alike in slender Don Morgan, who, while masquerading as the champion, was repeatedly being tagged with overhand rights.

"Don Morgan's not Sugar Ray Leonard," said the real Sugar Ray Leonard, "and Mike James isn't Roberto Duran. None of my sparring partners are here to imitate him. They're just here to get me in shape, and I'm not trying to embarrass any of them. I don't need any 'psyching,' but Duran does. When we first met in New York, he was perspiring so badly, I thought he was wearing a sweatsuit. He called me a 'clown' and said I haven't fought anybody. But I'm twenty-seven and oh. I guess they don't have any TV in Panama."

It was now showtime, and, in the grand tradition of Ali, Leonard was exchanging barbs with the crowd in the improvised gym. During a lengthy harangue, Leonard vowed he would destroy Duran. "And when I do, they will say he was too old, over-the-hill, or out-of-shape. They will refuse to admit that I'm the greatest."

Later, a newsman, seeking clarification, asked if Leonard would please identify "they" for the sake of his readers.

"Oh, that's just a figure of speech," the fighter laughed. "My father taught me that. After all, I couldn't say, 'You-all.' "

In the background, Charley Brotman, Sugar Ray's publicity man, was now bellowing, 'OK, everybody, line up on the right. Ray will have autographed pictures for all of you. Just wait your turn."

The press also waited. And a few frustrated feature writers on assignment from New York soon discovered that they would be afforded less time with the champion than the autograph hounds. Vic Ziegel, the veteran boxing writer freelancing for *New York* magazine, was granted a five-minute audience as Brotman, standing over his shoulder, reminded him, "One more question. Ray's got a lot of commitments today."

A question Leonard would hear quite often during the coming weeks was whether the enormity of the event and the staggering prospect of earning $10 million might prove overwhelming.

"No, it doesn't faze me," he said matter-of-factly. "I don't think about how big it is. I know how big it is, but I worked to get it. We all worked to get it," he added, nodding in the direction of his fast-growing entourage. "If anyone thinks it's easy, how come a lot more guys aren't trying to do the same thing?

"But it's a lot more than the money," said Leonard, taking on that serious look he affects for such deep thoughts. "I'm a perfectionist. My record may be perfect, but I'm not. I can look back at every fight I've had and find things I could have done better. That's the way I am. I want to be something special. Years from now, I want people to look in the *Ring* record book and say, 'and then there was Sugar Ray Leonard.' Even Ali, as great as he is. I didn't come all this way to stand in somebody's shadow."

In mentioning his inevitable comparison with Ali, Jane Leavy of *The Washington Post* wondered whether Leonard wouldn't like to follow Muhammad's example of going to the mountain top when it was time to prepare for a fight.

"Naw," said Sugar Ray, "I once tried cutting down a tree and got awful tired. The woods are nice, but I like it here in the hotel. The elevator, it goes up and down."

"What about eating raw eggs?" the lady reporter persisted.

"I tried that once, too," he laughed. "But all it did for me was give me a sourer look and stomach."

Instead, Leonard relied on the "in-house" cooking of his father and mother. Cicero Leonard prepared the breakfasts of cooked eggs, grits, and sausages and apple sauce, while mother Getha served up dinners of pork chops and fried chicken.

Almost every member of the Leonard clan had a special function in the fight camp. Brother Roger, an undefeated junior middleweight, and cousin O'Dell served as additional sparring partners when Ray wearied of knocking down Mike James. They would all join him at four in the morning for roadwork around Greenbelt Park with Leonard setting a fast pace while listening to the beat of soul music on his transistor radio.

"Listening to the sounds helps me tune out the other guys," Ray laughed. "I get tired of all their jabbering after awhile, but I still kill 'em on all the hills."

Before one of the sibling sparring sessions, Roger, a capable boxer minus a knockout punch, was asked where his smaller brother had acquired his superior punching power.

"I figure he got it from his grandfather, Bidge Leonard," Roger said. "Bidge was a tenant farmer down in South Carolina, a real tough old bird who liked his drink and tobacco.

"One night, he invited a bunch of his cronies in for a drink and they started out with three and a half gallons of corn liquor. After a few hours, they all conked out . . . everyone but Grandpa Bidge. He was still sipping that whiskey the next morning.

"Oh yeah, he could fight, too," said Roger. "They once bet him ten dollars that he couldn't knock out a mule. Well, Bidge hit that mule once and sent it kicking."

Grandpa Bidge, who died some time ago, was probably the only family member missing from the training camp scene that had begun to resemble an army depot. The champion's once intimate coterie of advisors and handlers had suddenly blossomed into a task force of muscular young men all uniformly dressed in red and white jumpsuits with "SUGAR RAY LEONARD" emblazoned across their broad backs. For a close-up look at the star attraction, a dutiful reporter had to pass through more checkpoints than the spy who came out of the cold.

When the constant crowds and fawning attention grew tedious, Sugar Ray escaped the frenzy and pressure by joining his wife, Juanita, at a dance studio where he was learning to boogie and tap dance. Otherwise, he could be found in his hotel suite, using his Betamax to play and replay films of Duran's fights with Vilomar Fernandez, Edwin Viruet, and Zeferino Gonzalez—three talented boxers who found a way to frustrate their ever-charging rival.

When someone queried Duran about Leonard's devoted film-watching, the Panamanian snarled, "Any fighter who has to watch films is either confused or a coward."

A day before Leonard is prepared to leave his Maryland camp for Montreal, Ray Didinger of the *Philadelphia Bulletin* asks the fighter if he ever thought what he might be doing now if he had pursued his original plan to quit boxing after the Olympics and attend college.

"I'd still be under pressure, only a different kind," he said. "I'd be a senior at the University of Maryland and getting ready for my final exams, wondering what I was going to do after graduation. I'd be plain, ol' Ray Leonard again, and I wouldn't have to worry about looking at Roberto Duran's ugly face next week. Besides," he roared, "I'd be a whole lot poorer."

✯ 18 ✯

THE MAN IN THE MOUNTAIN

Roberto Duran, the vicious Panama street brawler, the prince of darkness, was sitting in the beauty shop at Grossinger's Hotel in the Catskills having his "hands of stone" manicured by a blonde with a beehive hairdo.

Suddenly, the room filled with the throbbing beat of salsa music and Roberto's vivacious wife, Felicidad, glided across the floor with fluid grace. His nails cleansed, Duran started feverishly tapping his bongo drums and timbales, his wild black mane flying everywhere and his coal-black eyes flashing as he caught the rhythm. It was a happy interlude in his uncharacteristically long and arduous training preparations for Sugar Ray Leonard. Soon, the tedium would settle in again.

"When you go to camp, it's like going to jail," said Freddie Brown, the seventy-three-year-old trainer with a face like a battered boxing glove. "In the old days, most of the good fighters trained in New Jersey at Pompton Lakes, Greenwood Lake, or Esham's. We'd spend a lot of time listening to the radio. Now it's TV.

"But the fighters always found ways of making their own

fun," Brown added. "One time, Rocky Graziano and Terry Young, two dead-end kids, picked up Joe Baksi, a big heavyweight, and tossed him in the lake. Baksi starts screaming, 'I'm drowning, save me!' and the water wasn't even up to his belly button.

"Duran gets into mischief, too, but he ain't nearly as bad as he used to be. Before, he was always sneaking out to chase the women or grab extra food. I felt more like a private cop than a fight trainer."

The old New Jersey training sites have long since been forgotten. Grossinger's, an 800-acre hotel and resort some ninety miles from New York City, has since become the favorite retreat for fighters seeking fresh air and relative solitude while preparing for a major fight. The hotel is located in the heart of what has become known as "The Borscht Belt" because of the area's popularity with Jewish clientele.

Over the past forty years, such celebrated fighters as Barney Ross, Max Baer, Rocky Marciano, Randy Turpin, Billy Conn, Nino Benvenuti, Ingemar Johansson, and Ken Norton have flexed their muscles at Grossinger's, each leaving their personal stamp on the guests, but seldom joining them in sampling the blintzes, borscht, and gefilte fish that lured the tourists from the city.

The hotel's colorful link with boxing began with Barney Ross in 1934 when he was getting ready to challenge Jimmy McLarnin for the welterweight title.

The late Jennie Grossinger was perusing the paper one day and noticed a feature story about Ross, who followed the strict precepts of the Jewish faith.

"Why don't you ask him to come up here?" Jennie asked Milton Blackstone, the hotel's social director. "Our good kosher cooking will make him stronger for his next fight."

"Good idea," said Blackstone, "but let's take it a step further. Let's get Ross to train here, too. We've never had a fighter here before, and this way, we'll get the boxing writers from the New York dailies filing their stories with a Grossinger's dateline."

Jennie Grossinger's enthusiasm for the plan, however, was hardly shared by her mother, Mulka, the matriarch of the big hotel who ruled the kitchen with an iron hand and will. Extremely devout, Mulka regarded all prizefighters as unrefined savages.

His first day at the hotel, Ross innocently wandered into the kitchen and began humming a Jewish folk song while sticking his nose into the steaming pots and pans.

"My mother taught me that song," he told Mulka before introducing himself. "She was very religious and saw to it that I had a good Jewish education."

Mulka began singing along, before finally asking the visitor's name.

"I'm Barney Ross, the fighter," he said.

"You, Ross, the barbarian?" Mulka screamed, lifting a giant soup ladle and making threatening gestures.

For the first time in memory, Ross retreated. As a peace offering, he told Mulka, "Look, I'll give part of my purse from the McLarnin fight to your favorite Jewish charity, but please drop that ladle."

Somewhat mollified, Mulka said, "Okay, sit down. You look undernourished. I'd better fatten you up before that other man breaks you in half."

Paul Grossinger, who now operates the hotel, laughs at his grandmother's introduction to boxing. Every picture on the walls of his paneled office revives another story of a famous fighter who had once been a hotel guest.

"There's Max Baer and his trainer, Ancil Hoffman," Grossinger said, pointing to a picture almost fifty years old. "Max was quite a ladies' man, always looking for a fresh conquest. When Hoffman brought him here to train in 1935 for the Joe Louis fight, he must have checked every inch of the place. He checked every room and every exit. Ancil found a room on the second floor, looked out the window and said, 'That's got to be about twenty feet to the ground. I don't think Max will try it.' But he posted a cop outside that door for two weeks. It didn't help Max, though. Louis killed him."

A picture of the smiling Swede, Ingemar Johansson, rekindles another story. "Ingo was a little bolder than Baer," Grossinger said. "He brought his own girl friend, lovely Birgette, to camp with him before his second fight with Floyd Patterson.

"Well," the hotelkeeper continued, "after Ingo finished his morning roadwork, he'd go and have a 'talk' with Birgette. And he'd 'talk' with Birgette after lunch, after sparring, and after dinner. Even the day before the fight, Ingo was having a long 'talk' with Birgette. No wonder he lasted only five rounds."

Grossinger remembered the brief stay of lightweight Lew Jenkins, who got his kicks by racing motorcycles like a Hollywood stuntman.

"He was here about two weeks before his fight with Henry Armstrong when his wife showed up and "kidnapped' him. The writers tried to say that's why he lost the fight, but don't believe it. Jenkins could have lived in a monastery for a year, and he still wouldn't have licked Armstrong.

"Oh, yes, we had some colorful writers back then, too. People like Damon Runyon, Ring Lardner, Jimmy Cannon, and Hype Igoe. When one of them would get soused, the others would write his copy for him. One time, Igoe got drunk and missed an early deadline. Someone filed a piece for him. But when Igoe woke up, he dashed off a quick story and called his desk in New York, 'It's OK, Hype,' the copy editor told him. 'But your first one was better.' "

Now Lou Goldstein, the hotel's athletic director the past thirty years, picked up the storyline.

"One of the real colorful characters we had train here was Nino Benvenuti, the middleweight champ," Goldstein said. "Every night was like an Italian festival—wine, women, and song. One night, Antonino Rocca, the wrestling champ, showed up. He looked like he was ready for a match—no shoes, real scruffy clothes, and a heavy beard.

"Rocca must have finished every bottle of wine in Benvenuti's cottage. And now he's leaping and jumping around the place like he did in the wrestling ring. Tables and chairs are flying everywhere. Finally, Benvenuti screams, 'Throw the bum out of here!' "

But Goldstein's favorite fighter was the late Rocky Marciano, who would spend months training at Grossinger's. "You know," Goldstein said, "Rocky loved to play baseball. He was a minor league catcher for the Cubs' organization before he became a fighter.

"Well, one time, Rocky was training here and a bunch of the Yankees—Don Larsen, Yogi Berra, Hank Bauer, and Andy Carey—came up to see him. They start fooling around and Yogi gives Rocky a catcher's mask. Now Larsen is burning them in, and Rocky's having a ball until Charley Goldman, the little gnome that trained him, comes walking by the ballfield. 'Whadya tryin' to do,' he screamed, 'kill the heavyweight champ?'

"I loved Rocky, but I've got to admit he was a little light with a buck. One time, he came into my room and starts grabbing shirts and ties out of my closet. He picks out my best silk shirt and says, 'I like this one,' and starts throwing it over his arm.

" 'Rocky,' I said, 'my arms are four inches longer than yours. It'll never fit you.' But he just keeps walking toward the door. 'Don't worry, Lou,' he said, 'my mother can make them all into short-sleeve shirts.'

"Yeah," laughed Goldstein. "Almost all the fighters are the same, whether they have short or long arms. They all have tiny pockets."

Duran had spent a relatively tranquil two weeks at Grossingers; on every count he had been a model guest, even agreeing to leave his pet lion behind in Panama. The only real problem, insisted Freddie Brown, had been monitoring the fighter's eating habits and calorie count. Between fights in recent years, Duran had, on occasion, taken on the proportions of a light-heavyweight while gouging himself on all the delicacies he had missed as a street urchin.

So, almost daily, Brown and Duran would engage in a private game of "One potato, two potato." Duran would choose a baked potato as big as a boxing glove and Brown would quickly try and replace it with one of less epic dimensions.

Back and forth the potatoes would roll like a game of marbles until Duran finally chose one that met his trainer's stern approval. But the fighter would make amends by burying the potato in a mountain of sour cream.

"I had to give up fifteen fighters to take Duran," Brown said. "But I wouldn't have taken just any fighter. It was the difference between $5,000 and $500 paydays. But with Roberto, you earn it."

Brown and his even more venerable sidekick, Ray Arcel, had long ago discovered training Duran was about as easy as taming a lion. They have been forced to use the combined wisdom of their 154 years to make a point with the stubborn and strong-willed Panamanian.

Truly, Arcel and Brown were living dinosaurs from a forgotten era when talented boxers were a dime a dozen. "They're older than water," cracked Dundee, who once served an apprenticeship as their bucketman. If there were tricks of the trade, the two "wise men" in Duran's corner had probably invented them.

"When I first agreed to train Duran," said Arcel, "he was right-hand crazy. I kept trying to tell him that he had to use his left to set up the right, but it was like talking to a deaf man.

"One day, I grabbed him by the scruff of the neck and said, 'Roberto, I want you to hit Freddie with the best right hand you have.' He looked at me like I was crazy. 'I no hit an old man,' he said, and started walking out of the room. So I started flapping my arms like a chicken. That got him mad, and he threw a wild right at Freddie, who was right in front of him. Freddie ducked, and slapped him on the face three times before he knew what had hit him.

"Now he was really mad," Arcel said, "and he almost took the door off the hinges. But the next day in training, he threw some of the most beautiful lefts you've ever seen. And he grabs me later and smiles, 'Now I have nothing to worry about. Now I am a man with two hands.' "

Arcel is a product of New York's Lower East Side. "We lived in a really tough neighborhood," he recalled. "Everybody fought to survive, especially me. I was the only Jew on the street. Somebody would call me a 'dirty Kike,' and a fight would start."

His boxing baptism had taken place in the company of a couple of wily old pros named Doc Bagley and Dai Dollings. One day, Bagley invited Arcel to help him with one of his fighters.

"I'd learned this one trick from Bagley," Arcel said. "He'd use a chaw of tobacco to stop a cut from bleeding. I was almost hoping that my fighter would get cut so that I could try it. Well, around the fourth round, my guy gets cut around the eye and I start chewing the tobacco real fast. The next thing I remember was a doctor giving me smelling salts. I must have swallowed the tobacco. And, you know, I've never used tobacco the rest of my life."

A few years after his less than auspicious debut as a cornerman, Arcel discovered his first champion—a ghetto kid named Benny Leonard.

"That was like *Golden Boy* or John Garfield in *Body and Soul*," Arcel laughed. "You know the plot, how the Jewish kid has to sneak out of the house to fight so his parents won't find out.

"Well, that's just what happened with Benny. He must have had almost thirty fights before an old washerwoman tells his mother, 'I saw your boy, Benny's picture on a fight poster.' That made Mrs. Leonard hysterical. She called a family summit meeting and they were all ready to pounce on Benny when he returned from the fight.

"Benny walked in the door and he's surprised to see all his relatives waiting for him. But before anyone says a word, he tossed a big wad of bills on the dining room table. His father took one look and said, 'Nu, Benny, when's your next fight?' "

Over the next half-century, Arcel would tutor eighteen world champions, including Leonard, Barney Ross, Jim Braddock, and Ezzard Charles. Despite his huge success, Arcel had to live down the nickname, "The Meat Wagon," for the days he mastered the clean and jerk technique in lugging victims of Joe Louis's "Bum of the Month" club back to the corner.

"It got so bad," Arcel laughed, "that I remember walking down the aisle with Buddy Baer before his second fight with Louis, and a guy at ringside turned to his girl and said, 'Here comes The Meat Wagon.' And she's looking everywhere, and saying, 'Where? Where? I don't see any wagon.' "

For several years, Arcel tried his hand at promoting fights, competing against the then octopuslike International Boxing Club. For his troubles, he woke up in a Boston alley one night with a large bump on his head.

Arcel turned his back on boxing for the next eighteen years (1953–71) while working as a purchasing agent in a foundry owned by former fight referee Harry Kessler.

"In the time I was away, I became quite aloof about boxing," he said. "The sport was dying. All the small clubs were going under. They couldn't compete with TV. I don't want to sound vain, but I didn't see any class among the fighters, even the champions."

Curiosity brought Arcel to Madison Square Garden in 1972 to view Ken Buchanan, a Scotsman who had won the lightweight crown and was being hailed as the most gifted boxer since Willie Pep. Buchanan won a convincing decision over Ismael Laguna that night, but Arcel was less than impressed.

"But I saw a kid from Panama named Duran fight in the semifinal," he remembered. "He was just like a tiger. He destroyed a tough club fighter named Benny Huertas in ninety seconds. He reminded me of a little Jack Dempsey—RIP, RIP, RIP. A real strong kid who loved to fight."

A few months later, when Duran was offered a title match with Buchanan, Arcel got a call from his old friend, Carlos Eleta, the Panamanian millionaire, who was seeking help to refine the natural talents of the young roughneck Arcel had watched at the Garden.

"I told Eleta, 'Look, Carlos, I've worked with your fighters before and I like this kid and his fighting spirit. But at my age, I don't think I have the patience to train him. You're trying to put me on an uncontrollable colt who nobody's been able to handle. He'll knock me out of the saddle a hundred times before I get through to him.' "

It seemed like the most unlikely of boxing unions. As columnist Larry Merchant noted, "Getting Ray Arcel to teach Roberto Duran how to box is like Andres Segovia trying to show a rock musician how to tune up." They spoke different languages over different eras, but somehow Arcel was able to deliver his message.

"Today, we're just like father and son," Arcel said proudly. "Roberto understands me when I tell him, 'You're like my own son, and I love you.' He reminds me of a wild animal. If you keep petting him, sooner or later you'll have him eating out of your hand."

Like Professor Higgins laboring with Eliza Doolittle, Arcel's tutoring of Duran was a long and often frustrating battle. "Roberto didn't know the first thing about conditioning his body," the venerable trainer said. "I even had to show him how to do roadwork. But it was like starting from point 'A.'

"Here was a headstrong kid who had always had his

own way. It was like trying to teach something completely foreign to him, like getting a kid to try spinach. So, instead of being a trainer, I became a teacher."

Arcel, of course, was in Duran's corner the night he lifted the lightweight crown from Kenny Buchanan. Before the fight, he had needled Roberto, "I suppose you know you won't be able to go back to Panama if you lose tonight."

And the then twenty-one-year-old Duran replied, "If I lose, I commit suicide."

It took Duran's lone defeat—a non-title bout with DeJesus in 1972—to teach Roberto a valuable lesson.

"In that first fight, DeJesus slipped a right and dropped Roberto with a hook," Arcel remembered. "I knew when we made the rematch that DeJesus would figure that Roberto would just come charging after him, winging wild rights.

"So I tell Roberto, 'Box him early. Jab, move, and counter. Wait 'til I tell you to throw the right.' Well, Roberto boxed like a champion for ten rounds. He had DeJesus completely befuddled. In the eleventh, I yelled, 'Now!' and Roberto nailed DeJesus with a picture right hand. They could have counted to one hundred."

"Is Duran an old fighter at twenty-nine?" a reporter inquired one morning in the hotel coffee shop.

"No," Arcel said. "Age is no factor. With a fighter, it's not a question of losing his foot or hand speed. It's the desire he loses first. I once had a great young fighter named Tony Janiro. He was washed-up at twenty-two.

"But Roberto wanted this fight with Leonard more than anything in the world. And when Leonard told him in New York, 'I'm going to kill you,' he made a grave mistake. If he had said that to Roberto out in the street, Mr. Leonard would still be stretched out in an alley."

This same belligerent attitude was clearly evident that afternoon as Duran whipped his sparring partners unmercifully in Grossinger's Ski Lodge. Watching the little assassin bludgeon lanky Teddy White, publicist Bobby Goodman smiled mischievously and said, "He's just an animal when he's in the ring. I remember the time he knocked out Pedro Mendoza in one round. Some woman, I think it was Mendoza's wife, jumped in the ring and makes a beeline for Duran. He just whirled around and flattened the broad with a right hand, better than the one he starched Mendoza with.

"And what about when he had finished knocking the bleep out of Carlos Palomino at the Garden last year?" Goodman continued. When the final bell rings, he walks up to Palomino and says, "You're finished. Quit now. You have no more heart for fighting.' "

But Duran was now smiling. He was finished working for the day, and he playfully tossed his huge gold medallion around Freddie Brown's neck. "I love Freddie Brown," he said. "He is my father."

"That's why you can't stay mad at him," Brown confides. "One time, we were making a plane trip from Panama to New York. They gave him a lot of greasy food, and I told him not to eat it. So he gets real angry, and tosses the tray across the aisle. The food flew everywhere. But an hour later, he came back to apologize. He's got a big heart. That's why I love him. Otherwise, I'd quit."

"Is Roberto really fearless?" someone asked.

"Yes," said Arcel, joining the conversation. "He respects no one. But that's both good and bad. Benny Leonard always said, 'I'd rather fight a cocky fighter than a guy who's a little yellow. It's the scary fighter who's unpredictable, not the bully.' "

"Roberto would fight anyone, anytime," chimes in Luis Henriquez, the fighter's advisor and interpreter. "One time, he was training in Miami the same time as Ali. After Ali watched him for a week or so, he told me, 'I'm glad he's not a heavyweight.' "

But Dave Anderson of *The New York Times* pressed the point. "What would happen if Ali and Duran got into a street argument and had to settle it right there?" he asked Henriquez.

"Roberto said he would beat the hell out of Ali," Henriquez replied. "As a kid, he always beat up bigger guys."

Is Roberto Duran always itching for a fight?

"Oh, no," said Duran's close friend, Rubin Blades, an entertainer of note in Panama. "He's a nice man, a real nice man," Blades assured Dave Kindred of *The Washington Post.*

"It's just too bad Roberto doesn't speak English. Americans would love him. He's a natural wit. Next to Roberto, Ali is nothing in saying funny things.

"Roberto is what I would categorize as a knowledgeable innocent. Fame and money have not changed him, and that is why Panamanians love him. They have respect for his innocence. It's not a plastic thing, Roberto's life. The more attention he gets, the less complicated he is. He doesn't travel with people to make him feel good by saying, 'Yes, yes, yes, Roberto.' He doesn't need them or want them. When a fight is over, he spends the time with his wife and four children at the beach or in the interior. Nothing glamorous."

For diversion, Roberto plays dominoes or spars with his pet lion. "He's had that lion since it was a cub," Blades explains. "Even when there are children around, the lion is not chained up. The lion respects Roberto."

No doubt, it is a very smart lion.

"Duran the Dark" proves he is only human three weeks before the dream match in Montreal. A camp visitor strikes up a casual conversation with a member of the fighter's entourage, whose face is not familiar. The man introduces himself as "Dr. Keith Holder. I'm a neurosurgeon in Panama. I'm here to check Roberto's back," he said. "He's been having spasms. We're going to have him take some tests at Jewish Memorial Hospital in New York City."

This was, of course, the first public acknowledgment of

Duran's delicate condition. And when the ubiquitous Luis Henriquez overheard the doctor's conversation with a reporter, the subsequent shock waves echoed through the hotel dining room.

"No, no, no!" screamed Henriquez, shaking dinner plates and glasses. "We must not have a story. It will start riots in the streets of Panama. It will put the fight in great peril. In Panama, they would not permit such a story."

The reporter, bearing the brunt of Henriquez's mounting rage, assured the Panamanian vice-counsel that this only made him more thankful to be a member of the American press.

"But people will think Roberto is dying," Henriquez insisted.

"I'm not a doctor," the reporter interrupted. "I only plan on writing that Duran is having his back examined at the hospital. I'm not making any prognosis. Besides, you can't throw a blanket over Duran. Someone is sure to recognize him at the hospital, and then the rumors will start. It's better they know the truth."

Henriquez was hardly mollified. His tirade continued through dessert as publicity man Bobby Goodman began to sink lower and lower in his chair to escape the crossfire.

As it developed, Duran's nagging backache was only a minor spasm. He would be back the following day, wreaking havoc against his sparring partners. The mental strain among his handlers had been far more severe. As Henriquez later confided to Phil Pepe of *The New York Daily News*, "Naturally, we watched Roberto closely, and had the pain persisted, we were seriously considering postponing the fight. We kept him under wraps with the heat and only allowed light workouts. After three days, the pain subsided and we were all finally able to get some sleep."

The first scare was over. But there would be a far greater one in Duran's camp a few weeks later in Montreal.

✯ 19 ✯

MEMORIES ARE MADE OF THIS . . .

Montreal, and a floodtide of memories for Sugar Ray Leonard. "I remember standing on the Olympic victory stand. 'The National Anthem' began to play, and I felt completely numb. The whole world seemed to be spinning around in my head. I was so fatigued and emotionally drained that I almost fell off the pedestal."

For a moment, the recollection made Leonard breathless.

"It's hard to explain the feeling I experienced unless you're a fighter," he told a roomful of reporters who had just watched his last serious workout at the Paul Sauvre Arena in the Montreal suburbs. "Winning an Olympic medal was like a dream come true—a beautiful feeling of having reached a level of excellence few attain. But you work so hard to achieve that goal that it leaves you mentally and physically exhausted."

Sitting in this arena, so close to where he had won his gold medal four years earlier, Leonard was asked to compare the pressure of that night he met Cuba's Andres

Aldama in the Olympic final to the fast-approaching showdown with Roberto Duran.

"The pressure is really the same," he said. "When it came time to fight Aldama, all the critics were saying, 'The Cuban's too tough, too strong, too experienced for this kid Leonard.' Now I'm hearing the same thing, 'Duran's mean, too experienced, a destroyer. Leonard is all flash.' But, believe me, the outcome will be the same with Duran as it was with Aldama."

Nothing else could ever be the same, however, for Sugar Ray, his family, and friends, who were now encamped in sixty-dollar-a-night luxurious rooms at the ultramodern Regency Hyatt Hotel—an army of thirty men and women enjoying "*la dolce vita,*" Montreal-style.

It was a striking contrast to their last visit to Montreal. Packed like so many sardines in a rented van that was parked across the street from the Olympic fight site, only the ladies in that traveling party—Ray's mother; his sisters, Sharon and Linda; and his girl friend, Juanita—enjoyed the comforts of a low-budget motel room. The men would take turns sneaking in and out of the room for free showers. All the meals were cooked and devoured community style in the cramped van, but no one ever complained.

"That was the only way we could all make it to the Olympics to see Ray fight," said the portly Jacobs, who had been affectionately dubbed "King Sardine." "But it was worth it," Jacobs added. "Looking back, I think the pressure was even harder on Ray back then. Remember, he was not fighting for himself, but also his country. Even I could feel the pressure. It was everywhere. But now Ray's already the world's champion. He's proved himself. Besides, he's fighting Duran on a Friday night. Same as Aldama. All the omens are with us."

"That's right," interrupted Leonard. "I remember it was a beautiful night in a beautiful city, but I'd been real homesick for a couple of weeks. I kept calling home, but nobody answered. I found out later that my grandmother had died, and no one had wanted me to worry."

Leonard had spent two weeks in the cramped quarters of a small apartment in the Olympic Village with four other fighters. "They made me the room captain, so I got to sleep in the bedroom," he laughed. "We hardly had room to turn around, but we all got along fine."

Returning to the city where he had first gained international acclaim, it was expected that the charismatic Leonard would be passionately embraced by the populace of Montreal. But, surprisingly, it would be Duran whom the French Canadians took to their hearts.

When the clowning Panamanian worked out in the promenade of Complex Des Jardins, a magnificent five-tiered shopping mall, over five thousand well-wishers turned out in midafternoon to lavish their affection.

"I thought Leonard would be the hero here," said Freddie Brown, "But Roberto's fooled everybody. He's taken their hearts away. He's got the kind of personality the Frenchmen go for. They appreciate his warmheartedness. Roberto loves the attention and the crowds. He's what you call a born entertainer."

And Duran, the poor man's Maurice Chevalier, knew how to cultivate his audience. He wore a T-shirt emblazoned "BONJOUR, MONTREAL" and before each public workout, he walked through the crowd blowing kisses and pressing flesh like a politician in a last-ditch election pitch.

There had been great concern by the promoters that ticket sales would suffer because Duran, the Latin who spoke only faltering English, could not attract enough supporters north of the border. "If there were one hundred places to put this fight," said veteran matchmaker Teddy Brenner, "Montreal would have been last on my list."

But, surprisingly, it was Duran who was causing the excitement in a proud sports town still trying to live down the boxing exploits of "Pretty Boy" Felstein.

"Een wan week," a Canadian with a thick accent said, "Duran has won zee city."

"He's a Latin," another Montrealer explained, "and they're a lot closer in temperament to us than the Americans. He's not very good at it, but at least Duran tried to speak a little French, and the people here appreciate that. And he's a simpler man than Leonard. To many of our people, Leonard appears a show-off."

Now Duran was in the ring, drawing "oohs" and "aahs" from the crowd for the ferocious way he was attacking sparring partner Don Morgan.

"It's always the same," said Colonel Ruben Paredes, the Panamanian strongman, who looked like just another fan maneuvering along the ropes to get a better look. "I saw Roberto fight as a sixteen-year-old. He was singing to himself while he was punching his opponent. He'd sing out, 'Left,' and deliver a left. Then he'd sing, 'Right,' and paste his man with a hard right. It didn't matter. There is no defense for Roberto Duran."

Now a needler in the huge crowd began shouting, "Leonardo! Leonardo!" Duran fixed the man with a menacing stare with his stone black eyes, but then began a comical pantomime of Sugar Ray flying around the ring like a chicken. He clearly had the crowd in the palm of his right glove.

"The only time Roberto is serious," noted Paredes, "is when he's sleeping and in a real fight. Right now, Panama is paralyzed. And nothing will move again until the fight is over and they raise Roberto's hand."

Carlos Eleta laughs in agreement. "It is true," said the Panamanian millionaire who has become Duran's surrogate father. "No one is a bigger hero in our country than Roberto. He knows how much the people love him. That is why he will give Leonard a worse beating than he gave Buchanan. For Leonard, this is his *first* professional fight."

"And what would happen," a man inquires, "if, by some quirk, Roberto should lose?"

"It will be a national tragedy," Eleta said gravely.

"No Man's Land" had been clearly established on a ribbon of turf in downtown Montreal known as University Avenue. It separated the two enemy camps—Leonard's entourage encamped in the Hyatt Regency, and Duran's retinue boarding at the fortresslike Hotel Bonventre. All that was missing from the scene was a United Nation's peacekeeping force.

Both camps, to be sure, exuded confidence. When Colonel Paredes happened upon Ray Arcel in the lobby, he hugged the ancient trainer and whispered in his ear, "On Friday night, you shall bring Panama back its champion, and we will not forget you."

Across the street, Mike Trainer, who had made Leonard the corporate envy of executives of IBM, Coca-Cola, and General Motors, was already plotting Leonard's three or four next title defenses.

As he told Jerry Izenberg of *The New York Post,* "We will have at least three big matches after Ray beats Duran—Cuevas, Hearns, and a rematch with Benitez.

"Right now, Duran's the money fight," the attorney added. "We had to get him while everyone still thinks he can fight. We had to get him while everyone still thinks he has 'hands of stone.'

"Duran was a big lightweight," Trainer continued, "but he was really a junior middleweight training down to 135 pounds. The guys he was terrorizing were natural lightweights."

Someone reminded Trainer that Duran had knocked out a pair of welterweights—Joszef Nsubaga and Wellington Wheately—in the last two fights.

"Nugubugu, or whatever his name was," snickered Trainer, "wouldn't fight Leonard. The same for Wheately.

The World Boxing Council would never sanction it. Duran took our rejects. Duran has always had trouble with good boxers. Edwin Viruet made him look real bad, and Viruet couldn't punch a bit. Ray will frustrate him, and Ray can punch, too."

While the powerbrokers made plans, the two fighters sought relief from the monotony of their training regimen. Leonard and his wife, Juanita, paid a short visit to Regine's, the ultra-chic disco for the jet-setters.

Duran, on the other hand, spent most of his time playing dominoes and spinning the TV dial, hoping to catch his favorite program, "The Incredible Hulk."

"Roberto deals only with winning," offered Henriquez. "Even when he loses at dominoes, he studies the cubes and wonders how they betrayed him."

While Leonard and Duran grew restless, the Canadian promoters secretly hoped for additional time to hype the lagging ticket sales. Only four days before the fight, less than 30,000 had been sold for the 78,000-seat arena. A crowd in excess of 45,000 was needed to reach the break-even point.

"Somebody should have told 'em about 'Gainford's Law,' " an old-time promoter from the States said.

To the boxing community, "Gainford's Law" held as much truth as "Einstein's Theory" to the world of science. First propounded by Ray Robinson's cagey manager, George Gainford, some thirty years ago, it stated quite simply: "It don't mean bleep how many seats you have in the arena. The only thing that matters is how many derrieres you have in those seats."

Gainford would put his theory to practical use repeatedly. When Robinson was booked for a fight, he would check advance sales like an accountant combing the books of a dubious creditor. If the fight appeared in financial trouble, Robinson would suddenly develop the flu or some other poorly-defined malady.

Canadian promoters of the Leonard-Duran match quickly became familiar with "Gainford's Law." They had no difficulty getting the high rollers to buy out the 2,200 ringside seats priced at $500 per copy. The $20 seats went just as quickly. But tickets ranging from $75 to $300 proved harder to sell than the Shah's likeness in Iran.

"The trouble with this promotion is that they won't let the old pros run it," said an old pro. "The Canadians want to run their own show, and they know as much about boxing as my Grandma Hanna knows about Greco-Roman wrestling.

"First of all," the old pro noted, "this fight belonged in New York, Las Vegas, New Orleans, or somewhere in the Southwest where you could draw a lot of Latins. The Canadians really get excited about only two things—hockey and separatism. They haven't had a fighter to cheer about since George Chuvalo, and he was a journeyman heavyweight with a concrete chin. Sure, they followed Leonard in the Olympics. But they didn't have to pay five hundred dollars a seat to see him then, did they?"

Except for the fans' enthusiasm at the free public workouts, there was little evidence that the Canadian metropolis was getting ready for what the papers billed "Le Combat de la Decennie." No fight souvenirs, buttons or T-shirts featuring the portraits of the two combatants were being hawked in the souvenir shops of Vieux Montreal, the most popular tourist area. The only thing to catch the eye were the ubiquitous separatist slogans, "*Tout le monde est importeur*" chalked on the walls in the graffiti-style of New York subway artists.

Inevitably, Bob Arum, never one to fret about international relations, fired a broadside at the way the Canadians had promoted the fight.

"First of all," Arum said, "ticket prices were way out of whack. They could have sold a lot more ringside area seats at $300, rather than $500. Then I would have scaled the tickets down to $200, $100, $60, $40, and $20.

"They also didn't market the fight properly," he said,

continuing his seminar. "They should have tied the tickets in with a hotel package to attract the Americans and the fans from Latin America. Now, I understand, they're trying to discount tickets to the big Canadian companies in exchange for Stadium advertising privileges."

But Arum would not lose any sleep over the problem of selling the "live" fight. He was too busy counting money in anticipation of record crowds and revenue at closed-circuit television outlets around the world.

"The Super Bowl is no comparison to this fight. Not even a seven-game World Series," he said. "At this moment, we're selling tickets at the fastest rate in the history of closed-circuit TV. The demand has been so big in New York, that we were forced to add sites at Aqueduct, Shea Stadium, and the Nassau Coliseum.

"We're adding new sites all over the country," he added. "At first, $30 million seemed like a high estimate, but now we may even exceed that. It's going to be the biggest closed-circuit event of all time, easily surpassing the first Ali-Frazier fight."

Arum was doing all the talking in the absence of his co-promoter, Don King, who was in Minnesota desperately trying to drum up business for Larry Holmes's heavyweight title match against journeyman Scott Ledoux. Arum seemed almost relieved that King, the master of circumlocution, was not on the scene.

"We've got a great fight here," Arum said. "We don't need any phony hype. It's like an apprentice jockey riding a great horse like Secretariat. All he's got to do is hang on for the ride.

"But we're also seeing the beginning of a boxing revolution with this fight," he said, sounding a warning to the three major commercial TV networks. "We're moving very close to the day when almost all boxing will be seen on pay TV. We've seen the last of the big fights on the networks. They know they've got only two years left with boxing."

Arum, in fact, was already making future plans for Leonard. Like Trainer, he rattled off the names of Cuevas, Hearns, and Benitez. "But we've also got to be thinking about the middleweights," he advised. "Whoever's the middleweight champion in 1981 could have an opportunity to make millions of dollars defending his title against Sugar Ray."

Instead of the future, muckrackers in the Montreal press were looking into the past. They kept comparing the costly Leonard-Duran promotion with the 1976 Olympic Games debacle that incurred a staggering deficit of $1.4 billion. Four years later, white papers were still being issued to assess the blame with Montreal Mayor Jean Drapeau as the favorite scapegoat.

With the Olympic cloud still hanging over Montreal, a visiting reporter wondered if the provincial government hadn't had second thoughts about risking $6–8 million in the promotion of the Leonard-Duran fight.

"No, not at all," said Jean Legault, press coordinator for the Olympic Installation Board. "The public is solidly behind Mayor Drapeau. The last election, he got seventy-eight percent of the vote.

"Besides," Legault noted, "that billion-dollar Olympic deficit is very misleading. We're still using most of the Olympic facilities. The Stadium is used for both professional baseball and football, and the Olympic Village is a public housing project with a long waiting list.

"Our problem is that this is our first professional boxing venture, and we still don't have a true profile on the boxing consumer. But we've had tremendous crowds attend the public workouts, and we expect a big boost in ticket sales the last few days."

But the Olympic Board was still taking precautionary steps against another financial disaster. At a cost of $600,000, they purchased an insurance policy that would wipe out any losses below the estimated break-even point of $5.1 million. (Despite the insurance, the promotion would still finish some $500,000 in the red, even though the live crowd of 46,195 exceeded expectations).

Only seventy-two hours before the fight, the promoters had much greater cause for alarm. On Tuesday, Roberto Duran had celebrated his twenty-ninth birthday, sticking his fingers into a huge cake with sparklers balanced on the ring apron while a crowd of over five thousand spectators broke into a spontaneous rendition of "Happy Birthday."

The following morning, Roberto Duran was feeling much older than twenty-nine. He had spent the last four hours at Montreal's Institute of Cardiology taking extensive tests after a routine examination a week earlier had indicated a possible heart disorder. Duran's millionaire manager, Carlos Eleta, made a hurried call to Dr. Guillermo Gonzales, a leading heart surgeon in Panama, to give the fighter another EKG reading.

With a smile on his face, Dr. Gonzales reported, "The tests Duran received at the Institute were the most extensive in the world, and he passed them all. He is perfect."

Not fully satisfied, reporters pressed Bob Arum, the poor man's Dr. Welby, for further details.

"The first time," Arum explained, "he just had a couple of squiggly lines where they shouldn't be. We had to find out if there was anything wrong with his heart. Now all the squiggly lines are in the right places."

"Why?" a reporter from Montreal persisted.

"How the hell should I know?" Arum snapped. "All I know is that this latest examination gave Duran an 'A-plus' bill of health. He's in absolutely perfect shape. He was so strong," the promoter added with a sly grin, "that he broke several doctors' instruments. The fact that we're here candidly telling you what happened proves that there are no medical secrets. This is a big fight, and we didn't want rumors spreading like wildfire."

While Duran was pronounced fit for combat, his

handlers were still suffering severe palpitations of the heart from the latest scare.

"I can laugh now," said Henriquez, "but watching Roberto take all those tests in the hospital, I admit I was scared half to death. He kept running from room to room shouting, 'Don't worry, there'll be a fight.' That is Roberto for you. He has the heart of a lion."

Leonard, of course, was not to be outdone by Duran's repeated hospital bulletins. Before beginning training in earnest, he had stretched a tendon in his right foot playing in a pick-up basketball game and was reduced to walking with a cane. After the foot healed, Leonard gashed his right forearm when his speed bag shattered an overhanging fluorescent light and brought down a shower of glass.

Now, only two days before the fight, Sugar Ray revealed at a press conference that he had been suffering from a virus that had kept his weight hovering at 143 pounds, causing him to curtail his training program.

"Are you still running a fever?" a man in the press gallery asked.

"No, nothing like that," Leonard assured him. "I've just had a little sore throat. I think it's just a matter of getting used to the change in surroundings here. I'll just eat a few juicy steaks and get my weight back. Right now, I feel great."

Almost everyone in Leonard's entourage voiced surprise over the "virus" story. "That's the first I heard of it," admitted trainer Dave Jacobs. "If it had been bad, I'm sure I would have known. But there's been no doctors. No medicine. Nothing."

The latest medical scare had little effect on the eight-to-five odds favoring the champion, who, when pigeon-holed by a Washington sportscaster about his health, winked mischeviously and said, "You guys are my friends. I don't have a cold. I'm just talking."

Both fighters continued talking and taunting each other

right up to the opening bell. They would have a brief confrontation two days before the match at an unofficial weigh-in ceremony in the bowels of the Meriden Hotel complex. Duran, in fact, would make a mockery of the proceedings by weighing in wearing jeans and saddle boots while a commission official gravely intoned, "One fifty-three-point-nine."

Once more, as it had happened in the Waldorf Astoria ballroom six weeks earlier, Duran made a macho motion to start the fight right then and there.

"Two more days, two more days," he bellowed, while Leonard, dressed only in blue briefs, weighed in at 147 pounds. When the champion responded by blowing a kiss and quietly mouthing an "I love you" at his tormentor, Duran's face turned red and he started to mount the four-foot steel barrier that separated them.

Several reporters, desperate for an angle, compared Leonard's "insult" to the way Benny Paret had incited Emile Griffith by calling him a homosexual before their welterweight championship fight in 1962 that ended with the tragic death of Paret, following a brutal beating.

But Duran's burst of anger seemed as calculated as Ali's tantrum before his first fight with Liston. And the show continued as Leonard's coterie of well-muscled bodyguards quickly formed a protective wall. "Those guys aren't going to help you Friday night," said Duran, in a parting shot.

There was no sign of fear in Leonard's eye as he held yet another press conference following the mock battle.

"He could fight Duran right now," Jacobs whispered to a friend in the crowd. "He's razor sharp."

With the prospect of earning $10 million, a man wondered if Sugar Ray had considered making this his last fight.

"Financially, I could quit today," he said. "I've never been one to need a lot of money to be happy. But I'm only twenty-four, and that's too young to quit fighting."

But with so much money in the bank and in blue-chip investments, wasn't there the danger of Leonard losing his killer's instinct in the ring?, another man wondered.

Leonard furrowed his brow for a moment and then said thoughtfully, "Truthfully, I feel there is more pressure on me now than when I had only a few bucks in my pocket. But I've always been geared to be ambitious since the time I was wearing my brothers' hand-me-down clothes. I've always made new goals for myself. That, and a sense of pride. But I still enjoy fighting, being competitive, and being challenged."

"And how do you expect to be challenged by Duran?" a reporter asked.

"I respected Duran the first time I saw him fight," he said. "I respect his determination in the ring. It glows on his face. I respect him," he repeated slowly, "but I'm not in awe of him."

Muhammad Ali, an athlete everyone once held in awe, provided comic-tragic relief as a sideshow freak to the "main event." He was in Montreal, ostensibly to appear at a fifty-dollar-a-plate dinner in his honor—"*une occasion unique*"—but, in reality, the former heavyweight champion was anxious that his once-adoring public would not totally forget him amid all the hubbub created by two glorified welterweights.

The day before Leonard and Duran squared off, Ali called a press conference at the Bonventre Hotel. In typically grand style, he ordered a sumptuous buffet and free-flowing drinks for the working media and curious onlookers. But his generosity would backfire as the mob of free-loaders glutted themselves as Ali, appearing like an overblown Banquo, droned on and on over the incessant din of clinking glasses and dishes.

"We live in a country where people love to be mystified," Muhammad said, his brown eyes growing large in his now fleshy face. "Everybody's askin', 'Who's gonna win? Who's it gonna be, Leonard or Duran? Who gonna win, Ali or Holmes? What's on the moon? What's on Mars?

"People don't know. They're mystified. They worry more about this fight than some plane crash that just killed forty-five people. This fight gets more publicity than the Russian invasion of Afghanistan. Mystery," Ali said, affecting his stage voice. "*Star Wars. The Wolfman. Dracula. Wonder Woman. The Incredible Hulk.* All so mystifying," added the former champion, looking more like "The Incredible Bulk."

He talked once more about his comeback plans, how he would beat Holmes and claim the heavyweight crown a fourth time, etc., etc., sounding more and more like the boy who cried, "Wolf." Asked when and if the Holmes fight would happen, Ali replied, "It takes time. Lawyers fightin' other lawyers, promoters fightin' promoters. My fights are sooo big."

A supporter in the background yelled, "Right on, champ!" But the reporters took the shout as an invitation for another round of drinks and a renewed assault on the buffet table.

There had been the promise by the promoters of a star-studded cast of celebrities on the fight scene—Sinatra, Farrah Fawcett-Majors, Woody Allen, Jean-Paul Belmondo, ad infinitum. It was all part of the last-minute ticket hype. Unfortunately, Thomas Schnurmacher, entertainment editor of the *Montreal Gazette,* called their bluff. He diligently checked out the whereabouts and travel plans of each celebrity reportedly heading for Montreal and discovered not one of the show-biz people mentioned had any intention of attending the fight. Instead, Schnurmacher playfully began publishing the names of those celebrities who would NOT be on the scene.

Certainly, the most "visible" celebrity was a bearded 500-pound giant known as "Antonio the Great" who was in evidence at every press conference and free buffet, dragging a huge chain that he wore around his neck like love beads.

"I am the strongest man in the world," wailed Antonio, making the walls shake as he flaunted a ham-sized fist in the face of cameramen. Antonio bragged about towing five city buses at once, and other superhuman feats, and no one seemed prepared to question their authenticity.

But the fight promoters, more concerned with lagging ticket sales, wondered whether "Antonio the Great" might be able to drag an additional 30,000 customers, kicking and screaming, to the Olympic Stadium.

No effort, however, had been made to boost attendance by staging an attractive under-card. The only real name appearing in the preliminaries was former heavyweight champion John Tate, launching a comeback at twenty-four against an obscure Canadian behemoth named Trevor Berbick.

Tate, in some ways, appeared a more tragic figure than Ali, whose clowning and mugging at celebrity events had come to be expected. Tate, however, had become a clown quite by accident. In a fight that would become a nightmare, "Big John" for fourteen rounds had totally dominated dangerous Mike Weaver. But then, in one of the most stunning form reversals in boxing history, Weaver delivered a vicious left hook, and Tate pitched forward like a giant oak attacked by a chainsaw. By the time he regained his senses, both his reputation and confidence had been shattered immeasurably.

"Big John" would spend the next few weeks in seclusion, enjoying only the company of his bulldog, Tish, and the two mastiffs, Big Red and Atlas, war trophies he had carried home from Africa after winning the WBA heavyweight title from Gerrie Coetzee.

"He'll be champion again, I guarantee it," said trainer Ace Miller, while overseeing a Tate workout. "This fight with Berbick is no 'confidence builder.' John still believes in himself. He just wants to get back to fighting as soon as he can. He'll fight anybody. We heard 'Ali' and we heard 'Holmes,' but it was just talk. But John didn't die against Weaver. He just lost a title he wasn't prepared to keep."

After Tate had completed Miller's book-length list of prescribed exercises and training techniques, he was asked if he found it demeaning as a one-time heavyweight king to be fighting a preliminary to a pair of welterweights.

"I can't complain," he said, while toweling off his ebony-hued body. "I'm an ex-champion. Money and fame's not the big thing now. I just need a lot of work to get my title back.

"I can't be jealous of Leonard making $8–10 million, neither. He's in a different world now. He's a champion, and he deserves anything he gets. He paid his dues to get there."

"That's right," interrupted Miller, who had been timing the interview with a stopwatch. "Getting the title is easy. Keeping it is the hard part."

Tate nodded a silent accent. He knew all about it.

Keeping the title was something Angelo Dundee had uppermost in his mind as he formulated his "game plan" for Leonard's championship encounter with Duran. Sugar Ray, to be sure, had always placed great faith in Dundee's scouting reports, but this time, the world's most famous trainer had worked overtime.

Like Abe Lincoln scribbling his "Gettysburg Address" on the back of an envelope, Dundee had cryptically transcribed his fight strategy on a piece of rumpled notepaper. But Dundee was ready and willing to interpret his remarks for an inquisitive reporter.

It read:

Must move constantly to R (right) on Duran.
Don't lead with R. D. [Duran] will counter with uppercut.
Can't miss D with right. Slide, and stick with jab.
Duran switches to southpaw on ropes, then must move to left.

Beware of Duran grabbing L&H in clinches.
Duran likes to feint L and throw R.
Duran throws L to body, R to chin.
Don't fight with D on ropes or corners.

"There's a lot more we've talked about after watching Duran on films," Dundee confided, "but you can't program a fighter. What I do is give Ray all the options and then let him go to town."

Several ringside strategists had suggested in print that Leonard's only chance of surviving against Duran's relentless attack was to consistently use his superior footwork to put distance between him and his raging foe.

"Just the opposite," Dundee said. "Running is a definite 'no-no.' The worse thing you can do is try to run from Duran. You're playing right into his hands, heightening his aggression. Besides, running's not Ray's style. For Ray, boxing is like a game of chess—slip, move, and counter. That's the best way to kill Duran's momentum. We'll dictate the fight, not him.

"Duran says Ray's only weapon is a jab," the manager said, "but he'll be surprised when Ray nails him with a right hand or left hook. Duran is especially vulnerable to a hook. That's how DeJesus knocked him on his butt. But Ray can also hurt him with the jab. Remember how he decked Benitez with a straight left?"

While scribbling a few more reminders on the notepad, Dundee said, "But you can't underestimate Duran. And no one has more respect for him than I do. A lot of people are fooled by his style, but Duran's plenty smart. He's beaten a lot of good boxers, like DeJesus and Ray Lampkin, by outfoxing them. He knows how to set up a guy, and he's a great finisher once he hurts his man. I just have to question whether he's as great a welterweight as he was a lightweight."

His visitor mentioned that Duran had seemingly lost his desire since moving up in weight because of all the publicity afforded Leonard, forcing him back in the shadows.

"Oh, he'll be motivated for this fight," Dundee laughed. "Leonard's really gotten under his skin. Sure, he resents all the press Leonard gets. First, when he was lightweight champion, all he'd hear about was Ali. Now he's a welterweight, but Leonard is the new kid on the block, the one getting all the attention. That's got to stick in his craw.

"But I still think Leonard can take him out in the tenth or eleventh round. Duran has a style just suited for him. If Ray gets rolling, he can really do a number on him. Nobody's ever tried to attack Duran where he lives—the body. But you can bet Ray will, and he'll hurt him inside, too.

"Duran has never faced a multifaceted fighter like Leonard. He's going to be confused and frustrated. Besides, Ray is bigger and stronger. He's a legitimate welterweight. Duran is just a lightweight with added beef on his frame.

"The public didn't see the *real* Sugar Ray Leonard against Benitez," Dundee concluded. "He was too cautious and tentative trying to win the title. But now he's the champion, and Duran's aggressiveness will bring out the best in him."

Rest assured, Ray Arcel, the eighty-one-year-old guru of the Duran camp, had not been caught napping while Dundee plotted across the street. Boxing's living dinosaur had worked just as diligently scouting Sugar Ray Leonard and the skills that made him a champion.

"Undeniably, Leonard is an excellent boxer," Arcel conceded in one of his early-morning forays on the coffee shop. "He can do just about anything you can ask of a fighter. But can he withstand the pressure Duran will bring to bear against him in the early rounds?

"Remember, this isn't basketball or football. A fighter can't scream, 'Time!' when the going gets tough. And Duran will never let up. It's not his nature. His savagery in the ring is part of his being. He's a creature of the ghetto and lived in places worse than anyone could imagine. He slept with rats and had to steal to eat. All these things give Roberto the rage to live.

"And Roberto is especially vicious when he's fighting someone he dislikes. He does not like Leonard, and he has set his mind on destroying him."

But Arcel's optimism was blunted by the initial report that Carlos Padilla had been named to referee the fight.

"We're in the camp of the enemy," the ancient trainer said gravely, reminding a visitor how the Filipino-born referee had been overzealous in stifling the aggressive style of Vito Antuofermo in his middleweight title defense against England's Alan Minter. Antuofermo would blame Padilla more than Minter for losing his crown.

"I fear and dread Padilla not letting Duran fight inside against Leonard," Arcel said. "That's his fight. He can wear Leonard down. There is a question of Leonard's endurance after the sixth or seventh round."

Thus, Padilla became the focal point of all the whispered conversations at the official weigh-in ceremony the morning of the fight. Only when the two fighters arrived did the heated debate over the referee subside.

Both Leonard and Duran weighed in at an even 147 pounds, but it immediately spurred speculation among the crowd of onlookers as to the physical condition of the fighters.

"Personally," said Arum, "I think the scale is off. I think they both look heavy."

"Ray's perfect," said Dave Jacobs. "He dried out better than he did for the Benitez fight. There's not as much pressure this time. But I think Duran had to kill himself to make the weight."

Others, however, saw Leonard as "drained," "worried," and "fearful." "Leonard looks distressed," said WBC President Jose Sulaiman. "He looks like the pressure is getting to him."

"Yeah," echoed Freddie Brown, "he looks real nervous.

When you're not sure of yourself, that's not good. Roberto? He's great. The closer to a fight he gets, the meaner he becomes. Right now, he's real mean."

Teddy Brenner, matchmaker and raconteur, laughed at all the psychoanalyzing. "There's just such a difference in their personalities," Brenner said. "If Leonard went to the ghetto, he'd sign autographs in a shirt and tie. If Duran went to the Spanish ghetto, he'd start singing and dancing with the people. He'd dance all night.

"Acting cool is just Leonard," Brenner added. "If he came to the weigh-in and staged a tantrum like Ali, no one would believe it, anyway."

One man on the scene who had no doubts about the outcome of the fight was Wilfredo Benitez, who had lost his title to Leonard.

"Leonard will win easy," said the little Puerto Rican. "I know I can knock out Duran in four rounds. He is just a fat lightweight."

But Benitez's opinion was dismissed for its biasness. Wilfredo, actively seeking a rematch with Leonard, had already formed an alliance with Sugar Ray's sister, Sharon, who was seen sporting a king-sized diamond on her ring finger.

While everyone was busy expressing his opinion, the handlers engaged in the customary sparring over fight regulations.

"What will be the color of Leonard's trunks?" said Sulaiman, presiding at the meeting.

"White, with red and blue stripes," Dundee said. "I think it's some country's colors."

"And what color will Duran wear?" Sulaiman asked.

"White with red stripes," said Arcel.

"They must be different," Sulaiman said patiently. "They can be red with a white stripe, if you choose so."

"Must Duran wear red and white?" Luis Henriquez wondered.

"No," said Arum, wearying of the pettiness. "They can be blue, black, or purple."

"OK," said Arcel. "He won't wear white and red."

Next on the agenda, Dundee raised the question of Duran's six-week-old bristly, black beard.

"A beard is allowed," said Sulaiman, "if it does not provide a cushion or serve as a weapon."

"Yeah, but who's going to be the cushion-checker?" Dundee inquired.

Sulaiman assured him that a member of the Montreal Athletic Commission would dutifully measure the density of Duran's chin growth.

"Sure," said Dundee, "but I'm still bringing a barber."

Then, it was Arcel's turn, and another interminable debate ensued about the use of smelling salts in the corner. Arcel lost this round to Dundee. Next came seemingly endless rules about butts and disqualifications, etc., etc.

"What's going to happen?" a man asked Dundee, "if Duran hits Leonard low, as he was accused of doing in winning the lightweight title from Buchanan?"

"Duran's a 'low-ball hitter.' " said Dundee. "If he starts hitting south of the border, my client will respond in kind," the trainer added, sounding more like F. Lee Bailey.

The planning and plotting was over. It was now only hours to fight time, a quiet time for the boxers before their finely tuned bodies would perform the most meaningful dialogue of all.

Leonard would spend the time with his friends, family, and advisors, talking around the fight, talking mostly about his older brother Kenny's marriage, scheduled only eight days after the fight.

Across "No Man's Land," Duran's hotel suite was filled with politicians and Panamanian military brass, all of whom realized that, in Panama, they stood in the shadow of Roberto Duran.

Arcel's fertile mind, however, was figuring out all the

possibilities, down to just what kind of footwear Duran would need to walk from the dressing room to the ring if it should rain at fight time.

Dave Kindred, of *The Washington Post*, asked the grand patriarch of cornermen what it was like for a fighter the last few hours before the first bell.

"Consider the average actor," said Arcel. "He doesn't know if he's coming or going the last half-hour before the curtain goes up. It's the same with a fighter. It's my job to get him ready that last half-hour when he can't get ready himself.

"The tension has been building for months. Now comes the fight, the moment of anxiety. What if the fighter has to wait through three 'National Anthems' before the fight begins? For Christ's sake, he's waiting and waiting and waiting. And he's out there naked."

Two near-naked men—Roberto Duran and Sugar Ray Leonard—with a whole world watching and waiting for them to prove their manhood.

☆ 20 ☆

FIGHT NIGHT

The rain began to fall early in the afternoon and continued through the early preliminary bouts. Ironically, the fans in the cheap seats, including the main contingent of Panamanians, remained bone dry under the overhanging roof while the big spenders in the $500 ringside section were handed Hefty garbage bags to use as makeshift raincoats.

But their wild anticipation at the prospect of seeing Leonard and Duran square-off made the drenched fans overlook their damp surroundings. As the late Pierce Egan of *Boxiana* fame noted, "The weather, it is well known, has no terrors to the admirers of Pugilism of life."

The majority of reporters, some six hundred strong, however, preferred the comfort of the press room, where they could also be entertained by matchmaker-raconteur Teddy Brenner's wealth of rainy-day stories.

"Back in 'Forty-eight," recalled Brenner, "Tony Janiro fought Beau Jack at the old Griffith Stadium in Washington. There was a torrential downpour and they finally wound up fighting barefooted. Jack won the decision, but it figured. He probably didn't own a pair of shoes until he was sixteen.

"And remember when Ali fought Henry Cooper in England," Brenner continued. "It also rained like hell that day, and the guys in Ali's entourage were rolling this carpet in front of him every step he took from the dressing room to the ring. It was a heckuva sight.

"Cooper knocked Ali down early in the fight with a left hook, but it shouldn't have happened. Ali spotted Elizabeth Taylor at ringside, and when he turned his head, Cooper caught him flush on the chin."

Now Brenner was warming to his task with an audience more attentive to his tales than the preliminary bouts.

"The best rain story?" he said. "That had to be in 1935 when Joe Louis fought King Levinsky at Chicago's Soldier Field. Mike Jacobs was promoting the fight, and when Levinsky started shaking in his boots at the weigh-in, Jacobs started thinking, 'This King won't last until ten o'clock.'

"So Jacobs starts running around press headquarters, telling all the reporters that he just got word that a tornado was heading for Chicago, and it would probably hit just when the main event was scheduled to start. 'We're moving up the fight to nine,' he shouted, and ran out the door.

"A couple of reporters saw Jacobs outside the ball park at eight o'clock selling two tickets for the price of one. The fight went off at nine, just like he said, and Louis flattened Levinsky with his first right-hand punch. He could have breathed on him and knocked him over. The trouble was, hardly anyone saw it. Most of the big spenders were still back at the Palmer House finishing off their dinners when Levinsky was already in his bed, sleeping it off."

The laughter in the pressroom died quickly. For in the second fight of the evening, Cleveland Denny, a twenty-four-year-old lightweight from Guyana, was knocked unconscious by Canadian champion Gaetan Hart only twelve seconds before the final bell of their ten-round fight.

It had been a close fight until the last round and Denny, who had won the eighth and ninth on the judges' cards, told his manager, Dave Campanile, before leaving his corner for the tenth, "I'm going out there and giving it all I've got."

But Hart, who, ironically, had also sent his previous rival, Ralph Racine, to the hospital, had more to give in the last three minutes. Instant replay showed Denny, slumped against the rope, absorbing a dozen savage blows to the head before referee Rosario Baillargeon finally moved in to stop the slaughter. Amazingly, Baillargeon stood behind Hart waving his arms to signal the fight was over—arms Hart couldn't see as he continued to pummel Denny.

Dr. Ferdie Pacheco, who was at ringside preparing to serve as colorman on the telecast of the Leonard-Duran match, jumped into the ring to help the stricken fighter. But Denny's convulsions were so severe, Pacheco found he could not remove the mouthpiece from his clenched jaw.

"When I hit him with that first good right hand in the tenth," Hart would later recall, "I saw his eyes roll back into his head."

Denny was rushed to Maisonneuve-Rosemont Hospital and underwent emergency brain surgery while Leonard and Duran were having their hands wrapped for battle. But it was already too late. The brain stem had swelled critically, killing off all the lifelines. On July 2, Denny was declared in "a clinical state of death," and his wife, Clarine, was given the choice of suspending the life-support system. Instead, she prayed for a miracle. Denny died five days later, the fifth boxing tragedy of the year.

The Hart-Denny fight set the brutal and basic tone of an evening in which boxing would be reduced to its most elemental form. Shortly later, there was the comic-tragic spectacle of enigmatic John Tate, staging a painful rerun of his lightning knockout by Mike Weaver that had cost him his heavyweight crown.

After winning the first nine rounds against obscure Canadian heavyweight Trevor Berbick, Tate apparently taunted his rival. An enraged Berbick tore out of his corner at the start of the last round and caught Tate with a solid right. Now Tate surprisingly turned tail, running for a safe asylum. Berbick was in quick pursuit, beating the back of his head until Tate all but belly-flopped out of the ring, his head protruding on the apron. The referee counted to ten, but, in essence, he was tolling the end of Tate's boxing career.

Tate's fall from grace was quickly forgotten as the loudspeakers picked up the salsa drums heralding the arrival of Duran in the bowels of the Stadium. Panamanians joyfully waved their tiny red-and-white flags and chanted "Du-ran Campeon" in unison. Several others jumped on the apron and unfurled the flag of Quebec, prompting the French Canadians to join in tribute to the raven-haired warrior.

In the minute it would take Leonard to join Duran in the ring, the challenger's two ancient cornermen, Ray Arcel and Freddie Brown, sternly lectured referee Carlos Padilla, a man without a vote, but, in their eyes, the man who could most influence the outcome of the fight.

"*We were in the lion's den,*" Arcel said. "*We had to do something to protect our interests. I told Padilla that he was one of the world's best referees, and he was involved in a fight with the world's two best fighters. I urged him to let them fight on the inside and not break them too quick from a clinch. For the fans' sake, they should be allowed to fight. 'Give us a great fight,' I said, 'the whole world is watching.'* "

In retrospect, Arcel's impassioned plea greatly influenced Padilla's action, or, more accurately, his inaction. In no way would he stifle Duran's aggressiveness, and the free-spirited alley fighter became confident, as the fight progressed, that anything short of a public mugging would be tolerated.

Now the Latin beat changed abruptly to the soulful sound of "Hey, Sugar Ray," the theme song for the welterweight champion. His wife, Juanita, and his sister, Sharon, jumped on their ringside chairs and began singing and dancing to the music. Leonard slowly inched his way through the crowd, protected by a phalanx of bodyguards dressed in red jumpsuits. Caught in the spotlight, Sugar Ray's Cupie doll face appeared so fragile compared to the malevolent, bearded countenance of Duran.

The prefight confrontation would be conducted without incident, minus the intense eyeballing that had marked the Leonard-Benitez match. But the intimidation would begin with the sound of the opening bell.

Norman Mailer, in his book *The Fight*, on the first Ali-Frazier encounter, advised us, "The first fifteen seconds of a fight can be the fight. It is equivalent to the first kiss of a love affair."

For Sugar Ray Leonard, the early moments were like a "kiss of death." If it is possible for a fighter to demonstrate his superiority in a matter of seconds, than Duran put his indelible trademark on this fight from the very outset.

His coal-black eyes flashing, Duran moved instantly to the attack, clawing, punching, shoving, butting, elbowing, fighting the way he knew best. But Leonard would not run. As he had intimated before the fight, he would stand his ground and meet the Panamanian head-on. For fifteen rounds, he would wear Duran as a second skin, their bodies entwined in a feverish sweat bath, breathing almost as one in the cramped quarters they had chosen as their battleground.

No, this would be no *Invitation to a Dance*. Leonard, the Nureyev of the ring who had so often lifted his brutal sport to an art form, tossed away his ballet slippers to engage his angry tormentor in a fearful battle of nerves and strength.

In so many ways, it would be a replica of the Ali-Frazier "Thrilla in Manila" that ended with a physically exhausted Ali admitting it had been "the closest thing to death" he had ever endured.

And so it would be this night for Leonard, intent on proving to the world he was more than a pretty face, a veritable fist-fighter who could match macho and ego with the twenty-nine-year-old ringleader of anarchy. Tonight, Leonard would be John L. Sullivan reincarnated, challenging everyone in the bar to test his courage. Once and for all, Sugar Ray would be king of the hill.

Duran accepted Leonard's brave stance with untold joy. No man could beat him on his own terms—an all-out, no-holds-barred war with minimal supervision by the browbeaten referee. The pattern of the fight was clearly established in the first three minutes with Duran using all the tricks he had learned fighting for survival in the Barrio against a man who had been schooled in the boxing etiquette established by the Marquis de Queensbury.

Charging head down, fists flailing from every conceivable angle, Duran simply bullied Leonard into the ropes. Once trapped, the champion seemed incapable of escape. Unlike Willie Pep, the old boxing master who could spin his rival like a top to avoid a trap, Leonard was repeatedly forced to fight his way clear, expending tremendous energy in the process. It was clearly not the plan of battle he had chosen.

Early in the first round after catching a right-hand lead by Duran—a weapon he would make good use of time and again—Leonard borrowed a trick from Ali and shook his head to assure the crowd he was in no real danger.

But there were no such theatrics in the second round when a left hook by Duran caught Leonard high on the forehead, turning him into a rubber-legged mannequin, the imitation of the classic screen drunk.

"I can remember being hit as hard, but I can't remem-

ber taking quite so long to recover from a punch," Leonard said. "*Maybe it was the tension, I don't know.*"

The blow carried Leonard into the ropes but, surprisingly, Duran was slow to follow up his advantage. Buying time to clear the cobwebs from his brain, Leonard held on desperately. This one time, Padilla's reluctance to separate the fighters worked in Sugar Ray's behalf. But it was only a brief respite. Duran soon had his prey pinned again and, when the bell finally sounded, the champion's face was filled with doubt.

There would also be signs of doubt in the ringside section harboring the Leonard clan. Juanita's face was already tear-stained. Seeing Sugar Ray being bludgeoned was a new and frightening experience. She would faint dead away in the eighth round and be slapped awake again by Ray's sister, Sharon.

And there would be doubts expressed in the minds of Leonard's cornermen.

"*Of course, it was a mistake,*" Dundee would later surmise. "*Duran was being Duran and my guy was going along with him. You never fight a guy to his strength. But Ray wanted to beat him at his own game, to 'outstrong' him and when a fighter feels this way, it's tough to change him.*"

Leonard continued to play the bold gladiator in the third round and paid for his bravado by absorbing ninety seconds of unrelenting punishment from Duran's "hands of stone." In the final minute of the round, Sugar Ray mounted his first major counter-attack and, for an instance, Duran retreated from the force of the blows. By the end of the round, however, Leonard was again pinioned against the ropes, resembling an overmatched defensive back trying to tackle Earl Campbell under a full head of steam.

"*That showed a lack of experience on Leonard's part,*" Arcel said. "*I was surprised by his inability to cope and adjust to Duran's aggressiveness. But Duran followed our orders to a 'T.' He cut off the ring beautifully and took away Leonard's jab and movement. He wouldn't let Leonard do what he wanted. He was always the dominant one. Leonard's best chance was to try and outbox us, move and box. You don't change your style to impress an audience."*

The absence of a jab, Leonard's principal weapon in winning his first twenty-seven fights, was still glaringly evident in the fourth round as Duran continued to dictate the course of battle with his unyielding pressure. The Panamanian unleashed a four-punch salvo that forced Leonard to retreat to the ropes. The champion fought back gamely with several searing combinations, but not hard enough to discourage his tenacious foe.

By now, Leonard was already showing rope burns on his back, but Freddie Brown continued to admonish Padilla, "Let 'em fight, damn it, let 'em fight."

Duran was pitching a strong shutout after three rounds, and the general consensus on press row was that Leonard had little chance of lasting the distance. More puzzling, however, was Sugar Ray's choice of tactics.

"Why did Leonard fight Duran's fight?" Freddie Brown said in response to a post-fight question. *"Well, this was a lot like Ezzard Charles's first fight with Marciano. Charles wanted to box him, but it's hard to think when you're getting your brains knocked out. Same with Leonard and Duran. This ain't football, you know. And Duran, like Marciano, never gives you the ball."*

The fight took its first dramatic turn in the fifth round. Sensing his crown slipping away, Leonard carried the fight to Duran with uncharacteristic ferocity. For the first time in the endless night, he displayed his dazzling hand speed, connecting with a left-right-left combination before firing a wild right.

Duran sneered in contempt. But, if nothing else, the shadow of fear had vanished from Leonard's face. In the sixth round, he was finding more room to deliver his staccato punches. He chased Duran into the ropes with a solid left hook, but continued to miss his rival's ever-bobbing head with right hands.

"*I think I started to hurt him at that point,*" Leonard said. "*By the sixth round, I felt I was in control of the fight. The one thing that concerned me was Duran's head. He was using it as a weapon. Every time I moved inside, he tried to butt me.*"

It reverted to a war of attrition in the seventh round. Duran was again mauling Leonard on the ropes while Padilla looked on like a timid citizen afraid to get involved as a witness to a street assault. There would be few classic overtones, only the savage sounds of two men engaged in hand-to-hand combat.

"*Duran's got a unique way of throwing a right hand, then a left hook and a knee at the same time,*" said Dundee. "*My guy wound up with lumps all over him from punches, butts, and knees. Duran's had a lot of practice at fighting like this. When a guy comes at you from every angle, you counter and move. Ray didn't.*"

Signs of exhaustion were evident in both corners before the eighth round. It would be a time for sucking it up and summoning a hidden source of energy to survive the challenge of going the fifteen-round distance. It was now more a test of endurance and suffering than skill and power, and Duran carried the ninth and tenth rounds by sheer strength of will.

Leonard's courage, however, was undaunted. There would be no slackening of resolve. He would command begrudging respect by standing toe-to-toe with the prince of darkness.

The eleventh round was meant for the ring archives—three minutes of cruel and bitter brawling that will probably never be forgotten by future generations of fight fans.

Leonard started the angry hostilities with an overhand

right, followed by a blinding four-punch tattoo of Duran's glistening body. But an enraged Duran answered with a booming fusillade of his own. Back and forth. Ninety seconds of unrelenting combat, with no-clear cut winner, and no prisoners taken.

"*Leonard showed me tremendous courage*," Arcel said. "*Duran landed some body shots that would have shook Hitler's army, but Leonard kept fighting back.*"

Both fighters were shaken by lusty hooks in the twelfth round, but the judges favored Duran, the last round he would win on their scorecards.

The thirteenth would be even more spectacularly brutal than the eleventh, with Leonard reaching deep down into his soul in a futile attempt to reverse the fight's inexorable course. He would escape an early assault by Duran on the ropes, then catch his tormentor with three thumping lefts to the body and two rights to the head. The loud thunderclaps echoed around the vast arena, but in the end, Duran was standing as tall as ever.

Leonard continued his desperate uphill struggle in the fourteenth round. Once, twice, three times he scored with head-twisting combinations, but Duran instinctively forced his way inside to smother the firestorm while Dundee pleaded from the corner, "Why don't you break 'em, Padilla?"

"*From the twelfth through the fifteenth, I felt I was in control*," said Leonard. "*I was landing my combinations and wearing him down. By the fourteenth, he was almost out of gas.*"

Everyone expected the fifteenth round to be a fight to the death, a walk through hell. Instead, Duran, confident of victory, chose to show his playful side. The "Macho Man" would prove that he could box, dance, and boogie as well as the "Sugar Man." Despite Arcel's orders to "stick to fighting," Duran preferred to taunt his rival, thrusting out his bristly chin and daring Leonard to take his best shot.

Leonard would win the round, but he could not remove the mocking smile from Duran's lips.

When the final bell sounded, Sugar Ray took a playful swipe at Duran's glove, a congratulatory gesture for both having survived the holocaust. But Duran would have none of it. He spun his heels and turned his back, disdainfully flicking his right glove over his shoulder, a final defiant message to Leonard that he was not quite ready to celebrate his manhood. This unspoken arrogance said more than the forty-five minutes of savage fighting that had preceded it.

Duran would not wait for the official verdict. He began his celebration in advance, dancing joyously around the ring and giving victory salutes to the cheering crowd. Leonard stood grim-faced and motionless in the opposite corner, as if ready to acknowledge the end of his brief championship reign.

"*When I went back to my corner, it was strangely quiet,*" Leonard said. "*I was looking out in the crowd, but I was confident. But when it took awhile for them to add up their cards, I had a strange feeling come over me. It was the first time the thought occurred to me that I might not have won. I didn't show any real emotion. Nothing.*"

The cards of the three judges were announced first in French, than in English, prolonging the suspense. First, Raymond Baldeyrou, of France: "146, Duran; 144, Leonard." Then, Angelo Poletti, of Italy: "147, Duran; 147, Leonard, a draw." And finally, Harry Gibbs, of England: "Duran, 145; Leonard, 144."

Leonard, now visibly moved, dropped his head on brother Kenny's shoulder, while Duran took a mighty frog's leap into the arms of promoter Don King, who had championed his cause and forced the showdown with Leonard.

An hour after the decision, while reporters faced with final deadlines were ending their stories, Bob Lee, vice-president of the World Boxing Council, appeared in the press room to announce a mistake in the scoring. In fact, judge Poletti had favored Duran, 148–147, making it a unanimous decision for the new champion.

"To add up nines and tens is not very difficult," Lee confessed, "but I put down the wrong number. I felt a little embarrassed about it. But if it became necessary for me to stand on Mt. Everest and admit my mistake, I would. I don't want Jose Sulaiman (WBC president) to take the blame. The mistake was one hundred and fifty percent mine."

This unexpected announcement caused a few diehard Leonard supporters in the crowd to begin circulating rumors of a "fix." Their complaints grew more vocal after it was further revealed that Poletti had voted three rounds to Duran, two to Leonard, and ruled the remaining ten "even."

"Calling ten rounds of a fight even is a diabolical disgrace," said fellow judge Harry Gibbs. And Jay Edson, supervisor of the WBC officials, added, "Any judge who calls ten rounds even is very insecure. A qualified official should be able to discern some difference between the fighters."

But Leonard refused to join in the postfight controversy.

"I thought I did the best I could to hold on to my title," he said softly, holding a protective arm around his wife, Juanita, who had regained her composure. "I fought from the heart. I thought he won the early rounds, but then it became a close fight. This was the toughest fight of my career. I didn't want to take any hard punches, but I had no alternative. There are no hard feelings. I stood my ground. I gave what I had. I have no regrets. I felt I left the ring a champion."

"No alternative." It seemed an odd choice of words. Two words that would be thoroughly analyzed in the months to come. Did he indeed have no choice, or did he elect this particular night to prove to the world that he could take as well as give with the best of them? Even in defeat, no one would ever again question his courage.

Not even Roberto Duran. Asked after the fight what had proved the difference, the proud little warrior pounded his heart.

"Do you mean that Leonard doesn't have a heart?" the same man persisted.

"No," Duran shook his head. "If Leonard didn't have a heart, he would not be alive tonight."

While the wildly happy Panamanians carried their hero off into the night, a reporter grabbed Freddie Brown's arm and asked for a more graphic analysis of the memorable brawl.

Brown gave the man a quizzical look, but then answered slowly, as if explaining a lesson to a retarded student.

"Duran won the way he always does," the hoary trainer said. "By fighting."

The morning after. A day for crowing and rejoicing for Duran camp followers. At six A.M., a raucous band of flag-waving Panamanians after a full night of celebrating in old Montreal, stagger into the lobby of the Hotel Bonventre, somehow hoping to find their conquering hero waiting to greet and embrace them.

Across the street, it is a day for soul-searching and remorse among Leonard loyalists.

"I want him, I want Duran," says a bitter Roger Leonard, sporting scars of his own winning battle over Clyde Gray on the under-card the night before. "I want Duran next."

"Cool it," Roger," says Dave Jacobs, the father-figure who has trained both brothers for over a decade. "Everything's going to be real cool. Cool and steady."

Neither Duran nor Leonard would appear at the ten A.M. press conference. The ex-champion was already flying home to Washington when Don King, looking like the cock of the walk, began shaking the ballroom walls with his basso voice.

"Roberto had a very hard night last night," the promoter said. "To be truthful, he can't get up. He sends his regards, 'but me tired,' " King added, unaware that the new welterweight champion was at that very moment enjoying breakfast in the adjoining coffee shop.

Don King was not tired. He was burning with energy and renewed power after again finding himself at boxing's summit. Best of all, he could dissolve the awkward "Panama Pax" with Bob Arum. He was back in the driver's seat.

"We're ready to sign a rematch," he bellowed in behalf of Duran. "It's like a mirror, a reflection. Just turn all the numbers around on the old contract.

"Mr. [Mike] Trainer was quite adamant in his negotiations for the first fight and did a splendid job for Sugar Ray Leonard. I'm sure that Mr. [Carlos] Eleta and I can do the same for Roberto Duran. What's good for the goose is good for the gander. Roberto didn't worry about the *dinero* for the first one. He just wanted Leonard and the title. But now Duran's the champion, not the challenger. Fair exchange is no robbery."

Luis Henriquez, Duran's advisor and interpreter, was whistling a different tune. "We don't need Leonard next," he said. "Roberto deserves to make some easy money fighting 'tomato cans' like Davey Boy Green.

"But first we will have a giant celebration for Roberto in Panama. We have declared a national holiday in his behalf. The whole country will turn out to greet him. For them, there is only one Roberto Duran."

The welcoming committee would be considerably less numerous for Leonard when he arrived at National Airport. Some five hundred well-wishers turned out to offer their support and consolation.

Mike Trainer stayed behind to answer the inevitable questions.

"After this fight," the attorney said, "Ray doesn't ever have to fight again. If Ray decides to retire, there would be no problem at all, financially. He's cleared at least $5 million. If he were to ask me, I'd tell him to go enjoy himself. He doesn't have to keep fighting.

"But," Trainer added, "I think Ray's more popular this morning than he was yesterday. He's a little more human now in a lot of people's minds. He's found out that sometimes you spill out your guts and still don't win. It happens to all of us, all the time. Now it's happened to Sugar Ray Leonard."

Six days after the fight, Leonard appeared on "Good Morning, America" and hinted of retiring. Questioned by ABC's Tom Sullivan, he replied, "Yeah, I feel I pretty much accomplished what people said I couldn't do as far as the money is concerned, as far as being independent . . . bringing the same amazement and excitement to the ring as the heavyweights in the past . . . I feel I've fulfilled all the things they said I couldn't do. So, I guess, it's time for me to say, 'Let's cool out and try something else.' "

After the shock tremors had been recorded across the country, Leonard recanted. He explained that "cool out" was simply a slang expression, one that had been misinterpreted by the press, who were prepared to write his ring epitaph.

"I want my title back," he said. "After watching films of the fight, there's no question in my mind that I won. The judges just weren't used to seeing me fight that way. If I'd fought a Sugar Ray fight, I would have won for sure. But I wanted to beat Duran at his own game. It wasn't pride or anything. I just wanted to show him. Next time, I'll fight the way I know best, and I'll beat him clear. It won't be up to the judges. It will be up to me."

It was now a time to look back, and let the past catch up with him.

"Up to now," Sugar Ray told *The Washington Post*, "my whole career has been like a fairy tale: winning the Olympic gold medal, becoming a champion as quick as I did, and then being involved in a fight that created as much interest and intensity as the Duran fight did.

"In the script I've written, I become the champion of the world again, and that's it. The end. Fade-out."

Clearly, now Sugar Ray Leonard was orchestrating his own life. But while waiting for the indomitable Duran to play out the final scene, there would be times the fighter would seek out his closest friend, Janks Morton, for reassurance and reflection over how far they'd come together in such a short time.

They would pick the quiet, early morning hours to ride around the Capital Beltway, remembering where they had been, where they were going, and what was waiting over the next hill.

Come what may, Sugar Ray Leonard would be ready. After all, hadn't he written the script?

★ Epilogue ★

Indeed, on the night of November 25, 1980, in New Orleans, Ray Leonard wrote a different ending to the Roberto Duran chapter in his life. But, again, it wasn't wholly satisfying.

Months later, sportswriters and fans alike were still hotly debating the bizarre circumstances surrounding the Panamanian's impromptu surrender of his title. No one could fully accept the idea of an ornery, ferocious gladiator suddenly folding his tent and quitting in mid-ring like a frightened novice. And so, in effect, the skeptics were saying that Duran had lost rather than Sugar Ray had won the rematch.

It created a new game of intrigue for the sporting public. Instead of wondering "Who shot J.R.?" they now pondered the mystery of "What stopped R.D.?"

The fact that Duran had his $8-million purse waiting in escrow in a Panama bank prior to the Superdome battle only heightened speculation that Roberto, sensing his title was slipping away, took the money and ran, tainting Leonard's victory in the process.

"No, I don't think he's that bright," Leonard would say when this theory was offered to him. "I think he had built up such a personal hate for me that when he found I was going to outsmart him, he just decided he wouldn't let me humiliate him anymore.

"Duran's real problem was frustration. He's like a clock—you wind it too tight, and it'll break. His spring broke. That's what happened."

Leonard quickly dismissed the idea of a "rubber match" with Duran, insisting "it's not in my best interests or that of the boxing public." But it was more than a matter of ethics. There were sound economic reasons behind Sugar Ray's thinking. No promoter with common business sense would undertake such a match in the face of the financial disaster that befell the Hyatt Hotel Corporation in underwriting the New Orleans fight for $17.5 million.

Millions were lost in the undertaking as fight fans balked at the inflated ticket prices both at the Superdome and closed-circuit television sites. It had been a humbling experience for more than Duran.

"We paid too much for this fight," said Denzel Skinner, who books the attractions at the Superdome, but found himself caught in an expensive squeeze play between promoter Don King and the Houston Astrodome and Caesar's Palace in Las Vegas, both seemingly ready to meet King's $17.5 million price tag.

"It was either overpay or lose the promotion, but boxing may have reached the point of financial saturation. We squeezed every cent out of promoting and marketing the fight and took a beating. But we're big boys, and we knew what we were getting into."

Leonard, who had personally grossed over $16 million from the two Duran encounters, did not seem overly alarmed by the fight game's bearish financial picture. Instead, he was already thinking ahead to a lucrative engagement with Thomas Hearns, the Detroit "Hit Man" with the spectacular knockout record, who owned the

World Boxing Association version of the welterweight crown.

Only Hearns seemed attractive enough an opponent to inflame the passions of the fight mob and create another megabucks match. And already the fighters and power brokers were beginning to generate the prefight hype.

Leonard cast the first stone. When first asked to consider Hearns as a possible opponent, he said, "If I fight Tommy, I will physically destroy him, his family, and his manager."

"It took Leonard three days to prepare that little speech," Hearns's manager, Emanuel Steward, said bitterly. "But it would only take him a few seconds to sign a contract to fight us."

Even the usually reticent Hearns joined in the lively crossfire by openly questioning Leonard's courage.

"I watched Leonard's first fight with Duran and saw nothing but fear in his eyes," he said. "Leonard has skills, but not heart to go with it. He lacks the heart of a fighter. He's afraid to be hit, and if you're afraid of contact, you've got no business fighting. Leonard should quit before he gets hurt. He'd be better playing golf, or maybe Frisbee."

They had sparred once in 1977 when Leonard was preparing for his match with Hector Diaz in Washington. Hearns, then an amateur, was invited to his training camp.

"I was just coming off a shoulder injury," Leonard recalled, "and not really pushing myself in the gym. I worked a couple of easy rounds with Hearns and then we quit. But now the stories are getting better and better. First, his people said, Tommy really belted me around. Then, they said, he knocked me down. They probably would have said he had killed me, but I'm still here," Sugar Ray laughed.

Inevitably, Leonard would fight Hearns for the undisputed welterweight title, as soon as Mike Trainer felt the numbers were right.

"The money for the fighters will be there," the attorney said confidently, "but the middle men won't be getting their cut as before."

"How long will Leonard continue to fight?" a man asked.

"Ray could quit today and live comfortably the rest of his life on what he's already made," Trainer replied. "He's made sound investments and he's tied up commercially with a number of major companies. He also appears to have a bright future as a sports commentator.

"But as long as there's a personal challenge out there like a Tommy Hearns, Ray will keep fighting. He needs the motivation and the public telling him, 'You haven't beaten this guy yet.' Boxing is not only his livelihood, it's a big part of his life."

Juanita Leonard heard the lawyer's words and shrugged sadly. "That's the way it has to be," she said softly. "He knows I want him to quit, but I know he won't as long as there's a Tommy Hearns around. For Ray, there is always going to be one more fight."

Yes, it was time again. Time for Sugar Ray to answer another challenge. It's always that way when you're "King of the Hill."

✯ Appendix ✯

SUGAR RAY LEONARD'S PROFESSIONAL RECORD

Date	Opponent	Decision	Site	Attendance	TV
2–5–77	Luis Vega	W-6 rounds	Baltimore	10,170	CBS
5–14–77	Willie Rodriguez	W-6	Baltimore	6,826	ABC
6–10–77	Vinnie DeBarros	KO–3	Hartford	6,127	—
9–24–77	Frank Santore	KO-5	Baltimore	4,450	ABC
11–5–77	Augustine Estrada	KO-6	Las Vegas	4,500	ABC
12–17–77	Hector Diaz	KO-2	Washington	7,122	—
2–4–78	Rocky Ramon	W-8	Baltimore	7,217	ABC
3–1–78	Art McKnight	KO-7	Dayton	6,000	—
3–19–78	Javier Muniz	KO-1	New Haven	6,724	ABC
4–13–78	Bobby Haymon	KO-3	Landover, MD	15,272	—
5–13–78	Randy Milton	KO-8	Utica	3,876	—
6–3–78	Rafael Rodriguez	W-10	Baltimore	6,881	CBS
7–18–78	Dick Ecklund	W-10	Boston	5,000	HBO
9–9–78	Floyd Mayweather	KO-10	Providence	4,000	HBO
10–6–78	Randy Shields	W-10	Baltimore	10,061	—
11–3–78	Bernardo Prada	W-10	Portland, ME	6,280	—
12–9–78	Armando Muniz	KO-6	Springfield, MA	6,000	ABC
1–11–79	Johnny Gant	KO-8	Landover, MD	19,743	HBO
2–11–79	Fernand Marcotte	KO-8	Miami Beach	6,046	NBC
3–24–79	Daniel Gonzales	KO-1	Tucson	9,000	ABC
4–21–79	Adolpho Viruet	W-10	Las Vegas	2,100	ABC
5–20–79	Marcos Geraldo	W-10	Baton Rouge, LA	10,000	ABC
6–24–79	Tony Chiaverini	KO-4	Las Vegas	4,500	ABC
8–12–79	Pete Ranzany	KO-4	Las Vegas	4,500	ABC

9–28–79	Andy Price	KO-1	Las Vegas	4,500	ABC
11–30–79	Wilfredo Benitez	KO-15	Las Vegas	4,500	ABC
	(Won World Boxing Council Welterweight title)				
3–31–80	Davey Green	KO-4	Landover, MD	12,000	ABC
	(Title defense)				
6–20–80	Roberto Duran	L-15	Montreal	46,317	closed-circuit
	(Lost World Boxing Council title)				
11–25–80	Roberto Duran	KO-8	New Orleans	25,038	closed-circuit
3/28/81	(Regained WBC Welterweight Title) Larry Barnes KO=10	Syracuse	21,000	HBO	

Wins: 28 Losses: 1 KOs: 19